CONTROVERSIAL ISSUES in CRIME and JUSTICE

STUDIES IN CRIME, LAW AND JUSTICE

Series Editor: James A. Inciardi,
Division of Criminal Justice, University of Delaware

Studies in Crime, Law and Justice contains original research formulations and new analytic perspectives on continuing important issues of crime and the criminal justice and legal systems. Volumes are research based but are written in nontechnical language to allow for use in courses in criminal justice, criminology, law, social problems, and related subjects.

Studies are both contributions to the research literature and ideal text supplements, and are of interest to academics, professionals, and students.

Volume 1
Controversial Issues in Crime and Justice
Joseph E. Scott and Travis Hirschi, *editors*

Volume 2
Serial Murder
Ronald M. Holmes and James De Burger

Volume 3
**House Arrest and Correctional Policy:
Doing Time at Home**
Richard A. Ball, C. Ronald Huff, and J. Robert Lilly

CONTROVERSIAL ISSUES in CRIME and JUSTICE

EDITED BY

Joseph E. Scott

Travis Hirschi

STUDIES IN CRIME, LAW AND JUSTICE ■ Volume 1

SAGE PUBLICATIONS
The Publishers of Professional Social Science
Newbury Park   Beverly Hills   London   New Delhi

Copyright © 1988 by Sage Publications, Inc.

All rights reserved. No part of this book may be reproduced or utilized in any form or by any means, electronic or mechanical, including photocopying, recording, or by any information storage and retrieval system, without permission in writing from the publisher.

For information address:

> SAGE Publications, Inc.
> 2111 West Hillcrest Drive
> Newbury Park, California 91320

SAGE Publications Inc.
275 South Beverly Drive
Beverly Hills
California 90212

SAGE Publications Ltd.
28 Banner Street
London EC1Y 8QE
England

> SAGE PUBLICATIONS India Pvt. Ltd.
> M-32 Market
> Greater Kailash I
> New Delhi 110 048 India

Printed in the United States of America

Library of Congress Cataloging-in-Publication Data

Controversial issues in crime and justice/edited by Joseph E. Scott
  and Travis Hirschi.
    p. cm. -- (Studies in crime, law, and justice : v. 1)
  Bibliography: p.
  ISBN 0-8039-2912-9 : ISBN 0-8039-2913-7 (pbk.)
    1. Criminal justice, Administration of--United States. 2. Crime
and criminals--United States. I. Scott, Joseph E., 1943-
II. Hirschi, Travis. III. Series.
HV9950.C66 1987
364'.973--dc19   87-27333
                          CIP

Table of Contents

Introduction *Joseph E. Scott and Travis Hirschi*	7
Part I. Controversial Crimes	**15**
1. Medicaid Fraud *Gilbert Geis, Henry N. Pontell, and Paul D. Jesilow*	17
2. Pornography and Rape: An Examination of Adult Theater Rates and Rape Rates by State *Joseph E. Scott and Loretta A. Schwalm*	40
3. Organized Crime: Gangsters and Godfathers *John Dombrink*	54
Part II. Controversial Issues in Policing	**77**
4. Police Shooting: Environment and License *James J. Fyfe*	79
5. Police and the Modern Sting Operation *Carl B. Klockars*	95
Part III. Controversial Issues in the Courtroom	**113**
6. The Defense of Insanity *Rita J. Simon and David E. Aaronson*	115
7. Convicted But Innocent: False Positives and the Criminal Justice Process *C. Ronald Huff and Arye Rattner*	130
Part IV. Controversial Alternatives to Prison	**145**
8. Home Incarceration with Electronic Monitoring *Richard A. Ball and J. Robert Lilly*	147

9.	Probation Reform *Joan Petersilia*	166
Part V. Controversies in the Penal System		**181**
10.	Prison Crowding: The Dimensions of the Problem and Strategies of Population Control *Sandra Evans Skovron*	183
11.	Career Criminals and Selective Incapacitation *Michael Gottfredson and Travis Hirschi*	199
About the Contributors		211

Introduction

JOSEPH E. SCOTT
TRAVIS HIRSCHI

The chapters in this book were selected to illustrate controversial topics at various stages of the criminal justice system, beginning with types of crime, focusing on the police, the courts, and, finally, imprisonment and its alternatives. We have made no effort to provide exhaustive coverage of the many issues and areas of disagreement in criminology, nor have we attempted to represent in some balanced way the many points of view in the field. Even so, it seems to us that these chapters do address a good portion of the topics of active controversy in the field. Moreover, they do so with sufficient individual balance such that it is not hard to use them to introduce and consider the merits of alternative positions.

A standard way of presenting and thinking about controversial issues is to use the affirmative-negative or pro-and-con format of a debate, where one side, or viewpoint, is explicitly pitted against the other. This approach emphasizes irreconcilable differences in assumptions and values, and suggests that the best we can do with respect to criminal justice policy is to promote one set of values and then another in an endless cycle of conflict and reform. We are more optimistic than this. In fact, we believe that the purpose of controversy should be to state the issues with sufficient clarity that common or general interests can be recognized by all parties and a search for solutions can begin. Many of the chapters in the book have this quality, and several may even suggest to the reader basically noncontroversial "solutions" to serious problems. The one area in which our coverage could not hope to be complete or even remotely up-to-date is with respect to the many controversial crimes. The first article in this section addresses crimes committed by the elite, namely, physicians. The existences of white-collar crime is not new, but it has not received the attention it deserves. Nevertheless, Medicaid fraud is practically brand new, and the article on the topic by Gilbert Geis, Henry Pontell, and Paul Jesilow reflects this newness by its richly exploratory character.

Fraud, of course, is always possible when services are provided to people not qualified to assess the quality or at times even the quantity of services. But Medicaid provides unusual difficulties for those wishing to control fraud within it. For one thing, the service providers (doctors) are highly prestigious professionals and as such resent the institutionalized suspicion that would characterize an effective fraud control program. For another, the service receivers (poor and elderly patients) have no direct interest in controlling fraudulent claims concerning the services given them because they do not themselves directly pay for them. Moreover, Medicaid fraud affronts the stereotypes held by most Americans of "criminals"— poor, uneducated minorities that have few monetary opportunities of success other than crime. As more studies such as this one on Medicaid fraud become available, theories of criminal behavior may have to be revised to incorporate such findings. Still, we would guess, this too is a case where spelling out the sources of difficulty is itself a large step toward better regulating and controlling such abuses. While we would not expect Medicaid fraud to become one of the perennial problems of crime control in American society, the Geis, Pontell, and Jesilow article illustrates that when illicit profits are available with minimal risk of detection or sanctioning, even those in society's most trusted positions at times violate their trust.

As this introduction is being written, the Reagan Administration has announced an all-out war on drugs and attention of the media is just beginning to die down concerning the findings of a Federal Commission on the alleged connection between exposure to pornographic materials and violence against women. Two of the controversial crimes examined in this section of the book are "pornography" and "organized crime." The timeliness of these articles reflects not so much our good fortune as the fact that pornography and drugs are perennial issues, issues so old and so difficult to define and resolve that we may expect to have them with us for some time to come. The article by Joseph Scott and Loretta Schwalm examines what is referred to as a victimless crime — pornography. Many are critical of police efforts to control "victimless" crimes on the grounds that this distracts their attention from more serious offenses, such as serious violent and property offenses. Such criticisms are warranted, perhaps, if victimless crimes hurt no one other than the adults engaging in them. However, in the case of pornography, a number of feminists and fundamentalist groups have maintained that the consumption of such material encourages and facilitates some males to assault and rape women. If the availability and consumption of pornography has this effect, governmental intervention may be appropriate.

Scott and Schwalm examine the relation between the number of adult theaters and rape rates, state by state, controlling for a variety of other variables. The article reports findings of lower rape rates in those states with the most adult theaters per capita. This article thus argues that pornography may serve as a "safety valve" in society, rather than as a stimulus or catalyst with regard to assaults against women. Although Scott and Schwalm's findings differ considerably from the 1986 Attorney General's Commission Report, they are in line with the 1984 Canadian Commission on Pornography's findings, as well as the 1970 Presidential Commission's findings, both of which are considered by most academicians to be considerably more objective than the 1986 Attorney General Commission's report.

The article by John Dombrink on "organized" crime examines the various theories accounting for the structure of organized crime, and looks in depth at four organized crime enterprises: gambling, drugs, labor racketeering, and legitimate enterprises. Dombrink argues that prohibition policies of the United States government concerning alcohol, drugs, and gambling have been criminogenic and indeed the greatest contributor to the growth of criminal groups in American society. Of those three vices, Dombrink argues that drug trafficking has grown to be the largest and most profitable organized criminal enterprise. In other words, much of the strength of organized crime may be attributed to federal drug prohibition policies.

Dombrink's article is a unique examination of the role government has unintentionally played in the growth of organized crime. This article is perhaps the most thorough and in-depth examination of the strength and power of organized crime written in recent years. The article ends with an upbeat review of new legislation to deal with organized crime, namely, RICO statutes. Unfortunately, those acquainted with legal efforts to deal with drugs in this country—such as the passage of the Harrison Act of 1914, the subsequent Supreme Court decisions, the Boggs Act, the Narcotics Control Act, and other drug legislation—may not share Dombrink's optimism.

The second section of the book looks at controversies in policing. James Fyfe shows us that police shootings of citizens may be reduced by restricting the discretion permitted officers in the use of firearms. This solution has several notable attributes: It is likely to find favor with many parties; it is a product of well-designed research; it is remarkably inexpensive to implement; and it is easily "exported" from one jurisdiction to another. In fact, the Fyfe article describes a situation so rare in criminal justice policy that it should be studied carefully for further lessons on how the field might proceed to benefit from carefully focused research.

Fyfe's recommendations concerning police use of deadly force have recently been adopted in part by the U. S. Supreme Court in *Tennessee v. Garner* (1985). This decision was in reaction to the Memphis Police incident with a 15-year-old boy, who had stolen $10 and a purse from a home. When the police arrived on the scene, he ran and ignored their command to stop. As he was climbing over the rear fence the police shot and killed him. The U.S. Supreme Court held deadly force may not be used to prevent the escape of an apparently unarmed suspected felon unless the officer has probably cause to believe the suspect poses a significant threat of death or serious physical injury to the officer or others.

Carl Klockars's article on police sting operations offers good advice of a different sort. Read carefully, it advises us to think again when we read press accounts of successful sting operations that recover large amounts of stolen merchandise at little cost to the taxpayer. A recent newsarticle account of a sting operation in San Jose, California, was most complimentary of its success. It cited exotic items bought by police officers disguised as fences, such things as parts for military tanks, items that would seem to have little or no prospect for resale. The MiPorn sting operation in Miami was also hailed as a major police accomplishment. Here the government spent millions "wining" and "dining" and "living the good life" to impress and meet those involved in the x-rated video and explicit magazine manufacturing and distribution market. Ironically, they could have met these same "characters" and made similar orders and purchases by attending the annual adult video conference, which is widely advertised.

We regret that these accounts came too late for Klockars's comments, but his article raises clear issues about the limits of proactive policing and about the corrupting nature of such activities to the police, the prosecutor's office, and others who attempt to justify continuing such sting operations. Certainly Klockars's article should alarm conscientious citizens about the integrity of federally funded evaluations of federally sponsored programs concerning crime control, and about the use, or, perhaps better, misuse of the press by the police. It is probably fair to say that the most heated controversies in the criminal justice system center on the courts. With their concern for due process and other rights of the accused, the courts seem to many to be too often on the wrong side, too often protecting criminals from the rightful consequences of their acts, and not adequately concerned with victims' rights.

The two articles in the section on the courts come from the other side, emphasizing in both cases the symbolic significance of the courts' dealings with a tiny portion of those coming before them.

In the article by Rita Simon and David Aaronson, we learn that the insanity defense is rare and largely noncontroversial in the vast bulk of cases in which it is used. We learn further that the insanity plea receives enormous media attention and that the public is basically misinformed about the frequency of its use. Is the insanity plea then simply another example of the inclination of the courts to worry too much about the offender and too little about the crime he or she has committed? Simon and Aaronson might well say, "On the Contrary." Their analysis of the insanity defense traces its development to the present time. It includes the public reaction to John Hinckley's acquittal and the subsequent adoption of new standards to deal with the legally insane by numerous jurisdictions, namely, "guilty, but legally insane."

The article on wrongful conviction, by Ronald Huff and Arye Rattner, deals with a problem that may never go away and therefore one that should be systematically and regularly addressed. One might assume that there would be little controversy about the goal of reducing the number of wrongful convictions to zero (or, in practical terms, to the minimum consistent with other goals of the criminal justice system), and that our attention should therefore focus on how to reduce the number of such convictions and how to adequately document progress toward that goal (so that we can know whether our efforts have produced the desired effect). However, this begs the obvious! Our criminal system adopted the burden of proof in criminal cases to be "beyond a reasonable doubt." The logic of such a difficult burden was to avoid convicting the innocent. To paraphrase Justice Holmes, our system would rather have 10 guilty individuals go free than convict one innocent individual. Whether that is still a viable and desired goal of our system and one supported by the public, one can truly ponder. One might assert, here we have a problem where the solution is clear and simple. No one wants innocent individuals convicted and sent to prison. However, the difficulty is that the public wants individuals who break the law to be convicted and punished. The problem is to maximize the possibility of that goal without compromising the principle of protecting the innocent.

Probably the gloomiest article in the book is that by Richard Ball and J. Robert Lilly on home incarceration. Once advocates of home incarceration as an alternative to jail, Ball and Lilly have become disenchanted by the tendency to monitor offenders incarcerated at home using computers and electronic bracelets rather than limiting the use of such technology to people in the community. First introduced in 1964 (Gable, 1986), electronic monitoring appears to have moved far down the road toward acceptance and respectability. Whether this trend should be promoted or discouraged is a question best addressed, in our view, by careful evaluation of the costs and benefits of these monitoring methods relative to the costs and benefits of available alternatives. However, with the actual adoption of various electronic monitoring devices for home incarceration, we may be heading toward the use of implanted translucers and transducers, ploys many of us thought were strictly Orwellian fiction in the past.

The major alternatives, prison and ordinary probation, are the subject of the article by Joan Petersilia. She argues that as the prisons have become full, those offenders sentenced to routine probation have become all too often "a serious threat to the public." This leaves us no choice, Petersilia suggests, but to explore programs between prison and routine probation, programs that provide an acceptable level of control at an acceptable level of cost to the taxpayer. Not surprisingly, one of the programs she suggests is home incarceration with electronic monitoring.

Prisons may be set in stone, but new prisons can be built, available prisons can be used more efficiently, and methods of selecting and sentencing offenders can be improved. The chapters by Sandra Evans Skovron on prison crowding and by Michael Gottfredson and Travis Hirschi on selective incapacitation explore these alternatives. One conclusion from these articles might be that there are severe limits to what can be done at the last stage of the criminal justice system. Skovron reminds us of various sentencing devices available to reduce prison populations, including front-end strategies, back-end strategies, and capacity expansion. Each of these approaches will be attractive depending on one's "crime solving" orientation. Skovron points out that prison populations have skyrocketed at the very time the serious crime rate has decreased. She identifies a number of factors responsible for this and explores three strategies to reduce prison overcrowding. If one subscribes to a "hard line" in dealing with crime, the front-end approach of reducing the number of offenders admitted to prison or shortening the sentences of those admitted will not be appealing. Similarly, the back-end strategy will not be appealing because it increases the number of offenders released, typically by changes in good time credits or parole policies. Of the three strategies she suggests, only the capacity expansion will satisfy those who subscribe to "get tough" policies. Skovron's article on prison crowding demonstrates once again the controversial nature of most efforts to address the problems of the criminal justice system.

The final article in the book is a depressing review of correctional efforts in dealing with crime. Michael Gottfredson and Travis Hirschi review the criminal justice policy fads from rehabilitation, to deterrence, to incapacitation. Each of these approaches has been shown to be far from a panacea in meeting the needs of crime control. The rehabilitation approach fails because of its lack of positive impact. The deterrence perspective also fails because of its limited impact given the operation of the criminal justice system. Finally, Gottfredson and Hirschi conclude that current efforts to identify and incapacitate career criminals are not only doomed to failure, but that such efforts will not solve the problem of prison overcrowding or the problem of crime. They identify many reasons for the demise of isolating the "wicked" as a rational penal policy for this day and age. This conclusion brings us back to where we started, back to the criminal acts that make the criminal justice system necessary. Gottfredson and Hirschi remind us that all of the problems of the criminal justice system would be more tractable if there were less crime. They also suggest that it may be cheaper and better to concentrate our efforts on preventing crime rather than catching and punishing criminals. This too may be a controversial issue worthy of further discussion.

Hopefully, the chapters in this book lead the reader to rethink his or her perspective on the criminal justice system and on society in general. As a wise philosopher once said, "Every society has the criminals it deserves." Perhaps so. But the germane question is a little different. Do we have the criminal justice system we not only deserve but desire?

REFERENCES

GABLE, R. K. (1986) "Application of personal telemonitoring to current problems in corrections." Journal of Criminal Justice 14: 173-182.
Tennessee v. Garner 105 S. Ct. 1694. (1985)

PART I
Controversial Crimes

1

Medicaid Fraud

GILBERT GEIS, HENRY N. PONTELL, and PAUL D. JESILOW

Almost a decade ago, Harvey F. Pies (1977), assistant minority council of the Ways and Means Committee of the U.S. of Representatives, warned that more effective control of fraud and abuse in Medicare and Medicaid would be necessary before there could be further expansion of health programs financed by the government (Stotland, 1977). Obviously, we are no nearer a comprehensive national health program now than we were in 1977. Indeed, the federal government is in retreat from what once was lauded as a magnificent effort to bring the aged and the poor into the "mainstream" of health care (Stevens and Stevens, 1974). It is arguable that failure to control fraud and abuse in the benefit programs is significantly related to their distressed condition at the moment, but such failure speaks directly to endemic problems regarding the practice of medicine and the administration of medical benefit programs in the United States. The present article examines fraud and abuse in Medicaid, the program for the poor, where it is believed to be significantly more extensive than in Medicare, which serves the needs of the aged. Undoubtedly, a major reason for the higher level of violation in Medicaid, presuming that common understanding is accurate, lies in the considerably lower levels of payment accorded doctors under Medicaid. Physicians treating Medicare patients are paid 80% of what the government determines is a reasonable fee: They can collect the remaining 20% and any other unreimbursed charges directly from patients. Medicaid, state-operated with federal subsidy, typically pays physicians about

77% of what they might expect to collect from Medicare for the same procedures, and they cannot assess patients additional amounts (Buchberger, 1981: 18). States employ one of two systems to set physicians' fees under Medicaid: fee schedules or fee profiles. A fee schedule assigns a value for each medical procedure. A fee profile is based on the distribution of charges for a particular procedure by physicians in the area. States using the second approach generally compare a physician's actual charge against the level determined by the profile and pay whichever amount is lower (Buchberger, 1981).

Abuses of Medicaid also may be more extensive than those of Medicare because of attitudes held by some physicians toward welfare clients, and because the behavior of such clients sometimes irritates physicians. This view comes across pointedly in a statement by an obstetrician-gynecologist working in a metropolitan hospital:

> I like patients who are intelligent, responsible people, and I hate patients who are irresponsible slobs. The Medi-Cal (California's name for Medicaid) patients—the people on welfare—are the worst of the bunch. Since the government is paying for it, they just don't care about what's going on. They don't show up for appointments, and they never call to tell you. They don't take their medicine. They call you Saturday night, three in the morning, with a problem that could have been taken care of on Wednesday afternoon.
>
> Half of the problems these people have could have been avoided by just minimal precautions. Abortions, infections, venereal diseases, and all their complications. It's irritating to have to take care of people when they don't make the slightest effort to take care of themselves [Medved, 1982: 239].

Pay and prejudice by no means exhaust the roster of explanations for fraud by physicians against Medicaid. Medicaid is also notoriously vulnerable to fiscal exploitation, and the likelihood of being apprehended and punished for fraud and abuse appears to be extremely low. Investigators of Medicaid violations point out that the only malefactors they are likely to catch are "the fish who jump into the boat," and "the dopes." But with better resources, they believe there is so much lawbreaking that nabbing violators would be "like catching fish in a barrel."

The fact that Medicaid is federally authorized and subsidized, but state-operated, also complicates enforcement efforts. In addition, the uneasy relationship between government forces and private medical practitioners and their extraordinarily powerful lobby handicaps control of fraud and abuse in the Medicaid program. The practice of medicine is both a professional calling and a business enterprise, and any attempt to understand it exclusively as one or the other is to miss the point. For ages, doctors have traded services (of real or imagined utility) fundamental to human survival in a manner combining altruism and aggressive fiscal self-interest. The London College of Physicians was founded in 1523 primarily "to entrench a monopoly of medical practice in the hands of the few medical graduates that lived there": The motives of its founders, it has been noted, "were largely selfish" (Roberts, 1964: 221). In Puritan New England, Cotton Mather berated the only licensed doctor practicing in Boston during the 1721 smallpox epidemic for his failure to support inoculation. The doctor replied that he thought it "more natural to begin by reducing my smallpox accounts into bills and notes for the improvement of my purse" than to translate his medical notes into an agenda for the improvement of humankind (Silverman, 1984: 345). It should be remembered that the Hippocratic oath gives top priority to the payment and support of a doctor's teacher and his family, and not to the requirements of the patient (Jones, 1923: 291-301).

Difficulties in Medicaid enforcement associated with attempts to deal with doctors solely as commercial entrepreneurs, however, have been noted in a California study:

> Most of the procedures involved in the detection and recovery of inappropriate Medi-Cal expenditures are highly invasive of the traditional professional roles of physicians, hospital administrators, pharmacists, and other providers. Even though these techniques may be justified in terms of recovery of inappropriate payments, they also have the effect of driving providers—physicians in particular—out of the Medi-Cal program [Leighton, 1980: 60-61].

Such observations are reminiscent of Bentham's principle that punishment should never be so severe that its consequences outweigh the good derived from it. Bentham (1838) recommended, in such terms, that a foreign diplomat not be prosecuted for a petty offense if such a prosecution would antagonize his government (Geis, 1960). Doctors cheating Medicaid, unlike other thieves, find themselves in the position of being able to unnerve enforcers, who fear that their perceived heavy-handedness might drive these and other practitioners out of the benefit program in which their voluntary participation is essential. But what is particularly novel today is that doctors have been afforded an extraordinary opportunity to engage in one of the least traumatizing forms of fraud: stealing from an impersonal and faceless bureaucracy (Smigel and Ross, 1970).

SOURCES OF DATA

The primary source of data for the present article is from interviews with officials seeking to discover abuses of the Medicaid program. More than 50 such interviews were held, primarily in New York and California—the two largest Medicaid programs—and also in Florida, Illinois, and Indiana. Beyond this source, we have used an extensive literature on Medicaid fraud and abuse compiled by federal agencies, and numerous reports of Congressional committees.

Our aim is to identify crucial issues in the enforcement of the laws and regulations concerned with fraud and abuse in the Medicaid program. If Pies (1977) is correct, inadequate control has restricted expansion of health services, and has allowed loss of funds that might otherwise have been used for legitimate treatment of persons requiring such services. Our concentration on physicians does not imply that they are the worst Medicaid offenders. There is ample evidence of widespread fraud by pharmacists, ambulance companies, and every other group associated with Medicaid. Hospital expenses in particular have driven medical care costs beyond the fiscal tolerance of the government, and there is widespread belief that a significant portion of these expenses is legally unwarranted and, at times, criminally fraudulent. Physicians, however, stand at the heart of the medical treatment system; they are the linchpins of most Medicaid services. What Winsten (1983: 34) has noted about Medicare applies equally well to Medicaid:

> The doctor is the key decision maker recommending hospitalization and surgery, ordering laboratory tests, deciding when a patient is discharged and influencing adoption of new techniques. Typically, the physician is a private entrepreneur who mobilizes hospital resources yet bears no financial responsibility for the ensuing costs. In

no other industry are senior decision makers so unaccountable for the economic consequences of their actions.

CONTROLLING FRAUD AND ABUSE

The original legislative blueprints for Medicaid did not closely attend to questions of fraud and abuse. Passage of the law was so fraught with difficulty that any hint of distrust of physicians' behavior would have scuttled its hopes. For that matter, there was no warning from private insurance schemes, such as Blue Cross, that exploitation would prove to be a problem. There were two reasons for this: First, as programs based on actuarial calculations, systems such as Blue Cross were only passingly concerned about expenses since, at least within broad limits, premiums could readily be adjusted to cover payments; and second, a large segment of the private insurance field was controlled by the medical profession, which has been chronically disinterested in monitoring the business behavior of its members.

The guidelines for Medicaid in regard to fraud and abuse, as set out in the original act, noted that states must "provide such methods of administration... as are found by the Secretary to be necessary for the proper and efficient operation of the plan." Federal regulations later spelled out in more detail requirements that states were obligated to meet with respect to fraud and abuse. In practice, the precise delineation of violative actions, particularly the distinction between "fraud" and "abuse," would prove difficult. Some investigators would come to take a hard-nosed position: "I don't recognize the word 'abuse' as it applies to this. It's either fraud or it's not. You tell me what abuse is." Other commentators would make the effort to distinguish the categories:

> Fraud is generally defined as intentional deception or misrepresentation, with the intent of receiving some unauthorized benefit. In the health area, examples of fraud may include: billing for services not rendered, kickbacks, deliberate duplicated billing, and false or misleading entries on cost reports. Providers engaged in fraudulent activities are subject to criminal penalties. Program abuse is less clearly defined and includes activities wherein providers, practitioners, and suppliers of services operated in a manner inconsistent with accepted,

sound medical or business practices resulting in excessive cost to Medicare or Medicaid. Included in the area of abuse are the provision of unnecessary health services and the provision of unnecessary care in unnecessarily costly settings [U.S. Senate, 1982: 5].

Two circumstances drew particular attention to fraud and abuse as the Medicaid program developed. The first was the stunningly rapid rise in the program's cost. Total federal expenditures rose from $3.45 billion in 1968 to $8.71 by 1973. By 1978, the cost had climbed to $17.6 billion (Wing, 1983: 16). By 1985, the program involved expenditure of about $23 billion. Such huge increases were deemed unacceptable by officials faced with a huge deficit and a commitment to continuing heavy spending on the military (Bovbjerg and Holahan, 1982: xi).

In addition, not long after Medicaid was established, Congress began to concentrate on what became widely publicized hearings (Thomasson and West, 1973) about "Medicaid mills" (Mitchell and Cromwell, 1981; Cromwell and Mitchell, 1981), "small, for-profit welfare clinics that proliferate in the ghettos of our cities" (U.S. Senate, 1976: iii) with work involving "a conspiracy of several practitioners and the introduction of assembly-line methods to defraud the government" (U.S. Senate, 1976: 12). Some Medicaid mills employed "hawkers" to round up customers. Several catered to drug traffic (Goldstein, 1982: 42-43). Colorful terms were invented to describe their practices, including (1) pingponging—referring patients from one practitioner to another within the facility, though no medical need dictated such a procedure, (2) ganging—billing for multiple service to members of the same family on the same day, generally involving a mother and accompanying children, (3) upgrading—billing for a service more extensive than the one actually provided, and (4) steering—directing a patient to a particular pharmacy, in violation of the patient's freedom of choice (U.S. Senate, 1976: 18).

Undercover Congressional investigators visited about 85 Medicaid mill practitioners, usually pretending to be suffering from a cold. They underwent 18 electrocardiograms, eight tuberculosis tests, four allergy tests, as well as hearing, glaucoma, and electroencephalogram tests. Only once during the four months of investigation did a physician tell an investigator, "Get out of here, there's nothing wrong with you." (U.S. Senate, 1976: 44). More typical was the following summary of an investigator's experience:

His "head cold" was diagnosed as "sinusitis," he was given a general physical, an EKG, a TB test, told he had a severe heart murmur and that he probably had had rheumatic fever as a child. In addition, the doctor ordered a series of x-rays of the patient's sinuses and chest, and referred him to the heart specialist—all in the space of three minutes [U.S. Senate, 1976: 26].

The U.S. Senate committee, following its investigation and a review of other sources, concluded that Medicaid was "not only inefficient, but riddled with fraud and abuse" (1976: 1). Control of Medicaid fraud and abuse was seen as severely handicapped by the view that the agencies administering the programs thought of themselves as no more than "bill payers," with a "lamentable inability" to do anything about fraud and abuse (1982: 93). This was deemed by the Senate review committee as a consequence of their "hierarchy of priorities," which placed the delivery of services and the payment of providers and recipients in the preeminent position (1982: 107). Congress ultimately concluded that investigative, audit, and legal functions for Medicaid had to be combined in a separate office and that the office that conducted the investigations also would have to take responsibility for prosecutions. Creation of such agencies—Medicaid Fraud Control Units (MFCUs)—was authorized in 1981 by Public Law 95-142. Congress provided 90% matching funds for the initial years, but gradually cut back to 75%. Without federal subsidies, states were regarded as likely to be reluctant to mount effective enforcement efforts, since sums recovered largely went into federal coffers. In 1978, for instance, the Los Angeles District Attorney's office had attempted to create a Medicare/Medicaid fraud unit, but, according to one of our interviews, the County Board of Supervisors had vetoed the proposal because so little local money was involved in supporting the program.

The law called for MFCUs to be part of the state attorney general's office or another department of government that possessed statewide criminal prosecuting authority, and to have formal procedures for the referral of cases to prosecutors, if the state constitution did not provide the attorney general or another department of government with statewide criminal prosecuting authority. The MFCUs also were mandated to establish a formal relationship with the state attorney general and to institute procedures for referring cases to that office. Today, 30 states as well as the District of Columbia have

MFCUs certified by the federal government. Nebraska, Idaho, Colorado, and New Mexico have at one time had units, but no longer do. States not enrolled in the program primarily insist that they desire to retain their fraud control work within the state Medicaid agency. A Congressional report has been sharply critical of the failure of those states to form MFCUs. "The primary reason the 20 states have not applied for 90% funding," it noted "is the resistance of state Medicaid administrators who do not want to share their powers or have them taken away from them. . . . Political jealousies have interfered with the establishment of a viable national network and a national commitment to detect and prosecute those who commit Medicaid fraud." A number of states also had maintained that they were not interested in establishing a fraud control unit because they believed that few Medicaid violations existed in their jurisdiction, while others thought that investigative agencies already in place were perfectly capable of dealing with the issue (U.S. Comptroller General, 1980: 4).

In 1982, a staff study by the U.S. House of Representatives' Select Committee on Aging was sharply critical of the work of the MFCUs to that date. The report assumed that the Medicaid program was "fraught with fraud" (1982b: iii), and that virtually all such fraud was perpetrated by providers and not by recipients. The states were castigated for being "happy to accept federal funds [for enforcement], but not the responsibility to police Medicaid" (1982b: v). The number of convictions for fraud was declared to be "infinitesimal" compared to the presumed extent of such behavior (1982b: v). States were said to be having difficulty obtaining funds for their enforcement units from their legislatures, despite the fact that whatever sum was appropriated would be matched on a 9-to-1 ratio by the federal government (1982b: 19). The staff report also deplored the number of states whose units did not have independent subpoena power (1982: 22), but noted that most states, with the notable exception of California, had granted authority to use Medicaid cards for "shopping" potential violators (1982b: 23). During 1980, there had been 197 convictions for Medicaid fraud, with 13 resulting in prison sentences—the longest term, involving a physician, was for 2 1/2 years. The average fine imposed on violators was $1,000 (1982b: 31). MFCUs indicated in a questionnaire response that they had identified fraud and overpayments equal to about 40% of their own funding (1982b: 32).

In addition, the staff report faulted the Medicaid Management

Information System (MMIS), a computer program that had been heralded as the precursor to more efficient detection of fraudulent practices. The computer could readily pinpoint aberrant billings, such as performing a hysterectomy on a male, but the staff report found that its promised benefits had not been achieved, and that there were "very real problems in the system" (U.S. House, 1982b: 66). In all, the tone of the staff report was one of disappointment. "Convictions and jail sentences are the only hope the system has of deterring further fraud," it noted (U.S. Senate, 1982b: 101).

THE EXTENT OF FRAUD

The precise amount of fraud and abuse associated with Medicaid is a matter of uncertainty. Each year about 200 physicians are suspended from participation in Medicare and Medicaid because of fraudulent or abusive practices. Most of these acts take place in connection with Medicaid. A portrait of the violators through 1983 showed that family and general practitioners accounted for the greatest number (27%), followed by psychiatrists (18%), general surgeons (11%), and obstetricians and gynecologists (7%) (Pontell et al., 1985). Except for psychiatrists, these percentages roughly represent the portion of each speciality in the practice of medicine. Psychiatrists are apparently apprehended disproportionately more often because their violations are easier to detect and prove: Only they (and anesthesiologists) charge for time rather than for services. Surveillance can readily determine, for instance, that a psychiatrist is seeing a patient for 15 minutes but billing the government for 40 minutes of therapy (Geis et al., 1985). Blacks and foreign medical school graduates also were overrepresented in the ranks of violators, probably because they form a relatively large portion of the staff in inner-city Medicaid mills, where enforcement tends to be stringent (Pontell et al., 1985). Two statements appear to go hand-in-hand regarding the extent of infractions in Medicaid. First, there is a seemingly reflexive tribute to the general honesty of the medical profession as a whole: Almost invariably it is said that violations are the acts of an aberrant minority. The most impressive evidence of the possible truth of this point comes from a California fraud investigator who noted that before the advent of the MFCUs, "we would just kind of open the phone book and point and do random samples because we weren't set up yet for complaints and we needed to get going." Those included in this random audit process "usually came out clean," in contrast to the cases that had been initiated by a complaint, where "we found stuff."

Second, there are numerous speculations that the amount of Medicaid fraud is extremely extensive. "I would not be surprised that 85, 90% of all practitioners nickel and dime from time to time," a highly knowledgeable federal official maintained. There is widespread belief among enforcement personnel that physicians routinely "overutilize," that is, that they perform services that are not required. This sometimes is done to try to avoid malpractice actions—a strategy outside Medicaid guidelines. In appraisals that may be driven more by cynicism than facts, enforcers presume that numerous doctors calculate the likelihood of being discovered in a violation and, finding the risk virtually nonexistent if the act is done with even slight care and discretion, choose to pick up extra income from the government. The anecdotal information is difficult to interpret. One enforcement official maintained that "in the early days, the program was wide open and there was so much the providers could get away with and they certainly were getting away with it," implying a direct relationship between increasing enforcement energy and, perhaps, a less egregious level of violation. At the same time, another official insisted that since enforcement nets only the most blatant offenders, the program continues to be bled to death by overutilizers.

When a number is attached to the presumed amount of Medicaid fraud, it tends to be 10% (U.S. House, 1980: 78) or 25% (1982b: 10). No evidence that we have been able to locate permits the slightest credence to be accorded either figure. The most forthright statement on the issue was that of the Director of the Congressional Budget Office when she was asked in 1977 to comment on the financial implications related to the establishment of MFCUs. "The unknown magnitude of fraud and abuse presently extant in the programs," she wrote (U.S. Senate, 1977: 48), "makes it impracticable for the CBO to project the actual cost impact of this measure at this time." Estimates of the extent of Medicaid fraud undoubtedly have been influenced by the extraordinary, often bizarre nature of some of the violations. In Illinois, for instance, a psychiatrist was found to have billed Medicaid for 4,800 hours, or almost 24 hours each workday (Horoszowski, 1978: 151). Other doctors have been caught billing for services on persons who were dead at the time the alleged work was done. An optometrist sold patients cataract glasses for $35 and charged the government $180 for reading glasses. A California doctor billed Medicaid for $3,000 for a time period when he was in Africa on a safari. An opthalmologist performed unnecessary eye operations that left 14 persons with impaired vision in a scheme that defrauded the state of $14,000 (Eye Doctor Convicted, 1984), while a psychiatrist in California charged Medicaid for sexual liaisons with a patient, claiming that he had submitted the bills for professional services so that his wife would not become suspicious.

Another doctor billed for abortions on women who were not pregnant, including one who had had a hysterectomy. In 48 separate instances, he billed Medicaid for performing two abortions within a month on the same patient. Perhaps the most unusual case arose in Florida in the early days of the program. A physician was identified as the top biller in the state and was found to be requesting payments for such matters as treating a 22-year-old for diaper rash. Ultimately, the doctor received a 20-year sentence for fraud (Messerschmidt, 1982). Later, a life sentence was added when she was convicted of hiring someone to attempt to kill her partner to keep him from testifying in the Medicaid case (Katzenbach, 1982).

THE PROCESS OF DETECTION

The roster of cases noted in the previous section indicates one criterion by which fraud and abuse are detected: Physicians who engage in blatantly aberrant practices are marked for investigation. They cannot defend themselves by insisting that what they did involved medical judgment: No such judgment will justify bills for a 36-hour day or for extraction of more teeth than those contained in the human mouth.

The MMIS computer system is programmed to flag unusual practices. Further cases are generated by EOMBs and by patient referrals. On very rare occasions, a doctor will complain about a colleague; more often, office personnel or a disgruntled wife or lover is apt to tell enforcement authorities about illegal practices. Of employees, an investigator notes: "This happens because the doctor is too cheap to cut them in on the loot. They're doing the phony stuff for the guy and they're being underpaid, he's cheating them, too. That tends to breed a certain disloyalty." Of patients sexually involved, the same person says: "It's jim-dandy for a while, as they are flattered and impressed by it, but after a while they begin to feel cheapened and used and when that happens, they come in voluntarily. We filed on one guy and all of a sudden a couple more gals came in and told." Investigators also develop a sense of the patterns that represent cheating. A California investigator, for instance, notes: "I simply choose patients from the computer printouts. I look for common surnames. If I see four or five members of a single family being billed for one hour individually on the same day, I'm pretty sure it isn't happening."

As in other police work, the attitude of the person under suspicion plays a significant role in the reaction of those carrying out the inquiry (Westley, 1953). If a doctor says: "I didn't know that was what my billing clerk was billing—we'll change it right away," the enforcers note that they are apt to be indulgent. Truculence and hostility generate tougher enforcement responses. Investigations may be impaired, agents point out, because patients sometimes do not make good witnesses. "If you're talking about psychiatry-type cases, most of your patients are going to be borderline competent anyway. If they need psychiatric treatment, there's something wrong with them anyway. I maybe shouldn't say that, but they're not the best witnesses." Elderly patients, another investigator observed, "are a little forgetful like I am," and occasionally what appears to be fraud is a case of faulty memory.

"Patients, believe it or not," says a New York investigator, "have pretty good memories about when they went to the doctor and when they didn't." Many of them write their appointments on calendars, and some have to rely on calling a taxicab in order to get to the doctor, so that there is the possibility of a record check. Another agent thought physicians tended to be careless because they underestimated the intelligence of their Medicaid patients:

> They think that welfare patients are stupid, and I think that's their biggest mistake because there are a lot of bright people on public assistance and we go out and interview those people.

There are, in addition, structural barriers that inhibit the enforcement of the laws regulating Medicaid work. A Florida agent, for instance, pointed out that he is not regarded as a law enforcement officer and, therefore, under state law he cannot carry a weapon, has no arrest authority, and cannot use electronic wiretapping or carry a body bug. In this connection, one investigator noted that juries had been "spoiled" by the Abscam cases, and that they now were more apt to look askance at evidence that does not include a videotape of the charged behavior. Investigators also feel hamstrung in many jurisdictions by their inability to obtain information from private insurers. They maintain that if they could put together private and Medicaid billing patterns, they could more expeditiously obtain a complete picture of a physician's practice and more easily pinpoint violations.

To obtain records from private insurers involves issues of privacy and confidentiality and often requires a grand jury subpoena. Confidentiality questions bring into conflict two highly regarded values: that of the government to police the ways in which its funds are expended, and that of the physician to bar access to information revealed to him or her by patients. At times, agents have obtained the permission of patients to provide them access to a doctor's records, but their efforts often are thwarted by court rulings that insist either that medical confidentiality takes precedence over government attempts to detect fraud or that the government's mission could equally well be carried out by the use of other tactics (see *Commonwealth v. Kobrin*, 1985). Investigators feel frustrated because they believe that physicians sometimes use the cloak of confidentiality to camouflage wrong-doing, and they find it hypocritical and offensive to be confronted with high-minded defenses of mean-spirited behavior.

PROSECUTING MEDICAID CASES

The most common complaint of Medicaid investigators concerns the difficulty they experience getting prosecutors to go forward with cases they have developed. The law creating MFCUs insisted that the agencies be placed in a government niche that provided its own prosecutorial resources. Nonetheless, investigators must persuade attorneys to give precedence to their cases, which tend to be complicated and often hinge on proof of intent. One investigator noted cynically some of the difficulties in this connection:

> We can't prove intent for a number of reasons. One, no one would suspect this upstanding pillar of the community of any fraudulent intent. He has a tremendous education, makes a great appearance. He

is in that social order that is making the decision whether he is right or wrong—judges, prosecutors, etc.

The major complaint, however, is that prosecutors are concerned with glory-grabbing, and that they will not be bothered with low-profile matters such as Medicaid fraud. Several interview quotations convey the strength of the agents' views on this matter:

> White-collar crime calls for a lot of patience and most of the young attorneys want to go into a courtroom with John Dillinger by the nape of the neck. It just doesn't work that way.

An agent in Florida made these observations:

> These smaller circuits, all they're doing is rapes, robberies, murders, B-and-Es. You can try a good murder case in probably three or four days, whereas a white-collar crime could be taking three or four weeks. You can walk in with a wheelbarrow full of documentary evidence. They're apprehensive about trying them. They're complex, take a lot of time, a lot of preparation.

A federal official echoed several of the foregoing remarks:

> Most prosecutors are young people, relatively new out of school, and they break, you know, cut their teeth on gun cases and buy or bust drug cases. You're trying to build your record around the community as a good lawyer, and you go off on a two-year investigation, and people don't know you're around anymore. That's the down side of doing fraud cases.

The most common criterion for moving forward with a Medicaid case is the amount that the alleged fraud has involved. Federal officials believe that it's very difficult to get a U.S. Attorney to take a case that involves less than $20,000, so that "a lot of cases fall between the cracks."

Prosecutorial strategy generally involves selecting the easiest charges rather than placing all possible violations before the jury: "You don't list as a basis for a charge every single rotten thing the guy did, because you would bore the court and the jury to death." Similarly, the statute of limitations—generally five years—delimits the audit period. At the same time, there is some pressure upon physicians to plead guilty. "They don't want too much embarrassment, and they know they'll get light sentences."

PUNISHING MEDICAID FRAUD

There is a considerable behavioral science literature that insists that punishment of white-collar offenders is apt to be notably effective, both in deterring them from further illegal acts and in deterring others like them who might otherwise have been likely to commit such acts (Andenaes, 1971: 545; Braithwaite and Geis, 1982; Geerken and Gove, 1975: 509; Zimring and Hawkins, 1973: 127-128). Essentially, such conclusions are based on two suppositions: first, that white-collar offenders, such as physicians, have a great deal to lose by prosecution and therefore will be much more disinclined than street offenders to take the risk if they suspect that they will be caught; and second, that white-collar offenses, such as Medicaid fraud, are essentially rational behaviors and therefore are much more susceptible than many street crimes, particularly acts of violence, to utilitarian calculations on the part of those who might engage in them. The response of physicians to the Surgeon General's report on smoking provides inferential support for this theses. Well before the public had reduced its cigarette smoking, members of the medical profession showed a decline in usage. The probability that a physician was continuing to smoke related directly to the distance of his or her specialty from the lungs. Physicians dealing with lung cancer were quite unlikely to be smokers; so too were radiologists (Nisbett and Ross, 1980: 56).

A supervisor of New York investigators maintains that he has observed that "doctors' earnings go down when they realize they're being investigated," but this, at best, is only an intuition and could well represent, if accurate, prudence rather than a move toward law-abiding behavior: Both speeders and those traveling within the speed limit are apt to slow down when they spy a patrol car in their rear view mirror. Most investigators bewail the failure of courts to impose jail or prison sentences on convicted Medicaid offenders, and they believe that professional associations are notoriously indulgent of persons against whom Medicaid fraud has been proven. The associations rarely suspend the right to practice, and commonly regard such behavior as merely business-related and not a reflection of professional competence. A California doctor working with a licensing agency summarized the situation:

> Unless a guy has been blatant about his fraud, he usually doesn't lose his license. What we usually do is to put him on probation, restitution to the Department of Health. One of the most important terms in probation is an imposition of community free medical care and in some needed area, for a number of years, maybe for six to eight hours a week.

Even this seemingly straightforward resolution has not been without sardonic twists. In the same state, another official told about clinics billing the state for services provided by physicians who had been sentenced to provide free care at them.

Prison terms are believed to be exceedingly difficult to obtain from judges against doctors convicted of Medicaid fraud. In some instances, the physician is seen as providing a vital service that cannot readily be replaced, especially in small communities. In other instances, the incongruity of regarding doctors as "real" criminals appears to protect them from incarceration. In Memphis, one investigator noted, "a doctor... was convicted of a hundred and some odd counts of Medicaid fraud, and it was his second conviction, and he still got no jail time." On the other hand, like many other white-collar criminals, physicians proceeded against for Medicaid violations suffer from adverse effects that are not commonly associated with prosecution for street offenses. Their reputation is an integral aspect of their continuance in their profession and, as an official noted, "you put his nose on the front page of the article as a thief . . . you've destroyed him." The common tactic of excluding convicted doctors for a period of time—usually a few years—from further participation in Medicaid and Medicare seems to be a relatively benign consequence, though for doctors dependent on the programs for their livelihood the deprivation could be hurtful until or unless other sources of income are located.

The original Medicaid legislation provided only for recovery of overpayments and not for suspension. Suspension, however, became automatic in 1977 if a physician was convicted in a federal, state, or local court for defrauding the system (P.L. 95-142). A legal notice of suspension must be published in a local newspaper (and in a Spanish language newspaper, where appropriate) after a letter of notification is sent to the provider. The first claim received from a beneficiary who goes to a suspended doctor is paid, but a notice is sent to the beneficiary indicating that no further claim involving the particular provider will be honored. Most enforcement people—though they appear to be strongly in favor of tough penalties, and especially jail and prison terms, for Medicaid fraud perpetrators—have concluded that such outcomes are very unlikely except for the most flagrant offenses. Instead, the enforcement focus has begun to concentrate heavily on the recovery of monies and the imposition of further fines. In 1981, a civil money penalty intended to discourage fraud in government health care programs was established (Kusserow, 1983). The statute allows the secretary of HHS to impose a civil penalty of up to $2,000 for each fraudulent claim, and to impose an assessment of up to twice the amount of the fraudulent portion of the claim in lieu of damages. But such provisions can also be eviscerated by what investigators regard as overindulgent judges. Note, for instance, the following from a former director of the California MFCU:

> A classic case. We did a complete, comprehensive audit on a lab operator that established without any question $300,000 of bilking the state. We went in and got another one of these gutless judges who said, "Oh, he's a professional man, he's suffered enough having to go through the criminal process and therefore, even though he pleaded guilty, I am going to require him to pay only half of the restitution." So we get $160,000 from this guy, and we were outraged. The rest is profit. Who wouldn't go into crime?

WHICH WAY TO REFORM?

The most common remedial action proposed is a movement from fee-for-service programs to Health Maintenance Organizations (HMOs). HMOs differ from fee-for-service systems in at least three major respects. First, providers are at risk and are not reimbursed for each service they give; second, HMOs must either provide directly or have provided at their expense those services specified in their contract with the patient; and finally, a member of an HMO is not allowed, except under extraordinary circumstances of medical emergency, to seek care from physicians or other providers outside of the plan (Price, 1982: 1). Contracts between the government and HMOs for Medicaid services regularize and delimit expenditures, since the HMOs are paid a specified sum for each patient on their roster and any additional expenditure or saving is theirs to keep or bear. Fraud enforcement officials are skeptical about the likelihood that HMOs will reduce fraud notably, though they grant that HMOs might change fraud's form and say it probably will make the detection of fraud even more difficult. In past years, HMOs have been discovered enrolling persons who did not exist, and selecting for their rosters only persons with superior health. A California official told us of one such scam:

> The entrepreneur would send two recruiters to the neighborhood. The first would go through the poor neighborhood where there was going to be a high proportion of Medi-Cal patients. First they would go to the door and say, "We're doing a survey on the health of your family—how many people are there in your family, how healthy are they, have you had any diseases?" Then, if it turned out that this was a person or family that statistically was not likely to produce medical problems, then the next person who came through the neighborhood would sell them on joining the HMO.... So they got a higher proportion of well people at the HMO than the payments contemplated. Then, by eliminating the high cost operations, like emergency rooms, weekend service ... and sending these people to other hospitals, they increase the profit by that much more, and then when it began to look as if they were going to get caught, they declared bankruptcy and walked away with it.

Other suggested reforms include a proposal by one investigator for a central clearing source that would allow enforcers to see to it that violators do not migrate from one jurisdiction to another without the awareness of the agents in the second site. A Congressional Committee recommended that the Department of Justice establish a Medicaid strike force, and that a number of U.S. Attorneys be assigned to prosecute persons defrauding government programs (U.S. House, 1980: 101). In Hawaii, attorneys in the MFCU are deputized to serve as prosecutors, so that the reluctance of attorneys in other agencies to handle Medicaid cases is overcome.

ASSIGNMENT: THE PHYSICIANS' BLUDGEON?

All law enforcement ultimately depends upon the tacit consent or weakness of the enforcement targets. A notably efficient method for detecting tax fraud—with many thousands more investigators—would probably so infuriate the huge population of cheaters that a government inaugurating such measures would shortly find itself in political difficulty. Airport security can go only so far in hindering the pace of air traffic; and campaigns against theft can employ only a limited repertoire of techniques without running the risk of offending altogether too many persons. This condition is particularly pronounced with Medicaid fraud. Fear that physicians would not participate in the benefit programs was largely responsible for the many concessions granted to practitioners when Medicaid and Medicare were inaugurated: "There was," Marmor (1970: 15) notes, "the widespread fear, grounded in the bitter, hostile propaganda of the AMA, that physicians would refuse to provide services under a national health program." Continuing apprehension about such withdrawal constitutes one of the major points of tension in enforcement efforts.

In the early 1980s, one quarter of all primary care physicians were refusing to accept Medicaid patients, largely because of the low reimbursement rates (Buchberger, 1981; Davidson, 1982). Program administrators continually warn investigators, as one of them pointed out, "if you put doctors in jail, pretty soon none of the doctors will be in Medicaid." How reasonable are the fears that enforcement will so alienate Medicaid practitioners that it will become counterproductive? The best evidence seems to be that Medicaid now has become so intricately involved in medical practice that fears of massive physician withdrawal are only meaningless bluffs. In California, for instance, 15% of practicing physicians derive more than a quarter of their incomes from Medi-Cal patients (Jones and Hamburger, 1976). With competition for patients becoming more intense because of the "overproduction" of doctors in the United States, it seems unreasonable to expect that Medicaid would be abandoned wholesale by doctors because of decent efforts to combat fraud.

CONCLUSION

Physicians continue to enjoy extraordinarily high status in the United States. A 1985 Gallup Poll found them outpacing the clergy, college professors, lawyers, and business executives (in that order) in terms of designation as "very prestigious" (Maeroff, 1985). At the same time, a Harris Poll indicates that "the major group of concerns that physicians have about the future of medical practice relates to loss of autonomy, mainly as a result of regulatory interference and external intervention" (Harris, 1984: viii). Many physicians were worried about controls on such things as location and specialty (Harris, 1981: 96; Pruchansky, 1983). Only about half of the doctors surveyed said that they would recommend the practice of medicine today as highly as they might have 10 years ago (Harris, 1981: 74), and fewer than half of the physicians were satisfied either with their current incomes or with their financial prospects (Harris, 1981: 70). Obviously, there is a striking discrepancy between the fiscal self-image of a large number of the physicians and the state of public opinion about their earnings. Typical in our interviews, for instance, was the hostile remark of a federal investigator:

> [Doctors are] causing nursing home patients to lie in their own feces and their own bedsores and all of this good other stuff, because they're taking money that should be paying for food and nursing care and buying yachts and tennis courts.

Monitoring for fraud probably has contributed in some degree to the malaise expressed by physicians with their lot. As a prior condition, of course, the government had to invade the traditionally reserved enclaves of medical practice. It did so because there was a perceived (and real) absence of protection from fiscal disaster for large segments of the population and because sizable numbers of poor persons were unable to afford adequate medical care. It seems naive of doctors to have presumed, if they did, that the virtually open checkbook structure of the early days of the medical benefit programs would persist, especially in the face of escalating health care costs that far exceeded inflation figures. Government officials, traditionally beholden to the medical lobby, nonetheless have priorities that transcend obligations they might feel to a particular constituency:

They devoutly desire to continue in office. In terms of Medicaid fraud control, these and other considerations are shaping what seems to be a continuing diminution of medical autonomy and power and a gradual, rather erratic course of toughening enforcement against violators. It will be a complicated process to determine the long-run impact of this process on the health of citizens. In the meantime, it seems clear that doctors have been placed in what is for them an uncommonly discomforting position. That position can be illustrated by an observation gathered during our interviews. Enforcement officers, like the prototypical British servant, come to know their "betters" in ways denied to most outsiders. On the bases of her experience, one investigator carried on the following dialogue with us:

> Investigator: How do I feel about the medical profession personally? I'm afraid to go to a doctor. I don't trust any of them.
>
> Interviewer: You're into self cures now?
>
> Investigator: No, I'm into being well. I hope I never need a doctor. They scare me.

REFERENCES

ANDENAES, J. (1971) "Deterrence and specific offenses." University of Chicago Law Review 38: 537.
BENTHAM, J. (1839) The Works of Jeremy Bentham, John Bowring (ed.). Edinburgh: Tait.
BOVBJERG, R. R. and J. HOLAHAN (1982) Medicaid in the Reagan Era: Federal Policy and Stated Choices. Washington, DC: Urban Institute.
BRAITHWAITE, J. and G. GEIS (1982) "On theory and action for corporate crime control." Crime and Delinquency 28: 292.
BUCHBERGER, T. (1981) Medicaid: Choices for 1982 and Beyond. Washington, DC: Congressional Budget Office.
BUTLER, P. A. (1980) "Legal problems in Medicaid," in R. Roemer and G. McKray (eds.) Legal Aspects of Health Policy: Issues and Trends. Westport, CT: Greenwood.
Commonwealth v. Kobrin (1985) Supreme Judicial Court, Commonwealth of Massachusetts, No. SJC-3671.
Council of Economic Advisers (1985) Economic Report of the President. Washington, DC: Government Printing Office.
CROMWELL, J. and J. MITCHELL (1981) "High income Medicaid practices." Inquiry 18: 18.
DAVIDSON, S. M. (1982) "Physician participation in Medicaid: background and issues." Journal of Health Politics, Policy and Law 6: 703.

DAVIS K. and C. SCHOEN (1978) Health and the War on Poverty: A Ten-Year Appraisal. Washington, DC: Brookings Institution.
Eye Doctor Convicted (1984) Santa Ana (CA) Register, January 20: 14.
GEERKEN, M. R. and W. R. GOVE (1975) "Deterrence: some methodological considerations." Law and Society Review 9: 297.
GEIS, G. (1960) "Jeremy Bentham," in H. Mannheim (ed.) Pioneers in Criminology. London: Stevens.
GEIS, G., P. JESILOW, H. PONTELL, and M. J. O'BRIEN (1985) "Fraud and abuse of government medical benefit programs by psychiatrists." American Journal of Psychiatry 142: 231.
GOLDSTEIN, P. J. (1982) Prostitution and Drugs. Lexington, MA: Lexington.
HARRIS, L. and Associates (1984) Medical Practice in the 1980's: Physicians Look at Their Changing Profession. Menlo Park, CA: Kaiser Foundation.
HARRIS, R. A. (1969) A Sacred Trust (rev. ed.) Baltimore: Penguin.
HOROSZOWSKI, P. (1978) Economic Special-Opportunity Conduct and Crime. Lexington, MA: Lexington.
JONES, M. W. and B. HAMBURGER (1976) "A survey of physician participation in and dissatisfaction with the Medi-Cal program." Western Journal of Medicine 124: 75.
JONES, W.H.S. [ed.] (1923-31) Hippocrates, with an English Translation. London: Heinemann.
KATZENBACH, J. (1982) "MD charged in contract killing." Miami Herald, September 4, B: 1, 3.
KUSSEROW, R. P. (1983) "Civil money penalties law of 1981: a new effort to combat fraud and abuse in federal health care program." Notre Dame Law Review 58: 985.
LEIGHTON, R. (1980) Looking for the Monster: Description of the Problem of Medical Costs and Catalog of Cost Containing Strategies. Sacramento: State of California, Department of Health Services, Health and Welfare Agency.
MAEROFF, G. I. (1985) "Polls say Americans support raises and tests for teachers." New York Times (West Coast ed.) July 2: 10, col. 4-5.
MARMER, T. R. (1970) The Politics of Medicare. Chicago: Aldine.
MEDVED, M. (1982) Hospital: The Hidden Lives of a Medical Center Staff. New York: Simon & Schuster.
MESSERSCHMIDT, A. (1982) "Witnesses dispute doctor's claim." Miami Herald, January 16, B: 2.
MITCHELL, J. and J. CROMWELL (1981) "Large Medicaid practices and Medicaid mills." Journal of the American Medical Association 244: 2433.
NISBETT, E. and L. ROSS (1980) Human Inference: Strategies and Shortcomings of Social Judgment. Englewood Cliffs, NJ: Prentice-Hall.
O'SULLIVAN, J. (1981) Medicare and Medicaid Provisions of the "Omnibus Budget Reconciliation Act of 1981." Washington, DC: Library of Congress, Congressional Service.
PEAR, R. (1984) "Many states limit Medicaid program." New York Times, December 17: 1.
PIES, H. F. (1977) "Control of fraud and abuse in Medicare and Medicaid." American Journal of Law and Medicine 3: 323.

PONTELL, H. N., G. GEIS, M. J. O'BRIEN, and P. JESILOW (1985) "A demograghic portrait of physicians sanctioned by the federal government for fraud and abuse against Medicare and Medicaid." Medical Care 23: 1028.
PRICE, R. J. (1982) Health Maintenance Organizations. Washington, DC: Library of Congress, Congressional Research Service.
PRUCHANSKY, N. R. (1983) "Cost control and physicians: an examination of attitude and behavioral expectations." Medical Care 21: 508.
ROBERTS, R. S. (1964) "The personnel and practice of medicine in Tutor and Stuart England, part III: London." Medical History 8: 217.
SILVERMAN, K. (1984) The Life and Times of Cotton Mather. New York: Harper & Row.
SMIGEL, E., and H. L. ROSS [eds.] (1970) Crimes Against Bureaucracy. New York: Van Nostrand Reinhold.
STEVENS, R. and R. STEVENS (1974) Welfare Medicine in America: A Case Study of Medicaid. New York: Free Press.
STOTLAND, E. (1977) "White-collar criminals." Journal of Social Issues 33: 179.
THOMASSON, D. and C. WEST (1973) "Our multibillion dollar Medicaid scandal." Reader's Digest 110 (May): 87.
U.S. Comptroller General (1980) Federal Funding in State Medicaid Units Still Needed. Washington, DC: Government Printing Office.
U.S. House of Representatives (1977) "Medicare gaps and limitations." Subcommittee on Health and Long-Term Care, Select Committee on Aging. 95th Congress, 1st Session.
U.S. House of Representatives (1980) "Medicare: a fifteen-year perspective." Select Committee on Aging. 96th Congress, 2nd Session.
U.S. House of Representatives (1982a) "Medicaid fraud: a case history in the failure of state enforcement." Select Committee on Aging. 97th Congress, 2nd Session.
U.S. House of Representatives (1982b) News Release of March 27. 97th Congress, 2nd Session.
U.S. Senate (1976) "Fraud and abuse among practitioners in the Medicaid program." Subcommittee on Long-Term Care, Special Committee on Aging. 94th Congress, 2nd Session.
U.S. Senate (1977) "Medicare-Medicaid fraud and abuse amendments of 1977." Committee on Finance. 95th Congress, 1st Session.
U.S. Senate (1982) "Oversight of HHS Inspector General's effort to combat fraud, waste, and abuse." Committee on Finance, Special Committee on Aging. 97th Congress, 1st Session.
WESTLEY, W. A. (1953) "Violence and the police." American Journal of Sociology 56: 34.
WING, K. R. (1983) "The impact of Reagan-Era politics on the federal Medicaid program." Catholic University Law Review 33: 1.
WINSTEN, J. S. (1983) "Bailing out Medicare." New York Times, May 5 (1): 31, col. 5.
ZIMRING, F. E. and G. J. HAWKINS (1973) Deterrence: The Legal Threat in Crime Control. Chicago: University of Chicago Press.

2

Pornography and Rape

An Examination of Adult Theater Rates and Rape Rates by State

JOSEPH E. SCOTT and LORETTA A. SCHWALM

Pornography is anti-culture, anti-conscience, anti-God, anti-family, anti-child and anti-woman. Pornography brutalizes and insults society.

—Ellis, 1984: 8a

In 1970, the President's Commission on Obscenity and Pornography announced that they had found no evidence to link erotic materials with antisocial effects on behavior. With the release of this report, many felt that the controversy over "pornography" would end. Nothing of the kind transpired. In fact, there is perhaps more vocal opposition to the availability of erotic material today (albeit from a minority of citizens), than at any time in the recent past. The source of much of today's opposition is various feminist groups, which maintain that erotic materials degrade women and serve as a license to rape. These feminist groups have locked arms with the fundamentalists, who have opposed the availability of such materials for years. These groups appear to have had considerable influence on President Reagan's request that the U.S. attorney general appoint a new committee to "determine the nature, extent, and impact on society of pornography in the United States, and to make specific recommendations . . . concerning more effective ways in which the spread of pornography could be contained (Attorney General's Commission on Pornography, 1986: 215).

In October 1967, Congress passed Public Law 90-100 authorizing the president of the United States to establish a presidential commission to examine the traffic in obscenity and pornography and to determine whether such materials were harmful to the public. In 1968, President Lyndon B. Johnson appointed 18 members to the commission whose tasks were: "after a thorough study that shall include a study of the causal relationship of such materials to antisocial behavior, to recommend advisable, appropriate, effective, and constitutional means to deal effectively with such traffic in obscenity and pornography" (President's Commission on Obscenity and Pornography, 1970: 1).

The commission reviewed the evidence already available, commissioned considerable new research, and invited over 100 different groups to express their views on the subject. Basic scientific research techniques, including quasiexperiments, controlled experiments, and surveys, were utilized to ascertain the effects, if any, of exposure to erotic material and antisocial behavior. After spending approximately 2 million dollars and reviewing the evidence available, the commission concluded that there was no evidence "that exposure to explicit sexual materials plays a significant role in the causation of delinquent or criminal behavior among youth or adults" (President's Commission on Obscenity and Pornography, 1970: 32). It is noteworthy that the commission chose not to use the term "pornography" in its report inasmuch as they deemed it to have no legal significance and because it most often denotes subjective disapproval of certain material.

The commission's report expressed the view that much of the "problem" regarding erotic materials "stems from the inability or reluctance of people in our society to be open and direct in dealing with sexual matters" (1970: 53). The 1970 commission recommended, moreover, that "federal, state, and local legislation should not seek to interfere with the right of adults who wish to read, obtain, or view explicit sexual materials" (1970: 57).

The commission's report did not end the controversy over the effects of sexual material or whether they should be controlled. President Richard M. Nixon openly rejected the commission's findings and fundamentalists referred to the commission as the

"Commission on Permissiveness." Fundamentalists even issued their own report, *The Obscenity Report: The Report to the Task Force on Pornography and Obscenity*. In this report, they recommend, among other approaches, the establishment of a Federal Obscenity and Pornography Board. They went on to recommend that "anyone found to have been reading literature (or watching movies, and so on) determined beforehand by local juries to be pornographic or obscene would be compelled to register as a reader of pornography" with this board (1970: 114-115).

In the midst of this controversy, the U.S. Supreme Court in 1973 announced their decision in *Miller v. California* (1973), which established a new legal test for obscenity. In the 5-to-4 decision, the court held that a work may be subject to state regulations when:

1. the average person, applying contemporary community standards, would find that the work, taken as a whole, appeals to the prurient interests;
2. when the material portrays sexual conduct in a patently offensive way specifically defined by the applicable state law; and,
3. when the work, taken as a whole, lacks serious literary, artistic, political, or scientific value [1973: 24].

This novel definition not only did away with a national standard for obscenity but substituted the definition of "utterly without redeeming value" as previously adopted in *Memoirs v. Massachusetts* (1966) with "lacks serious literary, artistic, political, or scientific value." These changes were thought by many to favor the prosecution and substantially reverse the expansion of sexually oriented material.

OPPONENTS OF SEXUALLY ORIENTED MATERIAL

Fundamentalists reaction to the report of the president's commission was immediate. Charles Keating, founder of Citizens for Decent Literature and one of the 18 members of the presidential commission, totally rejected the report and abstained from even voting on whether to accept the report or not. Four additional commissioners dissented from the majority report. In their dissent, these commissioners argued that erotic materials are immoral. Their basic argument was that such material erodes public morality and respect for human life. They argued that government must regulate pornography through legislation to protect morality and our way of life.

Groups such as the Citizens for Decency Through Law, National Federation for Decency, Interdenominational Citizens Council for Decency, and Morality in Media have organized to combat the availability of sexually oriented material. Through their newsletters and national offices, they have lobbied and encouraged groups to speak out for "decency." They have been joined recently by various feminist groups in speaking out on the evils of erotic material.

Unlike the fundamentalists, who oppose the availability of erotic materials primarily on moral grounds, some feminist groups consider these materials antiwomen. These feminists argue that erotic material represent hate literature against women and serve as a support and manifestation of a culture that accepts and condones violence against females. These feminists believe pornography leads to violence against women and therefore support efforts to reduce its market. Groups such as Women Against Pornography conduct seminars to educate people about the harmful effects of pornographic images of women (Lederer, 1980), and encourage boycotts and demonstrations against establishments that carry such merchandise. Brownmiller (1975) and Dworkin (1981), two of the more recognized spokeswomen for the feminists, equate pornography with rape, viewing both as male tactics for expressing and ideologically encouraging hostility toward women. Erotic materials are considered the essence of antifemale propaganda to facilitate the subordinate role of women to men. Morgan (1980) and Diamond (1980) reflect the feminist views concerning sexually oriented material by identifying it as the medium for conveying male power and domination over women.

Such feminist groups have urged legislation that would ban erotic materials on the grounds that it is a violation of women's civil rights. This approach has shown some signs of success. Such pornography civil rights ordinances have been proposed in various forms by several communities, most notably in Los Angeles, California; Cambridge, Massachusetts; Minneapolis, Minnesota; and Indianapolis, Indiana. In fact, the city of Minneapolis hired feminist Andrea Dworkin to draft a local ordinance that would allow women to oppose pornography in court on the grounds it violated their civil rights on equality and free speech. Although this bill was vetoed by the Minneapolis mayor, the city of Indianapolis did pass such a bill in May 1984. The

Indianapolis ordinance identifies pornography as a "systematic practice of exploitation and subordination based on sex that differentially harms women" (City-County Council, 1984). That ordinance was ruled unconstitutional by the United States District Court in 1984, by the U.S. Court of Appeals in 1985, and by the U.S. Supreme Court in 1986. The federal courts ruled not only that the ordinance was vague, but also that it attempted to regulate material protected under the first amendment to the Constitution of the United States. Nevertheless, this approach at regulating erotic material through a claim of civil rights violation has received support not only from some feminist groups but even by the 1986 Attorney General's Commission on Pornography (see pp. 391-396).

The fundamentalists and feminists have had some success in their attempts to limit the availability of certain sexually oriented material, and they have received some support from researchers in recent years for their claims about the harmful effects of such material. As mentioned, some feminists have vociferously maintained that erotic materials encourage and facilitate rape.

RESEARCH FINDINGS SINCE THE PRESIDENT'S COMMISSION

As noted previously, the President's Commission on Obscenity and Pornography concluded that exposure to erotic materials is not a factor in the causation of sex crime or deviance. Since 1970, there has been considerable empirical research on this exact topic. Most of this research has been conducted in a laboratory setting by social psychologists using undergraduate students as subjects. The question that most of the recent research has attempted to answer is whether there is a causal link between exposure to erotic material with sexually violent themes and subsequent sexual violence or a greater tolerance for sexual violence.

A number of recent studies have reported that aggression levels in previously angered males are raised by exposure to explicit sexual material but that aggression is not raised in nonangered males (Baron, 1974, 1978; Donnerstein et al., 1975; Meyer, 1972). However, portrayals of violence without sexual content have been found to facilitate the expression of anger as much as portrayals of sexually related violence (Meyer, 1972).

Zillman and Sapolsky (1977) found that angered male college students exposed to simulated or explicit sexual material were no more likely to retaliate against the researcher when given the opportunity to do so than students exposed to nonsexual material. In fact, they concluded that men may be distracted from their anger by sexual material. Similar findings were reported by Baron and Bell (1977), who concluded that aggression by angered men was inhibited after exposure to erotic material. However, when exposure to erotic materials and anger are reversed (the subject is angered after having viewed erotic material), Donnerstein et al. (1975) found men attribute their arousal to anger, rather than the erotic material, which may then facilitate their aggression.

A number of studies have attempted to ascertain whether exposure to erotic materials lowers viewers' aggressive inhibitions. Donnerstein (1980) found that when male subjects were exposed to violent explicit sexual material, they were likely to exhibit more aggressiveness (as measured by intensity of electric shocks) toward men than women. This is in line with Baron and Bell's earlier findings as well (1973). Donnerstein's research did find that exposure to aggressive-erotic material elicited more aggression on the part of the subject after viewing such material than exposure to either neutral or simply erotic material.

Most of the studies that have attempted to examine a possible link between erotic material and aggressiveness have measured its effects within minutes after the subjects' exposure to erotic material. This is perhaps unrealistic if there is a relationship. Few would contend that after viewing sexually oriented material, males would immediately seek out a female and commit rape. Rather, the real question is what effect, if any, such materials have on viewers some time after having been exposed to them. Mann et al. (1973) examined this question in a study of married couples over a three-month period. They found that exposure to explicit sexual materials with violent themes produced no significant changes in the participants' sexual behavior.

Additional studies that have attempted to study the experience of rapists with erotic material have consistently found them to have had less exposure to sexually oriented material both during adolescence and adulthood than the general male population (Goldstein, 1973; Goldstein and Kant, 1974). Researchers have found that convicted rapists do become more sexually aroused by narrations of rape and violence than nonrapists (Abel et al., 1977). However, considerable research indicates that narrations of violent sex do not arouse rapists any more than do narrations of sex without aggression (Abel et al., 1977; Barbaree et al., 1979).

Additional research has found that subjects reporting a likelihood of committing rape if they felt they would not be caught was correlated with self-reported arousal to violent sexual depictions (Malamuth and Check, 1980) and that such subjects were more likely to believe rape myths (Malamuth, 1983). Exposure to films portraying violent sexuality has also been found to be related to male subjects' acceptance of violence against women.

In a major study outside of the laboratory, Straus and Baron (1983) examined the relationship between the consumption of erotic material and rape rates by state. They compiled statistics for the distribution of eight *male sophisticate magazines* (this is the term used by the trade industry) by state and compared them to states' rape rates. They found a rather high correlation between the distribution rates of these magazines (*Chic, Club, Forum, Gallery, Genesis, Hustler, Oui,* and *Playboy*) by state and rape rates. Although the magazines used for this analysis are certainly not of the explicitly sexually oriented type (in fact, *Forum* is almost exclusively narrative in nature), these findings do add some support to the feminist contention linking sexually oriented material to rape. Scott and Schwalm conducted a similar analysis of male sophisticate magazine consumption by state and rape rates (forthcoming). While their analysis is similar to that of Straus and Baron, they found that the ratio of single males in a state has a higher correlation rate to rape than does "girlie" magazine sales. This would seem to indicate that in states with a high percentage of single males, girlie magazines sell better and that the observed correlation between such magazines sales and rape is spurious.

However, research by Malamuth and Spinner (1980) found an increase in violent sexual portrayals in pictorials and cartoons in *Playboy* and *Penthouse* magazines from 1973 through 1977. They argue that since violence and sex may lead to violent sexual crimes, or at least lower males' inhibitions about such acts, that the increase in coverage of violent sexual portrayals may account for such crimes. However, a more extensive content analysis by Scott and Cuvelier (1987) of *Playboy* magazine from 1954 through 1983 did not find that the ratio of sexually violent pictorials or cartoons differed significantly from the 1950s compared to the 1980s. They did find that there were more sexually violent depictions in the 1970s. It may well be that

Malamuth and Spinners findings are an anomaly of the time period they examined rather than a trend. Moreover, inasmuch as rape rates have declined significantly nationwide for the past two years without any concomitant decline in sexually oriented material, the relationship between rape rates and the consumption of sexually oriented material must be questioned.

The research alone since the president's commission report does posit the possibility that exposure to sexually violent material under certain conditions may lower males' general inhibitions to aggress against females. The attorney general's 1986 commission seems to focus on violent sexual material as the "real" culprit and link to sexual aggression, although most research argues it is the violence per se, whether linked with sex or not, that may be responsible or even causative of violence. The 1986 commission seems almost to acknowledge that point, then ignores it and marches on.

ADULT THEATERS AND RAPE

This research examined the relationship between rape rates and adult theaters by state. The assumption was that if rape rates are affected by the availability of erotic material, and, more specifically, explicit material—and, at times, even violent explicit material—that those states with the most adult theaters per 100,000 residents should also have the highest rape rates. In order to test this proposition, rape rates for each state and the District of Columbia were recorded for 1982 from the Uniform Crime Reports. The number of adult theaters by state for 1983 was secured from the Adult Film Association of American, Inc. It was impossible to get the exact number of adult theaters broken down for every state. No information was secured for Arizona, and it was therefore not included in the analysis. A number of other states had the number of adult theaters listed only for that state and adjoining states. Those states and the adjoining states were (1) New Jersey and New York, (2) North and South Carolina, (3) Indiana and Michigan, (4) Oklahoma and Texas, (5) Kansas and Missouri, and (6) New Hampshire, Maine, Vermont, Rhode Island, and Connecticut. This required us to analyze the data for 41 areas, treating the above six grouping as new states. To do so, we combined the respective areas' other variables used in the analysis, including rape rates, and calculated them for the respective regions. This provided us 41 units of analysis (referred to as states, henceforth).

The states were trichotimized into those with the lowest, middle, and highest rape rates in order to examine the relationship between rape rates by the number of adult theaters. Table 2.1 indicates no statistically significant relationship between rape rates and adult theater rates.

As one can see, however, states with the lowest rape rates tend to also have the lowest adult theater rates and states with the highest rape rates tend to have higher rates of adult theaters, although the differences are so small as to be statistically not significant. The differences between states with low and high rape rates and adult theater rates is statistically not significant.

Inasmuch as previous research has found rape to be related to a number of other factors, additional variables were introduced into the analysis. These additional variables were the percent of a state that is classified as a standard metropolitan area (taken from the Uniform Crime Report), the alcohol consumption per gallon per capita (DISCUS, Wine Institute, USBA, U.S. Department of Commerce), the percentage of the state's population classified as nonwhite (U.S. Bureau of Census for 1980), the percentage of the state's population living below the poverty level (U.S. Bureau of Census), the status of women in each respective state (as calculated by Straus and Baron, 1983; based on 1977 data), the circulation rates of outdoor-type magazines by state (*Field and Stream, Sports Afield, Guns and Ammo, The American Hunter,* and *American Rifleman,* as provided by the Audit Bureau of Circulation for 1982), and the circulation rates of general readership-type magazines by state (*Reader's Digest, National Geographic, Time, Newsweek,* and *U.S. News and World Report,* as provided by the Audit Bureau of Circulation for 1982).

The logic in introducing these additional variables was their possible relationship with rape rates. Rape rates have consistently been higher in populated urban areas than in suburbs or rural areas; this justified including the percent of a state that is classified as a metropolitan statistical area. Several studies have found a high correlation between violent crimes, including rape, and alcohol consumption. Shupe (1954) found that 45% of the arrests for rape in Cincinnati involved offenders who had been drinking. Gebhard et al. (1967) found that two-thirds of child molesters had been intoxicated at the time of their offenses. Because of this high correlation between

TABLE 2.1
Analysis of 1982 Rape Rates and Adult Theater Rates

Rape Rates	Adult Theater Rates			
	Low	Med	High	Row Total
Low	8	3	3	14 34.1
Med	4	4	5	13 31.7
High	3	5	6	14 34.1
Column Total	15 36.6	12 29.3	14 34.1	41 100.0

$\chi^2 = 4.164 < 0.3842$

Regression Statistics with Rape Rates
Standardized Regression Coefficients

	X1	X2	X3	X4	X5	X6	X7	X8
Y =	.120	.460	.652	.237	.222	.352	.678	.073
P <	(.543)	(.058)	(.019)	(.171)	(.213)	(.119)	(.045)	(.777)

Y = Rape rates
X1 = Adult theater rates
X2 = Percent poor
X3 = Standard metropolitan statistical area
X4 = Status of women index
X5 = Alcohol consumption per capita
X6 = Percent nonwhite
X7 = Outdoor magazine circulation rates
X8 = General readership rates
R^2 = .49

intoxication and/or heavy drinking and sex crimes, the alcohol consumption rate per capita was included in the research.

The FBI's annual report has for years indicated a higher percentage of rape arrests of nonwhites than would be expected based on their percentage of the general population. For example, in 1980, nonwhites accounted for 49.4% of the total number of forcible rape arrests in the United States. For this reason, the percentage of a state's population that was nonwhite was included in this analysis. Several studies have also found that convicted violent offenders are more likely to come from poor backgrounds. For this reason, we included the percentage of a state's population living below the poverty level.

Feminists have maintained that rape, and the fear of rape, act to restrict women's options in society and thereby limit their participation. They have maintained that because women have inferior roles, they are viewed by men as "legitimate" rape targets. The assumption is that as the status of women increases in society, the rape rates should therefore decrease. The outdoor readership index was included in the analysis on the assumption that men who read these magazines may have a more "macho" orientation to life and this "macho" environment may indicate a culture more disrespectful of women and thereby more conducive to rape. The general readership index was included simply as a check on exposure to the mass media. For the last 30 years, the mass media has consistently devoted more coverage to the topic of sex (Scott and Franklin, 1973; Scott, 1986). Given this fact, those states where the readership of general circulation-type magazines is highest might reflect higher rape rates.

When the relationship between rape rates and adult theater rates is examined and other variables are introduced into the equation using regression analysis, the relationship between rape rates and adult theater rates is again not statistically significant and is almost nonexistent. The regression equation indicates that the percentage of poor, the percentage of a state that is a metropolitan area, the status of women, the alcohol consumption rate, the percentage of nonwhites, and the outdoor magazine circulation rates all account for more variation individually in rape rates than does the adult theater rate.

These findings may be surprising to many readers given the assumption that exposure to explicit sexual material may be related to rape rates. Certainly, movies shown at adult theaters are more explicit than the magazines examined by Straus and Baron (1983) or Scott and Schwalm (forthcoming). In fact, adult theaters, along with adult bookstores, have been targets for control or elimination by fundamentalist and various feminist groups. They have also been "busted" and prosecuted regularly for "pandering obscenity" by law enforcement personnel. Assuming that portrayals of violence may some way facilitate or engender a climate conducive to rape, the question is whether adult movies contain more violence than other types of movies. Research comparing violence rates for G-, PG-, R-, and X-rated movies has found fewer acts of violence in X-rated movies than any of the other types (Leyshon, 1981: 64). More recent research examining a random sample of video tapes released during the first six months of 1985 indicates that the G-, PG-, PG13-, and R-rated, as well as rock music and unclassified videos have over 30 times as many violent acts per video as the X-rated tapes (Scott and Davis, unpublished). This may partially account for the lack of a statistically significant relationship between rape rates and adult theaters.

Previous studies by Kutchinsky (1973) have found that sex offenses in Denmark declined after 1967, when the Danes repealed all bans on sexually oriented materials. From the various studies that have attempted to examine the long-term effects of erotic material and rape rates, as well as from our own research, there appears to be little if any relationship between the consumption of this type of material and rape. Rape rates do appear to be related to certain cultural climates. Those areas with high rates of violence (as measured by homicide, armed robbery, and aggravated assault) have high rape rates. To postulate that adult theaters or other forms of sexually oriented material are responsible for high violent crime rates would appear to be stretching the point. Rather, the proliferation of sexually oriented material would seem to be consistent with many other changes in our society in recent years (Winick, 1977) as it has become more tolerant of those desiring alternative lifestyles.

REFERENCES

ABEL, G. G., E. B. BLANCHARD, D. H. BARLOW, and M. MAVISSAKIAN (1975) "Identifying specific erotic cues in sexual deviations by audiotaped descriptions." Journal of Applied Behavior 8: 247-260.

ABEL, G. G., D. H. BARLOW, E. B. BLANCHARD, and D. GUILD (1977) "The components of rapists' sexual arousal." Archives of General Psychiatry 34: 895-903.

American Booksellers Association v. Hudnut (1984) 598 F. Supp. 1316 (S.D. Ind.).

American Civil Liberties Union: Public Policy Report (1986) Polluting the Censorship Debate: A Summary and Critique of the Final Report of the Attorney General's Commission on Pornography. Washington, DC: ACLU.

Attorney General's Commission on Pornography (1986) Final Report. Washington, DC: Department of Justice.

BARBAREE, H. E., W. L. MARSHALL, and R. D. LANTHIER (1979) "Deviant sexual arousal in rapists." Behaviour Research and Therapy 17: 215-222.

BARON, R. A. (1974) "Aggression-inhibiting influences of heightened sexual arousal." Journal of Personality and Social Psychology 30: 318-322.

BARON, R. A. (1978) "Aggression-inhibiting influences of sexual humor." Journal of Personality and Social Psychology 36: 189-197.

BARON, R. A. (1979) "Heightened sexual arousal and physical aggression: An extension to females." Journal of Research in Personality 13: 91-102.

BARON, R. A. and P. A. BELL (1973) "Effects of heightened sexual arousal on physical aggression." Presented to the annual convention of the American Psychological Association, Montreal, August.

BARON, R. A. and P. A. BELL (1977) "Sexual arousal and aggression by males: Effects of type of erotic stimuli and prior provocation." Journal of Personality and Social Psychology 35: 79-87.

BROWNMILLER, S. (1975) Against Our Will: Men, Women and Rape. New York: Bantam.

City-County Council, City of Indianapolis, Marion County, Indiana (1984) City-county general ordinance amending Chapter 16.

CUVELIER, S. J. (1984) "A longitudinal content analysis of violence and sexual victimization in a best-selling erotic magazine." (unpublished)

DIAMOND, I. (1980) "Pornography and repression: A reconsideration." Signs 5: 686-701.

DONNERSTEIN, E. (1980) "Pornography and violence against women: Experimental studies." Annals of the New York Academy of Science 347: 277-288.

DONNERSTEIN, E., M. DONNERSTEIN, and R. EVANS (1975) "Erotic stimuli and aggression: facilitation or inhibition?" Journal of Personality and Social Psychology 32: 237-244.

DWORKIN, A. (1981) Pornography: Men Possessing Women. New York: Putnam.

ELLIS, T. (1984) "We need tough laws to limit pervasive filth." U.S.A. Today, May 1: 8A.

GEBHARD, P., J. H. GAGNON, W. B. POMEROY, and V. CHRISTENSON (1967) Sex Offenders: An Analysis of Types. New York: Bantam.

GOLDSTEIN, M. J. (1973) "Exposure to erotic stimuli and sexual deviance." Journal of Social Issues 29: 197-219.

GOLDSTEIN, M. J. and H. S. KANT (1974) "Pornography and social deviance." Berkeley: University of California Press.

KUTCHINSKY, B. (1973) "The effect of easy availability of pornography on the incidence of sex crimes: The Danish experience." Journal of Social Issues 29: 163-181.

LEDERER, L. [ed.] (1980) Take Back the Night: Women on Pornography. New York: William Morrow.

LEYSHON, M. (1981) "Violence in motion pictures: A comparative study." Master's thesis, Ohio State University.

MALAMUTH, N. M. (1983) "Factors associated with rape as predictors of laboratory aggression against women." Journal of Personality and Social Psychology 45: 432-442.

MALAMUTH, N. M. and J.V.P. CHECK (1980) "Penile tumescence and perceptual responses to rape as a function of victim's perceived reactions." Journal of Applied Social Psychology 10: 528-547.

MALAMUTH, N. M. and B. SPINNER (1980) "A longitudinal content analysis of sexual violence in the best-selling erotic magazines." Journal of Sex Research 17: 226-237.

MANN, J., J. SIDMAN, and S. STARR (1973) "Evaluating social consequences of erotic films: An experimental approach." Journal of Social Issues 29: 113-131.

Memoirs v. Massachusetts (1966) 383 U.S. 413.

MEYER, T. (1972) "The effects of sexually arousing and violent films on aggressive behavior." Journal of Sex Research 8: 324-331.

Miller v. California (1973) 413 U.S. 15.
MORGAN, R. (1980) "Theory and practice: Pornography and rape," in L. Lederer (ed.) Take Back the Night: Women on Pornography. New York: William Morrow.
Obscenity Report: The Report to the Task Force on Pornography and Obscenity (1970) New York: Stein & Day.
President's Commission on Obscenity and Pornography (1970) The Report of the Commission on Obscenity and Pornography. New York: Bantam.
SCHWALM, L. A. (1984) "Violent sexual offenses and the availability, distribution, and consumption of erotic materials." Master's thesis, Ohio State University.
SCOTT, J. E. (1986) "An updated longitudinal content analysis of sex references in mass circulation magazines." Journal of Sex Research 22: 16-23.
SCOTT, J. E. and S. J. CUVELIER (1987) "Sexual violence in Playboy magazine: a longitudinal content analysis." Journal of Sex Research 23: 534-539.
SCOTT, J. E. and S. J. CUVELIER (1987) "Violence in *Playboy* Magazine: A longitudinal analysis." Archives of Sexual Behavior 16: 279-288.
SCOTT, J. E. and N. DAVIS (unpublished) "Violence in video tapes."
SCOTT, J. E. and J. L. FRANKLIN (1973) "Sex references in the mass media." Journal of Sex Research 9: 196-209.
SCOTT, J. E. and L. A. SCHWALM (forthcoming) "Rape rates and the circulation rates of adult magazines." Journal of Sex Research.
SHUPE, L. M. (1954) "Alcohol and Crime." Journal of Criminal Law, Criminology and Police Science 44: 661-664.
STRAUS, M. A. and L. BARON (1983) "Sexual stratification, pornography, and rape in American states." Presented at the American Society of Criminology annual meeting, Denver, November 11.
U.S. Department of Justice (1983) Uniform Crime Reports 1982. Washington, DC.
WINICK, C. (1977) "From deviant to normative changes in the social acceptability of sexually explicit material," in E. Sagarin (ed.) Deviance and Social Change. Beverly Hills, CA: Sage.
ZILLMAN, D. and B. S. SAPOLSKY (1977) "What mediates the effects of mild erotica on annoyance and hostile behavior in males?" Journal of Personality and Social Psychology 35: 587-596.

3

Organized Crime
Gangsters and Godfathers

JOHN DOMBRINK

According to authorized biographers of the late organized criminal financial mastermind Meyer Lansky, during interviews with them in Israel, Lansky reminisced about the influence in his early career exerted by noted gambler Arnold Rothstein, the man who fixed the 1919 World Series and was the model for the character Meyer Wolfsheim in *The Great Gatsby* (Fitzgerald, 1925). Rothstein, who was to be killed as a result of a gambling dispute even before the prohibition against alcoholic beverages was repealed in 1932, foresaw financial opportunities for Lansky and his youthful criminal entrepreneur colleagues beyond the limited returns of Prohibition-era bootlegging. Rothstein, his biographer wrote (Katcher, 1958: 351), "led crime into the business era. He had shaped it so it could survive in the new age." Rothstein's advice and planning were more than just the protestations of an Al Capone that he was "just a businessman," filling public demand for prohibited goods and services. Rothstein advised his protégés to adopt some of the rational planning aspects of legitimate business, to grasp the changing character of American society, and to plan carefully for organized crime's role in that society. Copy the methods and style of his business, Rothstein emphasized—departmentalize, diversify, be prudent, but, above all, create a good image (Hammer, 1975: 101).

This emphasis on the value of a good image was captured by the advice on bootlegging Rothstein reportedly gave Lansky. Because

Prohibition was largely an unpopular and unobserved legal reform, the chances for integration into legitimate society were great. According to Lansky, Rothstein laid down an important principle:

> We must maintain a reputation for having only the very best whiskey. In my opinion, we should sell the whiskey as it reaches us—in the original bottles, unadulterated and untouched. This way you'll be reaching a discerning clientele who will come and seek you out for more supplies. You'll be known as reputable merchants, for nobody really considers selling bootleg whiskey illegal or immoral. You'll find that the best customers will come pouring in with their orders, and they'll open their front doors to you as well. This is a very big opportunity for you to make your names—and your fortunes. You'll be introduced to America's most famous men. And a very important consideration is that no stigma will be attached to you as being real criminals, the sort of stigma you would get if you dealt in drugs or prostitution or other rackets. Believe me, it's the right way for you to set out on your careers. You can make a fortune for yourselves and at the same time become very popular with the people who count in this country [Eisenberg et al., 1978: 83-84].

In this story, Lansky pays attention to a notion—that of avoiding being stigmatized as a "real criminal"—that is central to any understanding of the function of organized crime in American society. Unlike the mugger or the burglar, the organized criminal depends on either demand for certain illicit goods or the susceptibility of certain industries to monopolistic control by organized crime-controlled unions or businesses. In 1986, it was estimated that annual organized criminal profits would probably reach $75 billion (President's Commission on Organized Crime, 1986). This fact creates a complicated set of policy prescriptions that must be considered when we evaluate the amount and type of resources we are willing to commit to control this unique form of criminality.

THE AMERICAN PUBLIC
AND ORGANIZED CRIMINALS

Historically, the connections between American citizens and organized crime have been complex, often contradictory, and occasionally cited as a main reason why organized crime has not been eradicated from American society. Citizens can fulfill a number of roles. They can be victims of organized crime, admirers of it, oblivious to it, customers for it, or organized against it. Such ambivalence has contributed to contemporary examples where organized crime is often tolerated, and where apathy is a common response.

The fictional American gangster, the paradoxical embodiment of ruthlessness and socially sanctioned upward mobility, burst into the consciousness of our society in a series of so-called "gangster movies" in the 1920s and 1930s. Even though a ruling by the Motion Picture Association later prescribed the inevitability of death for all movies of the gangster genre, lest they encourage lawbreaking, the popularity of the celluloid gangster was widespread. In the turbulent decades of the 1920s and 1930s in America, the gangster was the quintessential urban character in fiction and film. Like his counterpart the cowboy, he was basically individualistic in a society that demanded conformity to traditions and rules. He was his own man, living by his own code, one that superseded that of legitimate society. Michael Corleone, the fictional Don-in-waiting of *The Godfather* saga, explains this romanticized notion to his wife, when describing the career of his aging father, Vito:

> He doesn't accept rules of the society we live in because those rules would have condemned him to a life not suitable to a man like himself, a man of extraordinary force and character. What you have to understand is that he considers himself the equal of all those great men like Presidents and Prime Ministers and Supreme Court Justices and Governors of the States. He refuses to live by rules set up by others, rules that condemn him to a defeated life.... In the meantime he operates on a code of ethics he considers far superior to the legal structures of society [Puzo, 1969: 365].

As a hero of the Depression years, several film analysts write, the gangster ironically upheld some of our country's most revered myths about individual success (Bergman, 1971; Gabree, 1973; Rosow, 1978). "That only gangsters could make upward mobility believable," Bergman (1971: 7) writes, "tells much about how legitimate institutions had failed—but that mobility was still at the core of what Americans held to be the American dream. Both the bleakness and the determined faith of the early thirties are illuminated."

Some of the early customers of bootleggers were probably essentially law-abiding citizens whose main contact with the nascent organized criminal groups were as customers at a speakeasy, or illegal saloon. Others may have supplemented their meager incomes by participating in home distilling, keeping the fire burning under a home still that produced hundreds of gallons of raw alcohol a week. The "noble experiment," as Prohibition was called, had many unanticipated consequences, as numerous social theorists and legal scholars have observed (Schur, 1965; Kadish, 1967; Skolnick, 1968). Many of these developments have been viewed as the product of the unenforceability of an unpopular law. One of these certainly was the incentive given to otherwise law-abiding working-class citizens to break the law. As Nelli (1976: 147) concludes:

> Members of the working class and particularly those of immigrant background benefited from Prohibition in ways never anticipated by reformers. Someone had to produce and distribute the alcohol, which was still consumed in large volume. Many ethnics were willing to pay the price of possible imprisonment, personal injury, and even death in order to reap the money to be gained from supplying the public—that is, the middle and upper classes—with what it wanted.

These ties between organized criminals and lower-class citizens have extended to current times. Various enterprises have represented these connections while other businesses contain more elements of extortion, and still others monopolistic market control. In a broad sense, this integration of organized crime into legitimate society rested in some of the feeling that "they only kill each other," (Jennings, 1967), and threaten ordinary citizens far less than do common criminals, even most juvenile offenders. Indeed, the contemporary Little Italy section of New York City bears little graffiti and Pileggi (1985: 40) describes how a mobster-controlled neighborhood of Brooklyn is free of muggings, rape, and other common crimes that terrorize similarly situated urban neighborhoods.

SOCIAL SCIENCE AND ORGANIZED CRIME

Social scientists have struggled for decades with the problem of defining organized crime, assessing its impact on society, and determining the structure of individual organized criminal groups. One prominent contributor to a lively debate on such issues has divided the opposing camps into theorists of the "evolutional-centralization" school, and the "developmental-associational" school (Albini, 1971). Those in the former group support the findings of governmental bodies such as the Kefauver Committee (1950-1951) and the President's Commission on Law Enforcement and Administration of Justice (1967), which emphasize the conspiratorial elements of organized criminality. They are brought together by their belief in the intrinsically foreign nature of American organized crime, and the bureaucratic and centralized elements of its continued operations. Kefauver concluded that, behind the individual, locally based crime groups in major American cities lie both a national coordinating body and the international crime presence of the Sicilian Mafia. The 1967 commission, including the consultant paper by Cressey (1969), emphasized the bureaucratic and hierarchical nature of organized criminal groups, and supported the notion of a nationally coordinated syndicate.

In both cases, evolutional-centralization theorists have been accused of uncritically accepting the premises of law enforcement agencies, which have repeatedly asserted the existence of a nationally coordinated organized criminal structure (Albini, 1971). Developmental-associational theorists maintain that the bureaucratic centralized model does not conform to the reality of American organized crime, which they instead portray as indigenous, diffuse, and more a result of failed legal policies—such as Prohibition—than of an international criminal conspiracy. Ianni and Ianni's participant observation study of a Northeastern crime family led to their argument for a greater importance of informal ties and kinship factors in the structuring of criminal groups (Ianni and Ianni, 1972). They argue that some forms of organized crime have been found in American society since the nineteenth century, long before the wave of Italian immigration brought to America a sizable population that were responsive to Mafia-type extortion attempts (Albini, 1971).

Many of those who disagree with the evolutional-centralization school argue, as did Bell (1962), that the Kefauver Committee performed a disservice by equating gamblers with gangsters, thus overstating the extent of serious organized crime in America. W. H. Moore (1974) found parallels between the alien, conspiratorial view of American crime espoused by the Kefauver Committee and the concurrent hearings on Communist influence in American policy circles publicized by the McCarthy Committee. Others, like Reuter (1983: 4-5), contend that the Kefauver findings have been faithfully recited for three decades, even though evidence suggests the dissolution of such a monolithic model. To Reuter, the "Kefauver orthodoxy" emanates from those law enforcement agencies who overstate the lucrativeness and monopolization of illegal gambling in organized crime economies. A more reasonable view, from his perspective, would acknowledge the varying levels of violence, monopoly, profit, and corruptibility found in the diverse enterprises and regional economies of organized crime.

To some observers, one of the most troublesome aspects of attempts to assess and control organized crime in America has been the lack of an effective definition of organized crime. In fact, one governmental review body (General Accounting Office, 1977) criticized federal organized crime law enforcement agencies as being hampered by the lack of an effective definition of organized crime. The primary problem associated with effectively defining such a phenomenon lies with the issue of status offenses. Namely, are organized criminals those who commit certain "organized crimes," or persons who commit, in an organized fashion, crimes that are otherwise ordinary, or members of "organized crime groups" who commit any type of crime? One problem accompanying any such definitional attempt, whether legal or sociological in origin, is that our traditional definitions involve stereotypical elements—black shirts and white ties, talking out of the side of the mouth—from the bootlegging era long since passed. Probably the most highly regarded attempt to date is the second article by Maltz (1976, 1985), which identifies nine crucial components in the definition of organized crime.

Maltz elaborates his definition on the basis that overly broad definitions (organized crime is crime that is organized) and overly narrow definitions (organized crime = Mafia) are equally incomplete. The nine potential elements of a definition of organized crime are found, Maltz explains, in all types of organized crime, emerging groups as well as traditional or Mafia-like groups. They are corruption, violence, sophistication, continuity, structure, discipline, multiple enterprises, involvement in legitimate enterprises, and bonding. Maltz (1985) concludes:

> Corruption, violence, continuity, and involvement in multiple enterprises may be characteristic of essentially all organized crime groups... all have of necessity some structure, but no particular structure

characterizes all possible organized crime groups... most if not all are engaged in legitimate businesses as well as criminal enterprises, but this may not be a necessary characteristic... sophistication, discipline and bonding may be characteristic of some organized crime groups, but are neither necessary nor typical.

The next four sections examine key organized criminal enterprises at length. The four—gambling, drugs, labor racketeering, and legitimate enterprises—are not inclusive of all forms of racketeering, yet represent major forms of organized criminality that provide useful illustrations in the relationship between organized criminals and legitimate society.

GAMBLING

Illegal gambling has often been referred to as the most profitable activity engaged in by organized criminals in this country. Soon after Prohibition, many criminal groups that had amassed great reserves of cash from their bootlegging activities expanded into the gambling area. When Senator Estes Kefauver chaired the Senate Crime Investigating Committee in 1950, he focused upon the activities of illegal gambling across the country as the primary activity of organized criminals (Kefauver, 1951). This view of the importance of gambling has been attacked in recent years, particularly in one lauded study, as the enshrinement of an unchanging view of the lucrative nature of illegal gambling and its monopolistic control by major organized crime groups (Reuter, 1983).

In addition to enforcement limitations imposed by the fact that it is a consensual crime, gambling elicits contradictory responses from the public, a situation that complicates the effective deployment of law enforcement resources toward control of illegal gambling. Despite the fact that many law enforcement agents believe illegal gambling to be controlled by organized crime groups (Meeker and Dombrink, 1986), the public rates illegal gambling in seriousness to such infractions as playing a radio too loud in public, or truancy (Bureau of Justice Statistics, 1983). These findings corroborate the results of surveys taken in "Wincanton" by John Gardiner (1970) as part of his study of politics and corruption in that Eastern city. While the citizens of Wincanton were generally not in favor of devoting extensive resources to control of illegal gambling—viewing it as a tolerable vice—they were definitely concerned over potential corruption in the city, even where that malfeasance was the result of their tolerable illegal gambling enterprises.

Most illegal gambling in this country revolves around a limited number of games—numbers or illegal lotteries and bookmaking, involving sporting events and racing. Illegal casino games are relatively unpopular. While estimates of the aggregate amount of revenues derived from these games are understandably sketchy, the return rate for the games is not. Numbers, like lotteries, retain the highest, while bookmaking on single sporting events retains far less. Thus, while there are many more illegal dollars *bet* in bookmaking, the *revenues* are considerably less. It appears that legal gambling, for various reasons, has not competed especially well with the illegal variant. For reasons of convenience, credits, odds, or ambiance, illegal gamblers have stayed with their illicit purveyors, contributing to a side-by-side system of legal and illegal gambling of combined vitality.

Legal gambling provides unique problems for government regulators and opportunities for organized criminals. While fraud plagued the nineteenth-century American lottery and led to the dismantling of the popular Louisiana lottery, recent lotteries have been relatively scandal-free (Thompson and Dombrink, 1985). Horse racing has been more vulnerable to drugging and race-rigging schemes, and charitable gambling and bingo on Indian reservations have raised suspicions about some of their operators. However, the form of legal gambling most susceptible to organized criminal involvement has historically been legal casino gambling. When Las Vegas grew from a dusty town to a gambling resort in the late 1940s, one of Meyer Lansky's associates gave this account to Lansky's authorized biographers:

> Differences were ironed out peaceably in those early days in Vegas. For instance, when they were building the Stardust Hotel, which was the largest one then, Dalitz complained that it would give too much competition to his Desert Inn. The man behind the Stardust was Antonio Stralla, or as we called him, Tony Cornero, an old bootlegging friend. It looked like an old-fashioned war might break out, but Meyer suggested a meeting and we all flew in for it. I was there with Dalitz,

and his right-hand man, Kleinman, was there, and Longie Zwillman, and so forth. We worked out a deal that gave each group an interlocking interest in each other's hotels, and our lawyers set it up so that nobody could really tell who owned what out there [Eisenberg et al., 1978: 266-267].

For two decades, until corporate gaming and Howard Hughes brought a measure of respectability to Las Vegas gambling in the late 1960s, Nevada officials resisted federal government intimations that their state's primary industry was crime-ridden (Skolnick, 1978). The growth of legal gambling stock vitality in Wall Street in the late 1970s suggested that the strong association between organized crime and legal gambling may have been severed for good. However, a series of convictions in major organized crime cases involving mobster interests in Las Vegas casinos have blemished the road to respectability. In Atlantic City, ownership problems have been minimal, but organized crime infiltration of key peripheral services and industries, extending to the conviction for corruption of Atlantic City's mayor, have marred the success story of that revived resort's first decade with legal casinos. On the whole, legal gambling is not organized crime-infested, but serious invasions by important criminal groups indicate that the influence of organized criminal groups continues unabated.

DRUGS

Probably no single issue represents the frustrations of law enforcement in the organized crime area and simultaneously depicts the profitability of illegal trafficking in prohibited goods as does the business of illegal drugs. Social science and legal literature is rich with arguments that prohibition policies of government in the alcohol, drug, and gambling areas have been criminogenic, and the greatest contributor to the growth of criminal groups in American society (Geis, 1972; Schur, 1965; Skolnick, 1968). Of these three vices, illegal drug trafficking has grown to be the largest and most profitable organized criminal enterprise. Estimates of total revenues for illegal heroin trafficking in 1982 was $8 billion, with $11 billion for cocaine trafficking. Different drugs have historically taken different patterns of importation, distribution, and use. A Drug

Enforcement Administration official estimates that 49% of heroin in the U.S. market comes from Southwest Asia, 34% from Mexico, and 17% from Southeast Asia. While heroin and cocaine are produced predominantly outside the country, marijuana has significant internal production. Of the three, marijuana is the most legitimized in our society, with its use decriminalized in several states, and produced by groups with, historically, the lowest association with violence.

Heroin has for the longest time been viewed as an integral enterprise of traditional organized crime groups, despite protestations that narcotics trafficking was to be avoided, whereas the cocaine business has been operated by Cubans, and later Colombian "cocaine cowboys." Heroin has proven to be more hierarchically controlled, with careful attention to shielding important members of the organization from risk of detection and prosecution, and tributes paid to traditional crime families by leading heroin dealers, many of them Black New Yorkers, serving the large Black and Hispanic New York City heroin user community, which accounts for a large portion of the nation's estimated 500,000 users. Recently uncovered heroin importation by Sicilian Mafia members has resulted in prosecutions of members of the "Pizza Connection," so-called because they distributed heroin through pizza parlors.

Cocaine importation appears more diffuse, but both drugs share common features—their immense profitability and low levels of federal interception; "interdiction" of imported drugs rarely exceeds the 15% level. Given the enormous profitability of the drug business, such a low level of interception poses few disincentives for traffickers. Arguing that public policy choices in this area are not always without costs, Kleiman (1985) warns that the devotion of increased law enforcement resources toward marijuana control may prompt violence by traffickers, and increase the "reputational capital" of a group not known for its use of violence. Since even successful law enforcement efforts often nab only the drug couriers, or "mules," little disruption is inflicted on the ongoing criminal organizations. Federal authorities have recently sought to offset this situation by the aggressive use of civil and criminal forfeiture statutes, which attain for the government assets (money) that can be used for productive pursuits, instead of only contraband that must be destroyed.

Those who seek effective strategies against illegal drug use and trafficking can be separated into advocates of supply-side strategies— at the interdiction and high-level distribution level—and those who argue for enhanced attacks on the demand side. The latter group has supported the widespread adoption of drug-testing by private and public employers, a controversial policy, the recommendation of which has recently split the President's Commission on Organized Crime and generated vociferous outcries of "Big Brother"-type intervention into private habits and personal lifestyles. Continuing debates must naturally address these issues, and the extent of intrusion into personal privacy we are willing to accept in order to limit illegal drug use.

LABOR RACKETEERING

The recently completed President's Commission on Organized Crime identified four major ways in which organized crime uses unions. First, it converts union financial resources to its own use. Second, it uses unions to extort payoffs from businesses in the form of sweetheart contracts or strike insurance. Third, organized crime groups can use unions as a means of access to or protection from politicians and governmental processes. Finally, it uses unions as a way to influence an entire market, perhaps in the process utilizing sweetheart contracts or strike insurance.

While there are some contemporary organized crime schemes that utilize newly developed financial mechanisms, all of the current forms of labor racketeering are similar to rackets identified by the McClellan Committee nearly 30 years ago. Probably the single largest opportunity in the years since McClellan's hearings has been the increase in labor pension, health, and welfare trust funds. The leaders of the nation's largest union, the International Brotherhood of Teamsters, have long been suspected of being partners with organized crime (Brill, 1978). The President's Commission on Organized Crime went further, stating that national Teamster leaders "have been firmly under the influence of organized crime since the 1950s" (President's Commission on Organized Crime, 1985: 89). Recently, in testimony during a court case involving loans from the Teamster's Central States Pension Fund, former Teamster president Roy L. Williams—convicted on charges of conspiring to bribe a U.S. Senator—detailed how he acted at the behest of organized criminals during his tenure as president. Williams was one of a long line of

Teamster presidents—including James R. Hoffa—whose election was ensured when it was determined that he would be responsive to criminal organizations. It was not only at the national level that criminal groups exerted influence over the teamsters. In several key locals, organized criminal power was so strong as to constitute "capture," as in the case of Teamster Local 560 in Northern New Jersey. There a federal judge, under the innovative federal civil RICO statute, ordered all members of the Local 560's executive board removed and put the local into trusteeship. In New York, Ohio, Michigan, and elsewhere, the collusion between Teamsters officials and organized criminals has been substantial, and often intertwined with manipulation of the lucrative Teamster Pension and Health and Welfare Funds. Orchestrated by Hoffa, overseen by the late Allen Dorfman—victim of an unsolved murder when he appeared headed for prison in the bribery conspiracy case—the Pension Fund was used to funnel loans to criminal associates of the Teamsters. Blakey and Goldstock (1980: 343) explain the use of such loans:

> These illicit loans are of two types. First are those intended primarily as income for the racketeers. Sometimes these loans constitute simple embezzlement, circuitous ways of distributing spending money to fund insiders. The borrower functions as a 'bag-man,' and the loan is never repaid. More commonly, the borrower is solvent and well-intentioned, but the racketeer exacts a commission, or kickback, for arranging the deal. The second type of loan is designed primarily to underwrite the speculations of the borrower. While the fund racketeer may demand a kickback, the transaction is better understood as a contribution to capital, or even as a gift. Favored insiders, moreover, tend to have little difficulty in securing the desired loan.

After continued Labor Department litigation, the fund, which totalled over $1 billion in assets, was forced to alter its investment procedures and maintain serious financial accountability mechanisms.

Labor-management collusion, represented by the sweetheart contract, is pervasive in the construction and trucking industries in particular, but has common characteristics wherever it is found. The central feature is the low price of labor. "In return for a payoff to a corrupt union official," the President's Commission on Organized Crime (1985: 16) elaborated, "the employer can use fewer workers, pay them less, and assign and discharge them at will." Another strategy, also presented by the president's commission from testimony by the convicted former president of a security guard union, is used to keep legitimate unions from organizing in the affected workplace. The crucial element in the scheme was a "desk drawer contract," which resulted in kickbacks for the corrupt union official. As the convicted unionist explained (President's Commission on Organized Crime, 1985: 17):

> An umbrella or desk drawer contract is a contract that the employer of a particular company would call the union and say that he would like to place his people under a union, and he would like a favorable contract. And generally a contract would be drawn in most cases with the terms that the employer wants. And it would never be implemented. It would just sit in a file or drawer somewhere until such time as the employees would either look for a union to represent them or some union would come around and start organizing, and at that time the employer would pull out this contract and say, 'I'm already represented by a union.' And, in effect, it would be a bar from the union coming in to organize them because the people are already represented. So, in effect, an employer could pick up considerable amount of time without having to pay any union benefits and yet still be covered by a contract.

The third form of labor racketeering, strike insurance, is a form of extortion by which corrupt labor officials receive funds from management in return for the guarantee of labor peace. Particularly vulnerable to such demands are industries that can be damaged economically by delay tactics. Blakey and Goldstock (1980: 344-345) note that longshoreman unions and unions servicing meat retailers, the building trades, the garment trades (Leitcher, 1982), and the trucking industry most commonly engage in such practices. The prosecution of International Longshoremen Association Local 1814 president Anthony Scotto exposed widespread patterns of kickbacks, which flourished both in the physically constrained, historically corrupt New York harbor and, more recently, on South Florida docks. Scotto, a politically influential labor leader, had the benefit of character witnesses like the governor of New York and leading New York City journalists. To the president's commission (1985: 29), Scotto represented a "triple-threat racketeer"—someone who is a member of organized crime, an important business consultant or union leader, and a political kingmaker. In the commission's words,

"Scotto had cultivated political and charitable contacts which added to his aura of legitimacy and further increased his influence" (1985: 29). Thus the seemingly legitimate union, free to make public contacts to politicians and government officials, can simultaneously serve the needs of organized crime and enhance the respectability of the union.

Finally, as Blakey and Goldstock explain (1980: 345), a labor racketeer who uses illicit practices in legitimate enterprises—including the misuse of union power—enjoys several competitive advantages. Monopoly is a goal which can be accomplished through strategic use of sweetheart contracts and strike threats. Certain industries are particularly vulnerable to market corruption if, like the garbage industry, strike threats can create havoc for employers.

LEGITIMATE ENTERPRISES

Social scientists have differed in their interpretation of the dangers of organized criminal involvement in legitimate business. Some have proposed that violations of regulations and illegal operations in businesses owned or controlled by organized criminal groups or individuals might not be that much more likely than in legitimate businesses. The traditional law enforcement view, as presented in the 1967 president's commission report (President's Commission on Law Enforcement and Administration of Justice, 1967: 1) holds that organized criminal activity in legitimate activity tends to be aggressive and directed toward extracting extraordinary profits through illegal methods. Another view (Ianni and Ianni, 1972; Anderson, 1979:) is that increasing investment in legitimate business is essentially an effort to achieve respectability.

Anderson suggests, from a study of one traditional organized crime family, that involvement in legitimate businesses can serve several functions. First, it can provide establishment of a tax cover. Second, it can support illegal market enterprises. Next, it can assist in provision of services to members of the group. It can also contribute to diversification of the group's investments. Finally, the possibility of profits, whether sizable per se or enhanced by illegal or violent methods, exerts its own attraction (Anderson, 1979: 103-115).

Some of the investments of organized criminal assets in the

legitimate economy can increase profitability and legitimacy without any hint of illegality, save tax evasion. In many instances, it was the lead of Lansky, applying the advice of Rothstein, which prompted international currency movement, the use of offshore banks and corporations, and various laundering techniques. These methods represent a sophistication in financial matters that is certainly at odds with our stereotypical view of the crude and violent gangster.

However, areas of legitimate enterprise which utilize competitive advantages reaped through labor racketeering or extraordinary methods compel our attention, as they have attracted the scrutiny of federal prosecutors in recent months.

One noteworthy area of organized criminal activity in the New York City area has been in the construction industry, where bid-rigging and skimming have proved particularly profitable. There, it was estimated by the President's Commission on Organized Crime (1985: 232) that the gross "skim" revenue from 1981 through 1984 for New York's crime families from their control of the poured concrete business in the Manhattan building construction industry could be as high as $3.5 million. When one considers the other boroughs of New York City, and surrounding areas, and the other forms of construction beyond poured concrete, that figure could be much higher.

The poured concrete cartel, according to federal prosecutors, was conducted by representatives of New York's crime families. They operated this joint venture, the President's Commission on Organized Crime explains (1985: 228):

> By establishing a 'club' of contractors who poured concrete, allocated concrete-pouring contracts with a value exceeding two million dollars, controlled recalcitrant contractors by threatening labor and cement supply problems, and received payoffs from participating concrete contractors.

In other industries, such as the meat business, organized crime control of labor unions provides an opportunity to affect industry practices, and direct business to corporations either owned directly by their members, or influenced by their leadership.

ORGANIZED CRIME AND THE LEGAL SYSTEM: FROM ATTRITION STRATEGY TO AN ENTERPRISE FOCUS

At a conference on organized crime sponsored in 1979 by the University of Southern California, one respected career prosecutor observed in a speech that successful law enforcement efforts against organized criminals needed to be committed to a long struggle in the same manner that organized crime groups are structurally designed to ensure longevity, profitability, and avoidance of sanctioning by the criminal justice system (De Feo, 1979). Current successful efforts against well-entrenched crime families in major American cities ("The Thermonuclear Statute," *Time*, April 14, 1986) offer proof that complex and lengthy investigations against criminal groups can eventually lead to significant structural damage (Wilson, 1978). Goldstock's observation (while participating in a television panel on *The David Susskind Show*, April 26, 1986) that the "Peter Principle" of organizational incompetence and a loosening of discipline have come to characterize the contemporary American traditional organized crime groups portends an interesting decade ahead in organized crime control. Indeed, later in 1987, the federal government convicted four leaders of New York's five crime families as part of a conspiracy, an unprecedented prosecution that is representative of the recent successes against traditional organized crime (Giuliani, 1986). However, such newfound success does not characterize the history of law enforcement inroads against organized crime in America, and may not predict future success against more disciplined Asian gangs and other "emerging" organized crime groups (President's Commission on Organized Crime, 1985).

Essentially, the history of recent American law enforcement incursions against organized crime has not been a stellar one. For various reasons, criminal groups have proved particularly resistant to the effective use of legal sanctions against them. There are several reasons for this. The most well known, in a popular sense, has been the repeated use of intimidation, violence, and often murder against prospective witnesses. A representative example in recent years comes from the New York City trial of the reported head of one of that city's largest and most powerful organized crime families. In that trial, two earlier disappearances of witnesses and coedefendants was followed by a failure of memory by the victim of an assault charged against

John Gotti and another man ("Mr. Giotti's Day in Court," *New York Times*, April 13, 1986). Later, one of the codefendants was killed when a car bomb ignited. Such incidents, which are not uncommon in law enforcement files, support a theme in the history of organized crime, which Hobsbawm and Hess note in seminal essays on Sicilian mafioso (Hobsbawm, 1965; Hess, 1973). Unlike the bandit, or common criminal, the mafioso, when he commits his first major crime, does not flee to the mountains or another hideaway. Rather, it is the mafioso's ability to withstand scrutiny from the legal system, and emerge unconvicted after criminal prosecution, that differentiate him from the common criminal. Once he is seen as victorious in the legal setting, the mafioso's reputation increases, and persons with problems to solve or disputes to settle seek him out.

In our society, the sporadic successes and limited impact of governmental attacks on organized crime are also due to the secretive nature of most organized crime, the unwillingness of victims of commercial extortion to testify in court or otherwise provide information to authorities, the consensual nature of some forms of vice operated by organized criminals, the careful use of telephones and written documents, and general suspicion toward suspected informants or undercover government agents. What successes government prosecutors enjoyed against organized criminals from the days of Prohibition to the 1970s had been tempered by their acknowledgment that convicted criminals were either low-level operatives, or easily replaced, or, in the rare instance of a major crime family executive, able to conduct business from within prison.

The frustration that accompanies the prosecution of replaceable members of organized crime groups was identified by a high-ranking Justice Department official in the Carter Administration as an impetus which led to the deployment of an "enterprise strategy: "We have learned that the incarceration of individual criminals, even those of the highest rank, is generally not sufficient to immobilize or even to reduce the incentive of entrenched criminal organizations. As long as immense criminal profits remain available as operating capital, a convicted criminal's compatriots will be able to keep the organization functioning, and the prisoner himself may be able to resume business upon or even before his release" (Governmental Affairs Committee, 1979). This strategy, dependent upon lengthy and complex investigations, relies upon the unique statutory provisions of both the criminal and civil portions of the Racketeer Influenced and Corrupt Organizations statute (RICO), passed as part of the Organized Crime Control Act of 1970.

RICO has been described as potentially the broadest statute Congress has passed to combat the effects of organized crime. Prior to the enactment of RICO, federal prosecution of organized crime's use of a pattern of criminal acts was restricted to federal statutes of generally narrow applicability. In designing RICO, the Senate Judiciary Committee announced its purpose as "the elimination of the infiltration of organized crime and racketeering into legitimate organizations operating in interstate commerce... by the fashioning of new criminal and civil remedies and investigative procedures" (Committee on the Judiciary, 1969: 76).

RICO incorporates by reference more than two dozen federal and state crimes under the umbrella concept of "racketeering activity." The statute provides that anyone found to have committed two of these incorporated offenses within a 10-year period has undertaken a pattern of racketeering. RICO specifically makes unlawful four activities by any person:

1. using income derived from a pattern of racketeering activity to acquire an interest in an enterprise (18 USC § 1962 (a))
2. acquiring or maintaining an interest in an enterprise through a pattern of racketeering activity (18 USC § 1962 (b))
3. conducting the affairs of an enterprise through a pattern of racketeering activity (18 USC § 1962 (c))
4. conspiring to commit any one of these offenses (18 USC § 1962 (d))

In the words of a former assistant attorney general, "RICO's concept of a racketeering 'enterprise,' to which heavy penalties are attached, begins to address the central problems of organized crime—that an 'enterprise' gives the continuity needed to conduct and maintain the activities on which organized crime depends" (Heymann, 1980: 2). Currently, the use of RICO's civil sanctions in "garden variety" commercial fraud cases has generated arguments for amendments to the RICO statute. While the use of criminal RICO has been circumscribed (Meeker and Dombrink, 1984), potential for its abuse is present.

In 1981, a General Accounting Office study followed up a 1979 report on the effectiveness of Justice Department Organized Crime Strike Force prosecutors in securing convictions and lengthy incarceration for significant organized criminals. In the 1981 report, note was taken that RICO and its drug counterpart, the Continuing Criminal Enterprise statute, had contributed to an increase in average sentences imposed upon convicted organized criminals. This development, hoped for by drafters of the enhanced sentencing provisions of RICO, offset criticisms derived from the prior report, which found a majority of sentences in federal organized crime cases to impose either probation or imprisonment of two years or less.

In addition to increased criminal penalties, another recent development in the area of sanctions against organized criminals, that of criminal and civil forfeiture, is attracting attention, and should become among the most important legal developments in the organized crime field over the next decade. Criminal forfeiture provisions have been possible, if underutilized, in RICO and CCE prosecutions since those statutes' inception. Civil forfeiture actions, primarily against drug traffickers, have netted the federal government hundreds of millions of dollars in recent years. Recent changes in the law allow local police who contribute to eventual arrests and seizures to receive portions of the seized assets, hopefully furthering the often elusive goal of interagency and interjurisdictional cooperation in organized crime control. Appellate courts have generally upheld key provisions of recent statutes, promulgating innovative law enforcement responses in this area, and Congressional and judicial actions in the next decade should bear out the constitutionality of a group of aggressive statutes in organized crime control.

CONCLUSION

Some important forms of organized crime have been omitted from lengthy discussion in these pages. Unlawful toxic waste disposal has become an issue of great urgency, and important research on organized criminal involvement in it (Block and Scarpitti, 1985) has indicated the limits of legal sanctions in effecting compliance with public health and welfare demands of society. Traditional crimes like loansharking, prostitution, and pornography continue to supply significant profits to various organized crime groups. The four types of criminal involvement detailed above, however, represent the type of problems society faces in eradicating or controlling contemporary, sophisticated, and multifaceted organized crime. All four pose substantial strategic problems, even with the advent of strengthened federal and state statutes. All four depend upon some combination of public demand or indifference, or private sector acquiescence. To more than one observer, organized crime's unique position in American society has been that of tolerated crime. To fail to understand the extent to which organized crime in America has penetrated the legitimate social structure means to underestimate how much more difficult uprooting organized crime is in the 1980s than it might have been 20, 40, or 60 years ago.

REFERENCES

ALBINI, J. L. (1971) The American Mafia: Genesis of a Legend. New York: Appleton-Century-Crofts.
ANDERSON, A. G. (1979) The Business of Organized Crime. Stanford: Stanford University Press.
BELL, D. (1962) "Crime as an American way of life," in D. Bell (ed.) The End of Ideology. New York: Collier.
BERGMAN, A. (1971) "The gangsters," in A. Bergman (ed.) We're in the Money: Depression America and Its Films. New York: Harper Colophon.
BLAKEY, G. R. AND R. L. GOLDSTOCK (1980) "'On the Waterfront': RICO and labor racketeering." American Criminal Law Review 17: 341.
BLOCK, A. A. and F. R. SCARPITTI (1985) Poisoning for Profit: The Mafia and Toxic Waste in America. New York: William Morrow.
BRILL, S. (1978) The Teamsters. New York: Simon & Schuster.
Bureau of Justice Statistics (1983) Report to the Nation on Crime and Justice.
Committee on the Judiciary (1969) United States Senate, Organized Crime Control Act of 1969.
CRESSEY, D. R. (1969) Theft of the Nation: The Structure and Operations of Organized Crime in America. New York: Harper Colophon.
De FEO, M. (1979) Presentation at University of Southern California National Conference on Organized Crime, Los Angeles.
EISENBERG, D., U. DAN, and E. LANDAU (1978) Meyer Lansky: Mogul of the Mob. New York: Paddington.
FITZGERALD, F. S. (1925) The Great Gatsby. New York: Grosset & Dunlap.
GABREE, J. (1973) Gangsters: From Little Caesar to the Godfather. New York: Pyramid.
GARDINER, J. A. (1970) The Politics of Corruption: Organized Crime in an American City. New York: Russell Sage Foundation.
GEIS, G. (1972) Not the Law's Business? An Examination of Homosexuality, Abortion, Prostitution, Narcotics and Gambling in the United States. Washington, DC: Government Printing Office.

General Accounting Office (1977) "War on organized crime faltering: federal strike forces not getting the job done." Washington, DC, March 17.
General Accounting Office (1981) "Stronger federal effort needed on fight against organized crime." Washington, DC, December 7.
GIULIANI, R. (1986) United States Attorney, Southern District of New York. Interview, March.
GOLDSTOCK, R. L. (1986) Television panel participation on David Susskind Show, April 26.
Government Affairs Committee (1979) "United States Senate: illegal narcotics profits." Hearings before the Permanent Subcommittee on Investigations. 96th Congress, 1st Session.
HAMMER, R. (1975) Gangland U.S.A.: The Marketing of the Mob. Chicago: Playboy.
HESS, H. (1973) Mafia and Mafiosi: The Structure of Power. Lexington, MA: D.C. Heath.
HEYMANN, P. (1980) "Criminal division focuses on organized crime's vulnerability." Justice Assistance News, November.
HOBSBAWM, E. (1965) Primitive Rebels: Studies in Archaic Forms of Social Movement in the 19th and 20th Centuries. New York: W.W. Norton.
IANNI, F. and E. R. IANNI (1972) A Family Business: Kinship and Control in Organized Crime. New York: Russell Sage Foundation.
JENNINGS, D. (1967) We Only Kill Each Other: The Life and Bad Times of Bugsy Siegel. Greenwich, CT: Fawcett Crest.
KADISH, S. (1967) "The crisis of overcriminalization." Annals of the American Academy of Political and Social Science 157: 374.
KATCHER, L. (1958) The Big Bankroll: The Life and Times of Arnold Rothstein. New York: Harper & Brothers.
KEFAUVER, E. (1951) Crime in America. Garden City, NY: Doubleday.
KLEIMAN, M. (1985) "Drug enforcement and organized crime," in H. E. Alexander and G. E. Caiden (eds.) The Politics and Economics of Organized Crime. Lexington, MA: Lexington.
LANDESCO, J. (1929) Organized Crime in Chicago. Chicago: University of Chicago Press.
LEICHTER, F. S. (1982) "Sweatshops to shakedowns: organized crime in New York's garment industry." Albany: New York State Senate.
MALTZ, M. D. (1976) "On defining 'organized crime': the development of a definition and a typology." Crime and Delinquency 26, 3.
MALTZ, M. D. (1985) "Toward defining organized crime," in H. E. Alexander and G. E. Caiden (eds.) The Politics and Economics of Organized Crime. Lexington, MA: Lexington.
MEEKER, J. W. and J. DOMBRINK (1984) "Criminal RICO and organized crime: an analysis of appellate litigation." Criminal Law Bulletin 20, 4.
MEEKER, J. W. and J. DOMBRINK (1986) "Gambling and organized crime: further complexities." (unpublished)
MOORE, M. H. (1977) Buy and Bust. Lexington, MA: Lexington.
MOORE, W. H. (1974) The Kefauver Committee and the Politics of Crime, 1950-1952. Columbia: University of Missouri Press.
NELLI, H. S. (1976) The Business of Crime: Italians and Syndicate Crime in the United Stated. New York: Oxford University Press.

PILEGGI, N. (1985) Wise Guy. New York: Simon & Schuster.
President's Commission on Law Enforcement and Administration of Justice (1967) The Challenge of Crime in a Free Society. Task Force Report: Organized Crime. Washington, DC.
President's Commission on Organized Crime (1984) Organized Crime of Asian Origin. Record of Hearing III. Washington, DC, October.
President's Commission on Organized Crime (1985) The Edge: Organized Crime, Business and Labor Unions. Washington, DC, April.
President's Commission on Organized Crime (1986) Final Report. Washington, DC, April.
PUZO, M. (1969) The Godfather. New York: Putnam's.
REUTER, P. (1983) Disorganized Crime: The Economics of the Visible Hand. Cambridge: MIT Press.
ROSOW, E. (1978) Born to Lose: The Gangster Film in America. New York: Oxford University Press.
SCHUR, E. (1965) Crimes Without Victims. Englewood Cliffs, NJ: Prentice-Hall.
SKOLNICK, J. H. (1968) "Coercion to virtue: the enforcement of morals." Southern California Law Review 41: 588.
SKOLNICK, J. H. (1978) House of Cards: Legalization and Control of Casino Gambling. Boston: Little, Brown.
SMITH, D. C. and R. SALERNO (1970) "The use of strategies in organized crime control." Journal of Criminal Law, Criminology and Police Science 61, 1.
THOMPSON, W. N. and J. DOMBRINK (1985) "Riding the third wave: legal and illegal gambling policy." Prepared for the President's Commission on Organized Crime.
WILSON, J. Q. (1978) The Investigators: Managing FBI and Narcotics Agents. New York: Basic Books.

PART II
Controversial Issues in Policing

4

Police Shooting
Environment and License

JAMES J. FYFE

STUDYING THE POLICE

The 1960s are generally regarded as a turning point in the history of the United States. During that decade, the civil rights movement was at its peak, disorder erupted in many cities, antigovernment demonstrations became almost routine, crime rates rose dramatically, and Americans learned that attempts upon the lives of political leaders were not a phenomenon that occurred exclusively beyond our borders.

Until that period, debate and study of police issues were generally confined to members of that occupation and to a few local government officials and academicians. Because the police were so intimately involved with the social events and movements of the 1960s, however, they became the subjects of more widespread interest, debate, and study. Several presidential commissions studied crime, violence, criminal justice, and the police, and two of the three candidates for president in 1968 ran on platforms that promised returns to "law and order." The Congress appropriated unprecedented amounts of money to study and improve the criminal justice system, and encouraged scholars not previously associated with research in crime and justice to expend their energies there. So, too, did the Ford Foundation, which, in 1970, established the Police Foundation with a $30 million endowment and a mandate to improve the quality of policing.

Not surprisingly, these efforts have been criticized by people who point out that crime rates are presently higher than they were before these increased expenditures, and that most of the research has told us little about what programs are actually effective in reducing crime. Such arguments, however, overlook the naïveté of many of the assumptions upon which these various wars on crime were based. Often, the assumptions were simplistic, and treated "crime" as a univariate problem with a single cause and a single cure. If nothing else, the studies of the last 20 years—often conducted by researchers who began their work as naively as did those who encouraged it—have been valuable because they have shown that crime and the formulation of policies and practices to address it are far more complex than was originally thought.

Critics of recent programs and research also overlook the question of whether crime rates would be higher still without the efforts of the last 20 years. There is reason to believe that they would be. The research may not have produced a magic pill for crime, but it has demonstrated that many of the practices previously thought to be useful were ineffective or even counterproductive. As a consequence, we have stopped pouring resources into expansion of those practices, and have begun attempts to find and employ more effective means of using criminal justice resources.

Where the police are concerned, we have learned that the practice of assigning uniformed officers in marked radio cars to random "preventive patrol" apparently has little effect on rates of reported crime, victimization, or upon citizens' perceptions of police presence or safety on the streets (Kelling et al., 1974). As a result, police agencies have devised new means of deploying officers, such as "directed patrol," in which they are assigned to be present at the places and times at which analyses have identified problems amenable to police presence. We have also learned that assigning detectives to conduct investigations of all reported crimes is apparently counterproductive. That is so because many crimes (e.g., burglaries and thefts of easily disposable items that cannot be readily identified) are almost never solvable, and because requiring detectives to go through the motions of investigating these case diverts their energies from working on more promising cases (Greenwood and Petersilia, 1975).

Further, much of the most valuable research has not dealt directly with police crime-fighting techniques, but has instead been directed at development of fairer and more humane policies and practices.

Several studies (e.g., President's Commission on Law Enforcement and Administration of Justice, 1967) pointed out that police were often regarded by inner-city residents as an almost lily-white, all male "occupying army," the members of which had little understanding of the cultures or problems of the poor and minorities, sometimes acted in ill-considered manners that precipitated violence, and consequently received little cooperation from the people who most needed them. Since that time (and with encouragement from equal employment opportunity litigation and legislation), police have generally attempted to recruit minority officers, to sensitize all officers to the pressures and cultures of ghetto life, and to reassess their most abrasive policies and practices. If the comparative absence of urban riots and the more humane police responses to those that did occur over the last decade and a half are a fair indication, this research and the official responses to it have been quite effective.

Thus much of the study that followed the turmoil of the 1960s has had the effect of breaking down some of the parochialism and previously untested assumptions that formerly characterized American policing, and has helped to make police agencies more representative of and sensitive to the populations they serve. It has led to the beginnings of a scientifically based body of literature on policing, to dissemination of information that has enabled police agencies to benefit from the advances and mistakes of their colleagues in other jurisdictions, and to efforts to develop some degree of uniformity across America's 17,000 police agencies.

POLICE SHOOTINGS

An important part of the newly developing literature concerns police shootings of citizens. Prior to the 1960s, there existed little systematic information about police use of firearms,[1] and few questions were asked when citizens were shot by police. When presidential commissions reported that several of the riots of the period were immediately precipitated by police shootings (President's Commission, 1967: 189), however, questions were raised in many quarters, and there ensued a considerable amount of study of this most critical police power. It is not likely that any of this work has had direct effects on crime rates (except, perhaps, in helping police to avoid disorders like those that followed so many shootings of the 1960s), but it has probably helped police to do their jobs with less loss of life and with no less effectiveness. This article surveys some of the lessons and effects of that research.

Police Shooting Frequencies

Despite the shortcomings of available data,[2] the research suggests that, at least in the larger jurisdictions, police shootings have declined over the past several years. It has also shown that rates of police shootings vary significantly across American jurisdictions. Table 4.1 presents data on fatal police shootings from two separate studies. The table shows that, with some notable exceptions (e.g., Dallas, Los Angeles), rates of shooting per 100 officers and per 100,000 population have decreased in the 10 largest American cities during the last decade. Despite this general trend, the table shows also that police in some cities are far more likely to shoot and kill people than are their colleagues in other cities, and that citizens in some cities run far greater risk of death by police shooting than is true in other places.

During the early period included on the table, Detroit police officers were nearly two and a half times as likely to kill as Chicago police officers (rates = 0.40 and 0.17, respectively), while during 1983, they were about three times as likely to kill as Chicago officers (rates = 0.37 and 0.12). Similarly, in both periods, the Detroit police shootings per 100,000 population (1.63 and 1.08) were far higher than were the Chicago rates (0.74 and 0.50).

Explanations of Shooting Rate Variation

Environment. Several explanations of variations like these have been offered. Kania and Mackey (1977), who analyzed National Center for Health Statistics (NCHS) data on fatal police shootings across the 50 states, report that rates of "death by legal intervention of the police"[3] are closely associated with rates of "police exposure to threats and stress" (e.g., reported violent crime) and "rates of public violence" (e.g., public homicide rates). While the validity of their findings has been placed into question by subsequent findings that

TABLE 4.1
Annual Rates of Fatal Police Shootings in 10 American Cities

City	Rate per 100 officers		Rate per 100,000 population	
	1975-1979[a]	1/1-12/3 1983[b]	1975-1979[a]	1/1-12/3 1983[b]
New York	0.14	0.08	0.48	0.27
Chicago	0.17	0.12	0.74	0.50
Los Angeles	0.35	0.41	0.89	0.94
Philadelphia	0.21	0.06	0.94	0.25
Houston	0.58	0.43	1.10	1.01
Detroit	0.40	0.37	1.63	1.08
Dallas	0.35	0.78	0.83	1.78
San Diego	0.33	0.16	0.48	0.24
Phoenix	0.22	0.06	0.52	0.13
Baltimore	0.26	0.08	1.06	0.27
Means	0.28	0.18	0.66	0.52

a. Mean Annual Rate, 1975-1979. Source: Matulia, K. (1982: 80-81).
b. Standardized Annual Rate calculated from data for January 1 to December 3, 1983. Source: K. Merida and L. Samuels, "Dallas Third in Police Slayings," *Dallas Morning Herald,* December 11, 1983: 1, 22.

the NCHS data they analyzed are extremely inaccurate,[4] the general thrust of Kania and Mackey's work—that police who work in the most violent places are most likely to shoot others—is both intuitively and empirically sound. Fyfe (1980), for example, reports close associations among police shooting rates and rates of public homicide ($r = +.78$) and arrests for violent crime ($r = +.62$) across the geographic subdivisions of the New York City Police Department. In Chicago, Geller and Karales (1981: 160) report a strong association ($r = +.64$) between quarterly frequencies of police shootings and arrests for forcible felonies during 1974-1980. In both these places, then, there were found strong geographic and temporal associations between police exposure to community violence and police shooting.

Despite the findings of Fyfe, and Geller and Karales, it is clear that variations in external police working environments do not account for all—or even most—of the variations in shooting rates shown in Table 4.1. It would be difficult to argue that the general downward trend of police shootings is accounted for by diminished levels of violence and threats around the country. It is also unlikely that Detroit police officers are three times as likely as Chicago officers to shoot and kill people because they work in an environment three times as violent and threatening as that of Chicago officers. Further, no measures of public violence or threats to officers would support the hypothesis that the great decreases in Philadelphia police shooting rates between 1979 and 1983 (from 0.21 to 0.06 per 100 officers; from 0.94 to 0.25 per 100,000 population) are explained by sudden increases in "Brotherly Love" among the citizens of that city.

License. If external environmental influences do not explain these variations, we must look for explanations among variables internal to police agencies. In 1967, when the President's Task Force on the Police began its look at internal variables related to police shooting, it found great and troubling inconsistencies. In one case, when its staff asked a police agency what sort of limits it placed upon officers' authority to shoot, it was told that the rules on firearms were fully described by the following line from the department's manual:

> Never take me out in anger, never put me back in disgrace.

The task force characterized such rules as grossly inadequate, and suggested that the absence of more clear and definitive direction might account for many unnecessary police shootings (President's Commission, 1967: 188-189). Since then, there has developed considerable empirical evidence that internal police organizational variables independent of external working environments are a major influence upon frequency of police shooting. Uelman's (1973) analysis of shootings in 51 Los Angeles County police agencies led him to conclude that the varying philosophies of police chiefs regarding use of deadly force accounted for most of the variation in shooting rates among those departments. Fyfe (1979) reported that significant decreases in police shooting frequencies followed establishment and enforcement of a clear and restrictive deadly force policy in New York City. He found also that this restriction in shooting discretion had no effect upon violent crime rates, arrest rates, or police injury or death rates, as did Sherman (1983) in his study of Atlanta police shootings. Fyfe (1982) also reported that variations in departmental philosophies, policies, and practices, rather than environmental differences, accounted for differences between shooting frequencies in Memphis and New York City.[5]

The internal philosophical, policy, and practice variables found by Uelman, Fyfe, and Sherman to affect shooting frequencies might be broadly classified under the single heading of license: the degree of discretion officers are permitted in use of their firearms, and the degree to which they are held accountable for operating within the bounds of that discretion. License may be measured along several dimensions. As Uelman (1973) suggests, license includes general administrative philosophy, and is perhaps made most apparent through the public utterances and statements of those responsible for administering police services. The work of Fyfe (1979) and Sherman (1983) is more specific, and indicates that establishment and enforcement of formal policies that clearly define officers' shooting discretion have a direct effect on their field behavior.

No matter how clear their message, however, internal police philosophies and policies can affect the frequency of only some percentage of police agencies' shootings. That is so because some police shootings involve the defense of the lives of officers or others against immediate and unavoidable threats. The frequency of such shootings may vary depending upon how well officers are trained in tactics that help them avoid becoming vulnerable to potential assailants,[6] but they are not subject to reduction by mere administrative philosophy or fiat. Even the most restrained police chief cannot suggest or order that officers refrain from shooting when they have no other means of protecting their lives. Shootings in such cases are largely a function of environmental variables beyond the direct control of police administrators (e.g., officers' exposure to confrontations with armed and dangerous offenders). Thus, as long as police deal with a violent environment, and as long as that environmental violence is as immune to ameliorative police efforts as much of the recent research has indicated, it is unrealistic to think that they will be able to do their work totally without bloodshed.

The shootings that are subject to control by administrative philosophies and rule making are those that are *elective*. These involve situations in which officers shoot people who present no immediate risk to themselves or to other innocent persons. Thus, where officers have broad license to shoot, one would expect to find relatively high shooting rates, and to find that many shootings would be elective.

The discrepancies between the findings of Fyfe, and Geller and Karales and the data in Table 4.1 also suggest that license is an important determinant of police shooting rates. Fyfe, and Geller and Karales studied geographic and temporal variations in shooting rates within single police agencies in which license was a constant, rather than a variable. Table 4.1 includes 10 separate agencies among which license varies considerably, and within which internal organizational variables changed over time.

In Philadelphia, for example, variables internal to the police department changed dramatically between 1979 and 1983. During the 1970s, allegations and denials of excessive use of force—including firearms—were frequent and loud in that city. During that period, the Philadelphia Police Department abolished its formerly restrictive police shooting policy on grounds that it could not interpret the state's amended law on police use of deadly force. Thus it left officers with no written shooting policy.[7] The city's district attorney established a "Police Brutality Unit" to investigate complaints, and the Pennsylvania House of Representatives and the United States Civil Rights Commission held hearings on the issue. In 1979, the Civil Rights Division of the United States Justice Department took the unprecedented step of filing suit against the city, charging that it had encouraged and tolerated systematic police brutality. Frank Rizzo, the flamboyant and vociferous former police chief who became the city's mayor in 1972, was the focus of most of the criticism and controversy. Rizzo was compelled to leave office at the end of 1979, after failing in a referendum to change the law that limited him to two consecutive four-year terms as mayor. (See, generally, U.S. Civil Rights Commission, 1981.)

One of the first acts of the police chief appointed by William Green, who was elected mayor in 1980, was to promulgate an internal order that limited officers' shooting discretion far more stringently than had previously been the case (Philadelphia Police Department, 1980). Given this series of events, it is reasonable to speculate that the decrease in Philadelphia police shootings shown in Table 4.1 was more closely associated with changes in license afforded officers than with any major changes in the external environment of the police. With a stroke of his pen, the police chief could forbid elective police shootings; no such unilateral action could rid the city of those who present officers with situations in which they must shoot to save lives.

Assessing Effects of Environment and License

While the aggregate shooting rates reported in Table 4.1 give little real clue as to the reasons for the table's variations, we may learn something about the relative effects upon police shooting rates of environment and license if we examine the circumstances that prevail at the time officers shoot other persons. If one were to find that variation between two jurisdictions' shooting rates (or in temporal variations in the same jurisdiction) was accounted for by differences in the frequency with which officers confronted assaultive persons armed with guns, one might conclude that shooting rate variation was a consequence of differing external environments. Conversely, were one to find that officers in one jurisdiction shot unarmed, nonthreatening persons far more often than was true of those in another jurisdiction, one might conclude that differences were due to officers' license to shoot.

Such findings have obvious implications. In the former case, the police agency the personnel of which shot great numbers of armed people might seek to determine, perhaps by studying the other agency, whether it was possible to train officers in a way that better structures confrontations, so that violence is less likely to ensue. In the latter case, the police agency with the higher shooting rate might wish to determine whether there existed variations in organizational license, and to determine what, if any, effects these variations might have upon other areas of police operation (e.g., are officers in the agency with the lower shooting rate more frequently injured or less effective at fighting crime, maintaining order, or protecting themselves than are officers in the department with the higher rate?). Were one to find that the department that shot less often suffered no greater injury rates and no loss of effectiveness, one would conclude that the administrator of the police agency with the higher rate—whose primary obligation is to protect human life—was obliged to review and revise that department's officers' license to shoot.

A Typology of Police Shootings

Unfortunately, police shooting incidents—which generally must be reconstructed from officers's accounts and reports—are not so readily dichotomized into elective and nonelective incidents. Instead, the degree to which shootings involve danger to the lives of officers or others is best measured after the fact by use of a typology that provides some indication of threat to officers' safety. This article employs such a typology to assess the relative effects of environmental and license variables upon police shootings in New York and Philadelphia.

The typology employs as discriminators of risk to officers (or other innocent persons) two characteristics of the persons shot, as indicated on police reports. First, cases were separated on the basis of the weapons with which shooting victims were reportedly armed at the time they were shot. This resulted in types that included persons armed with guns (including handguns and long guns, as well as imitation guns and various "shiny objects" that officers reportedly perceived as operable firearms), knives and other cutting instruments, and "other weapons" (e.g., clubs, bats, chairs, vehicles), as well as people who were unarmed. Second, unarmed shooting victims were dichotomized on the basis of whether or not they had reportedly assaulted or attempted to assault officers or others.

Data Sources

The data analyzed in this article include records of all reported police shootings in which citizens were killed or nonfatally wounded by police in New York City (n = 907) and Philadelphia (n = 474) during the years 1971 through 1975.[8]

These are particularly interesting data because they may also help to explain the precipitous drop in Philadelphia police shootings discussed in Table 4.1. In 1979, Philadelphia police were operating under a vague unwritten shooting policy and under the leadership of a police chief who stated that he would defend their actions so long as they *felt* they were right. They were also much more likely to shoot and kill than were New York City officers (rates per 100 officers = 0.21 and 0.14, respectively; rates per 100,000 population = 0.94 and 0.48, respectively). By 1983, however, when Philadelphia officers were operating under a clearly defined and objectively enforced shooting policy very similar to that previously enacted in New York City (New York City Police Department, 1972), their shooting rates (0.06 per 100 officers; 0.25 per 100,000 population) had dropped below those of New York City officers (0.08 per 100 officers; 0.27 per 100,000 population). If, as stated earlier, police chiefs have little effect on nonelective shootings, the question that arises is whether the earlier shooting discrepancies between New York City and Philadelphia were attributable to differences in elective shooting rates.

Table 4.2 indicates that they were. In the aggregate, these data show that, during 1971 through 1975, Philadelphia police were

TABLE 4.2
Shooting Incident Types, New York City and Philadelphia 1971-1975[a]

Shooting Type	New York Percentage	Rate[b]	Philadelphia Percentage	Rate[b]
Gun assault	53.0 (n = 481)	0.32	39.0 (n = 185)	0.46
Knife assault	22.3 (n = 202)	0.14	9.7 (n = 46)	0.11
Other assault	11.7 (n = 106)	0.07	9.9 (n = 47)	0.12
Physical assault	4.5 (n = 41)	0.08	16.5 (n = 78)	0.19
Unarmed, no assault	8.5 (n = 77)	0.05	24.9 (n = 118)	0.29
Totals	100.0 (n = 907)	0.61	100.0 (n = 474)	1.18

NOTE: chi square = 151.771; $p < .00001$.
a. Includes all reported incidents in which police officers shot and wounded or killed others.
b. Mean annual rate per 100 officers.

approximately twice as likely to have shot citizens as were New York City police: The mean annual rate of police shootings in Philadelphia during these years was 1.18 per 100 officers, as versus a mean annual New York rate of 0.61.

The table also shows considerable difference between the patterns of police shootings in New York City and Philadelphia ($p < .0001$). More than half (53%) of those shot by New York City police officers during these years were reportedly armed with guns and attempting to assault officers or others, while the comparable Philadelphia percentage is 39%. On the other end of this continuum of danger to officers, nearly one in four (24.9%) of Philadelphia police shooting victims and one in twelve (8.5%) New York police shooting victims were reportedly unarmed and not assaultive at the time they were shot. Further, the mean annual rates per 100 police officers show that Philadelphia police (rate = 0.29) were nearly six times as likely to have shot unarmed nonassaultive persons as were New York City police (rate = 0.05). Table 4.2 indicates, therefore, that during the years examined, the difference between the police shooting rate of New York City and that of Philadelphia was largely attributable to a comparatively great number of Philadelphia shootings involving minimal danger to officers or other innocent persons. Indeed, it is apparent that the discrepancies between New York City and Philadelphia shooting rates increase as the threat to life posed by those shot (in terms of weapon and assaultive versus nonassaultive behavior) decreases: Philadelphia police were about 40% more likely to have shot reportedly assaultive persons armed with guns than were New York City police (rates = 0.46 and 0.32, respectively),[9] and were about 600% more likely than New York police to have shot unarmed persons (combined New York Physical Assault and Unarmed, nonassault rate = 0.14; Philadelphia rate = 0.48).

CONCLUSIONS

Because the research upon which this analysis of shootings in New York City and Philadelphia is based is still in progress, any conclusions related to it must be both tentative and tempered by the absence of data on more recent patterns of police shootings in those two cities. It is clear, however, that the earlier difference in shooting rates in those two cities was largely a consequence of the relatively high frequency of apparently elective shootings by members of the Philadelphia Police Department. Since that time, there have been dramatic changes in the operating philosophies and practices of the Philadelphia Police Department, and its officers' license to engage in elective shootings has, in effect, been revoked. By inference, therefore, it is likely that the more recent very similar shooting rates in New York and Philadelphia are an indication that Philadelphia officers presently engage in far fewer elective shootings than was previously true.

Without more information, it is impossible to define reasons for the differences in the aggregate shooting rates among the police departments shown in Table 4.1, and it is almost certain that they are affected by an enormous universe of variables (demographics, availability of handguns and other weapons among the general population, etc.). But, in addition to these external variables, it is also likely that variations in license more directly controllable by police administrators—operating philosophies, policies, and accountability—play a significant role in them as well. By determining the degree to which their department's shooting rates include elective shootings, police administrators can make some assessment of the effects of shooting license on their department's experience, and can react accordingly.

If, as occurred in Philadelphia, they restrict shooting license—by clearer policies or more objective enforcement of existing policies, for example—and there follows a great decrease in killings by officers, they will have achieved no minor feat. Further, if the research to date is generalizable to their agencies, they will do so without undesirable effects on rates of crime, arrest, or public or police safety.

By the standards of the critics of the police research of the past two decades, however, their efforts will have been insignificant because they will probably result in no measurable decrease in crime, and thus in no increase in "effectiveness." But these critics are shortsighted, and fail to recognize that police effectiveness involves more than suppression of street crime. The primary responsibility of the police is to protect life and, if they can effect great decreases in the frequency with which they *take* life without incurring any other costs, they will have become far more effective.

In five years, Philadelphia's police department changed from one that was frequently (and justifiably) accused of excessive use of force to a department whose officers are less likely to take lives than are police in almost any of the 10 largest American cities. That fact, and the general decreases in shooting by American big-city police, suggests that there has been considerable payoff from the study of police shootings that began when President Johnson's Task Force on the Police surveyed police shooting license almost two decades ago. At the same time, the continuing great shooting rate variation that characterizes even our most cosmopolitan police departments suggests that there is much more to learn and accomplish. Without the work of the last 20 years, however, all of our police would almost certainly still be operating under the assumptions of the early 1960s, and would be killing far more often than is presently true.

That work, therefore, is extremely significant and, like much other research into matters of crime and justice, it should not be denigrated because it has not shown us how to cure crime. Instead, it should be continued and disseminated to police agencies that continue to operate in the same manner that they did 30 or more years ago.

NOTES

1. Perhaps the earliest published empirical study of police shootings is Robin (1963).
2. There exist no systematic national data concerning police shootings. The Federal Bureau of Investigation collects information concerning *fatal* police shootings from police agencies that volunteer it, but does not publish it, apparently because its accuracy is highly questionable. No federal agency collects or publishes data on nonfatal gunshot woundings or other firearms use by police. Data analyzed in all the research to date has been collected on an ad hoc basis.
3. "Death by legal intervention of the police" is number 984 of the categories for causes of mortality used by NCHS (1967: 501).
4. Sherman and Langworthy (1979) report that statistics on fatal police shootings obtained directly from 32 major police departments reflect approximately twice as many deaths as do the corresponding NCHS data. In addition, Kania and Mackey's research may be faulted for its use of FBI Uniform Crime Report data as its measure of police exposure to threats and stress. The questionable validity of these reported crime figures has been amply documented.
5. Another environmental variable that one might reasonably expect to affect police shooting rates, of course, is state criminal law regarding police use of deadly force. Because these laws are generally so broad (Geller and Karales, 1981: 20-52), and because officers are so rarely prosecuted or convicted for violating them (Kobler, 1975), they have generally been supplemented (at least among the larger police agencies) with clearer administrative guidelines. Thus, except where such administrative guidelines do not exist, state laws have little real effect on officers' decisions to shoot or to refrain from shooting.
6. It is almost certain, for example, that police can reduce shootings by training officers to avoid placing themselves in situations that leave them no alternative but to shoot others in order to escape injury to themselves. Many police shootings with which this author is familiar involve situations in which officers put themselves in harm's way (e.g., by charging into the scene of a reported armed robbery), and were subsequently required to shoot themselves out of face-to-face confrontations with armed suspects. Training officers to approach such situations more cautiously seems a promising means of reducing the gunfire and bloodshed they produce.
7. In 1973, the Pennsylvania statute on police use of deadly force (18 Pa. Cons. Stat. Ann. sec. 508) was enacted, and authorized officers to use deadly force in defense of life, or to effect arrests of armed or dangerous suspects, or of persons who have committed "forcible felonies." Six years later, Philadelphia Police Commissioner Joseph O'Neill told the United States Civil Rights Commission that he could not recall whether his department had attempted to interpret the law (e.g., by defining "forcible felonies") for officers, and that he would have to be at the scene in order to make a determination of whether it was appropriate to shoot a fleeing suspect. In the interim, the Philadelphia Police Department suspended its regulation permitting officers to shoot only at persons suspected of "violent crimes," "such as rape by force, murder, armed robbery, assault with intent to kill by axe, etc." (Philadelphia Police Department, n.d.: 64-66), leaving officers with no administrative policy whatever. Further, O'Neill told the

commission that if one of his officers "did shoot, if he felt that he was doing that which is right, I'd most certainly defend him" (U.S. Civil Rights Commission 1979: 215-218)

8. These data are part of a larger study funded by the Police Foundation. The author acknowledges the assistance of Gilbert Branche of the Police Brutality Unit of the Philadelphia District Attorney's Office, and former New York City Police Chief of Personnel Neil Behan for assistance in obtaining these data.

9. Preliminary examination of these data suggests that a far greater percentage of the Philadelphia shootings of persons reportedly armed with guns involved shiny objects, toy guns, and other devices subsequently found incapable of causing injury or death. Future analyses of these data will distinguish between these and real guns, and are likely to show very little difference between New York and Philadelphia rates of shooting persons armed with working firearms.

REFERENCES

Commission on Accreditation for Law Enforcement Agencies (1983) "Standards for law enforcement agencies." Fairfax, VA: Author.
FYFE, J. (1979) "Administrative interventions on police shooting discretion: an empirical examination." Journal of Criminal Justice 7 (Winter): 309-324.
FYFE, J. (1982) "Blind justice: police shootings in Memphis." Journal of Criminal Law and Criminology 73 (Summer): 707-722.
FYFE, J. (1980) "Geographic correlates of police shooting: a microanalysis." Journal of Research in Crime and Delinquency 17 (January): 101-113.
GELLER, W. and K. KARALES (1981) "Split-second decisions: shooting of and by Chicago police." Chicago: Chicago Law Enforcement Study Group.
GREENWOOD, P. and J. PETERSILIA (1975) "The criminal investigation process, I: summary and implications." Santa Monica, CA: Rand Corporation.
KANIA, R. and W. MAKEY (1977) "Police violence as a function of community characteristics." Criminology 15 (May): 27-48.
KELLING, G. L. et al., (1974) "The Kansas City preventive patrol experiment: summary report." Washington, DC: Police Foundation.
KOBLER, A. (1975) "Figures (and perhaps some facts) on police killings of civilians in the United States, 1965-1969." Journal of Social Issues 31: 185-191.
MATULIA, K. (1982) "A balance of forces." Gaithersburg, MD: International Association of Chiefs of Police.
National Center for Health Statistics (1967) "International classification for diseases, adapted for use in the United States" (8th rev.). Washington, DC: Government Printing Office.
New York City Police Department (1972) Temporary operating procedure 237, August.
Pennsylvania Statutes Annotated (1973).
Philadelphia Police Department (1980) Directive 10, April 2.
Philadelphia Police Department (n.d.) "Duty manual."
President's Commission on Law Enforcement and Administration of Justice (1967) "Task force report: the police." Washington, DC: Government Printing Office.

ROBIN, G. (1963) "Justifiable homicide by police." Journal of Criminal Law, Criminology, and Police Science 54 (May-June): 225-231.

SHERMAN, L. (1983) "Reducing police gun use," pp. 98-125 in M. Punch (ed.) Control in the Police Organization. Cambridge: MIT Press.

SHERMAN, L. and R. LANGWORTHY (1979) "Measuring homicide by police officers." Journal of Criminal Law and Criminology 70 (Winter): 546-560.

UELMAN, G. (1973) "Varieties of public policy: a study of police policy regarding the use of deadly force in Los Angeles County." Loyola of Los Angeles Law Review 6: 1-55.

U.S. Civil Rights Commission (1979) "Hearings before the U.S. Commission on Civil Rights." Philadelphia, April 16-17. Washington, DC: Government Printing Office.

U.S. Civil Rights Commission (1981) Who is Guarding the Guardians? Washington, DC: Government Printing Office.

5

Police and the Modern Sting Operation

CARL B. KLOCKARS

Both Egon Bittner and Peter Manning have argued that much of what police work is or is promoted to be may be understood as efforts to reconcile the realities of policing with norms of conventional respectability (Bittner, 1971; Manning, 1977). Bittner's thesis is that the police role, the core of which is the right to use coercive force, is fundamentally at odds with modern democratic societies' aspirations to achieve peace through peaceful means. Hence, Bittner finds, the police role must be wrapped in concealments and circumlocutions (e.g., crime fighting, military, or professional rhetoric) to make it palatable to the policy that authorizes it. Manning's contribution, in the same vein, has been to bring the perspectives and powers of "dramaturgical" analysis to the exploration of the rituals, roles, symbols, mystifications, deceptions, appearances, and stagings through which the police reconcile their behavior with public norms of respectability and create impressions of efficiency.

The modern "sting" operation, wherein police pose as thieves and as dealers in stolen property, fences, in order to induce thieves to bring stolen property to them, appears to be an especially inviting example for both the Bittner and Manning theses. The core of the police role in sting operations is packed with behaviors that go against conventional norms of respectable behavior: lies, deceptions, concealments, and betrayals. At the conclusion of the sting operation, these behaviors require public revelation and accounting. Both the Bittner and Manning theses advise, under such conditions, to be especially alert to counterconcealments, circumlocutions, and deceptions. The analysis of sting operations that follows operates on a hypothesis consistent with both the Manning and Bittner approaches: *The more successful police are in appearing really bad, the more successful they must be in appearing really good.*

THE COSTS AND DANGERS
OF MAINTAINING AN IMAGE AS A FENCE

Unlike conventional detective policing, running a sting operation requires a considerable investment in equipment and materials to create an environment in which the image of a fence can be sustained. In addition to the rental of a location that will serve as the front; videotape equipment to record transactions; storage space where purchased goods can be kept secure and out of sight; merchandise supporting the impression that the front also carries on legitimate business; cars, trucks, and vans that undercover personnel can operate full-time; and money for field expenses, "flash," and buys. A considerable investment is required to install monitoring equipment, build bulletproof walls and counters, wire alarms and install silent triggering devices, and fit them to the architecture of the rented front in ways that will not arouse suspicion at the same time they will ensure the safety of the officers who work the counter. All of this work that must be done before a sting front opens its doors incurs costs that are typically hidden in two ways. First, most of the work is done by police officers from the agency running the sting operation. During the time these police officers are searching for an appropriate location then doing the carpentry, electrical, and construction work necessary to turn it into a working front, purchasing materials to outfit it as a business, finding undercover vehicles, and leasing or purchasing the other equipment necessary to sustain their image, they are not employed at other police duties; however, no accounting is made of the loss of their manpower while they are employed, sometimes for months, in preparations. Second, these preliminary image-sustaining and -generating costs, most of which cannot be recovered after the sting goes public, are also not included, either as capital expenditures or as salaries, in the typical police public relations accountings offered for public consumption; if any cost-benefit information is provided at all, it consists of reporting buy money expended in relation to the value of property recovered.

An allied problem associated with meeting and accounting for the costs involved in generating a fence image involves securing the money for such expenditures while preserving the proposed operation. In dealing with an agency such as LEAA, this means that obtaining a grant for a sting operation cannot be handled through the same funding channels or be reviewed by the same accounting procedures as can conventional, nonclandestine grants. We have reason to believe that in order to maintain the clandestine image of sting operations, some of them have been funded in advance of ever submitting a written request for funds.

Aside from the hidden economic costs and dangerous accounting practices involved in generating an image of a fence, there are a variety of costs and risks associated with maintaining and managing that image that are not easily measured in economic terms. A first set of such difficulties is associated with making the fence image attractive enough to entice thieves to trade with it. One way of managing this problem is to offer thieves better prices than competitors are paying. This strategy is available to sting operations but, should the price offered become "too high" or too far out of line with the prevailing market for the stolen goods in question, the authenticity of the fence image will be endangered. There is an analogous problem in undercover narcotics policing where drug dealers are sensitive to the fact that narcs are typically willing to pay more for drugs than genuine users.

Whether or not a sting fence is willing to pay prices at or above the going rate, the problem of getting that message out to prospective customers remains. Sting operations seem to approach this problem of advertising their disreputability in two rather different ways. The first seems to involve the creation of some preposterous story. A Washington, D.C., sting operation advertised themselves as a group of Mafiosi come to town to take over the stolen property business in the nation's capital (Shaffer et al., 1977). This sting, which promoted employees with names like "Rico Rigatoni" and "Angelo Lasagna," demonstrates the level of subtlety such stories need to attain to secure the confidence of thieves at the level of sophistication dealt with in this instance.

A second strategy that sting operations sometimes employ to secure a more plausible image of illegitimacy involves the purchase of a genuine criminal reputation or at least someone with some real experience in playing the role of a bad actor. In four sting operations of which we have inside knowledge, this second strategy was employed by hiring a professional criminal. In one of the cases, the criminal was a fence who had been arrested and given a plea bargain deal wherein the charges against him would be dropped if he allowed his real fencing operation to be used as a sting for a period of nine months (Buffalo, New York, 1976). In the other three (the names of which cannot be revealed because doing so would compromise my informants), a three-time loser was given the option of going to jail for the rest of his natural life under a habitual criminal prosecution or joining the staff of a local sting. After working one such operation and finding the work to his liking, the man became a professional informant and was salaried by sting operations in two other states.

Whether the fence image of the sting operations is enhanced by imaginative police officers spinning stories to explain its presence or by employing former criminals under coercive plea bargains, the object of these tactics is to bring thieves into the fence front, where their sale of stolen property can be taped and recorded. The focus on this front stage scene in the sting drama has a tendency to divert attention from the fact that unless the sting's reputation for paying higher than normal prices spreads through the subculture of theft and attracts thieves on that basis alone, the real work in generating, cultivating, and maintaining an enticing image of the fence is done by those undercover operatives who work the street and bring thieves to the counter where their transactions are recorded.

This type of work—which is never photographed, hard to describe in the saturated detail that makes it sensible, and, when challenged, becomes an issue of whether one believes the account of the undercover officer, professional informant, or the thief—is highly varied. In our experience, it begins by frequenting places where bad actors congregate and staging performances likely to impress them with the illegitimacy and connections of the undercover operatives. This may mean hanging out in certain bars, pool rooms, coffee shops, and luncheonettes, getting in on gambling games, horse parlors, and bookie joints, offering stolen property for sale in these places, picking up hitchhikers late at night and telling stories to them about one's own criminal exploits, attending parties, after-hours clubs, and other establishments frequented by people "in the life," and so forth. Once such activities succeed in sponsoring the impression that the undercover operatives are thieves themselves, "street reps" for a good fence whom they have dealt with themselves, or traffickers in other kinds of criminal endeavor, it is not unusual in our experience for them to be asked to participate in the commission of thefts and burglaries, taking more active roles than mere receivers or connections for stolen property.

Sometimes it is possible to arrange for the arrest of thieves and burglars in the act, but often there is no time to set such a trap and the undercover operative must become a participant in the crime. The officer could, of course, reveal his or her identity as an undercover agent and make an arrest at the scene of the crime, but doing so would run a substantial risk of destroying the fence image, which may well have required months of work and many tens of thousands of dollars to generate. Of course, the danger in such participation, necessary though it might be to preserve the image of the fence, is that in addition to such preservation it may also promote crimes that would not have occurred without the undercover operatives' image preserving participation in them.

A final series of risks and costs associated with generating and maintaining the fence image that are not usually calculated in the evaluation of sting operations involves the toll that the work requires upon those who do it. Here again, the burden does not fall most heavily upon the officers who work the counter and whose work is usually the evidentiary core against the thief but on those operatives who work the street, build the fence's image in the eyes of thieves, and entice them into the front to make a transaction that can be recorded. It is hard to imagine a more morally corrosive environment than that of the working world of the "ropers," as they were called on one sting operation with which we were familiar. The seductions of the undercover life, the drugs, the drinking, and the sex, present one sort of problem, while the exposure to people whom one can grow to like, who do favors for one, and whom one eventually will betray, presents to the best of undercover police a problem of quite a different sort.

THE COSTS AND DANGERS OF MAINTAINING AN EXEMPLARY POLICE IMAGE

Because sting operations involve risks that are far greater those of conventional detective policing and are constantly in danger of being overwhelmed by the disguises and deceptions sting work requires, the precarious adoption of the role of fence demands, at some point, that it be counterbalanced with a police image of even larger and more dramatic proportions. Stings make good press—they need to do so.

However, the demands of producing and maintaining an exemplary police image tend to encourage practices, procedures, ways of working, and manipulations that puff the image beyond proportions, lay it open to dramatic deflation, and encourage doctoring and cover-ups that further complicate an already complex scene. In part, of course, sting operations engage in these practices as part of the syndrome that has beset many "exemplary" projects drawing federal funds: A granting agency that spends enormous sums of money and is hungry for some successes to legitimize its spending grants money to an agency that promises to produce some result. To keep its promise, the receiving agency produces an evaluation of its work designed to emphasize its successes, findings that the funders, not about to argue that they made a poor investment, are not likely to dispute, unless the puffing is conspicuous or transparent.

Although this syndrome has marked many federal projects, most that were "great successes" but that folded after the federal monies for their support disappeared, it takes on some special properties, some of which are rather risky and potentially dangerous, when added to the already deceptive and clandestine operation of a sting. The first set of such problems can be discerned from a careful reading of the two documents that currently summarize the "successes" of some 62 sting operations in 39 American cities since 1974: *Taking the Offensive* and *What Happened* (U.S. Department of Justice, 1978, 1979, respectively). The latter volume is the more systematic and comprehensive volume and is subtitled, "A Special Report to the Commissioner." Its summary, printed in boldface type, seeks to establish the exemplary character of sting operations with the following review of findings:

(1) Subjects who sell stolen property to undercover operatives in antifencing operations are considerably older than individuals arrested nationally for property crimes.
(2) Nearly one in five of the subjects apprehended and/or identified in antifencing operations have been classified as a fence.
(3) Most subjects have a prior arrest record and many have lengthy criminal histories, while some had long escaped police attention because of their cautious approach to criminal activities.

(4) Prosecutors enjoy a very high conviction rate for subjects arrested in antifencing operations.
(5) The antifencing projects examined showed decreases in property crime at the termination of their operations.
(6) Further analysis focusing on the impact on incidence of the individual types of property crime is strongly indicated.
(7) The assumption that the impact is maximized at termination may be questionable, since education and sentencing often take place over an extended period of time.
(8) Undercover personnel have paid a very small percentage of fair market value for the stolen property recovered.
(9) The recovered property usually has been returned to the victim or insurance company.
(10) The property recovered in antifencing operations has ranged from small auto parts to Rembrandt paintings.

As this summary includes many but not all of the dimensions along which architects and advocates of sting operations seek to construct an exemplary police image, each of the claims, the evidence, and the work necessary to support it deserves careful attention.

(1) *Subjects who sell stolen property to undercover operatives in antifencing operations are considerably older than individuals arrested nationally for property crimes.*

The premier finding of the *What Happened* summary is supported by data gathered on 20 sting operations that produced 1693 arrested subjects. The age distribution of sting arrestees is compared with 1977 national arrest data—which we compiled from the 1977 Uniform Crime Reports (UCR)—in Table 5.1 (Webster, 1979).

If we assume that, for the three varieties of property crime in Table 5.1, the UCR arrest data accurately reflects the age distribution of perpetrators of those crimes, we are presented with a rather curious finding: Sting operations manage to arrest most people from age categories least responsible for property crimes. In fact, the age group most responsible is rarely (3%) stung at all. In order to understand this finding and the policy it mirrors, we must ask ourselves how it would look and what it would do for the sting's exemplary police image to report that half the people brought into the front, enticed there by undercover policemen and informants, and subsequently arrested, were juveniles. Hardly the kind of heroic thief-taking results sufficient to warrant the deceptions, illusions, efforts, and expenditures that stings necessitate.

TABLE 5.1
Age Distributions of Sting Arrestees and Burglary, Larceny, and Auto Theft Arrestees Nationally, 1977
(Percent of Total)

Arrestees	17 and under	18-20	21-25	26-30	31+
Stings	3%	13%	30% (21-24)	25% (25-29)	29% (30+)
UCR burglary	51.5%	19.8%	12.7%	7.9%	9.1%
UCR larceny-theft	42.9%	16.8%	13.0%	9.7%	17.6%
UCR auto theft	53.0%	18.5%	11.9%	7.6%	9.0%

Consequently, it is our experience, based upon inside knowledge of four separate sting operations and the inference we are obliged to draw from the data above, that most sting operations avoid arresting juveniles, even though they are most likely responsible for nearly half of all property crime. This is not to say that the informants and undercover agents whose job it is to bring thieves into the front do not meet these young thieves or are not approached with offers of stolen property by them, but rather, when they are approached with such offers, by and large, they pass them up in order to forestall possibly hostile public opinion.

(2) *Nearly one in five of the subjects apprehended and/or identified in antifencing operations has been classified as a fence.*

If the premier finding of *What Happened* must be understood as masking a policy of ignoring juvenile property crime, the second seeks to sponsor the impression that the targets of sting operations, while less common than juvenile perpetrators, are more important, more serious, and more professional criminals than their juvenile counterparts. Some rather unusual stretching and shaping is required to make this point.

First, if we take the statement above at face value, it asks us to consider sting operations as *antifencing operations* on the basis that nearly one in five subjects *apprehended or identified* in them has been classified as a fence. Even if this statement were faultless, it would be hard to defend understanding sting operations as antifencing operations on the basis of the fact that fewer than 20% of the people involved in them have been classified as a fence. Sting operations are not *antifencing operations.* They are *antitheft operations.*

Second, were we to take the second major finding of *What*

Happened at face value, we would miss at least three face-making manipulations that rest beneath the surface and support the second finding above. The first is that the only data in *What Happened* dealing with the proportion of fences encountered in sting operations establishes that 16%, *one in six, not one in five,* subjects were classified as fences. Second, decisions to classify such subjects as fences were "subjective judgments made by operational personnel," "personnel," we might add, employed in "antifencing operations." Finally, it must be emphasized that both the one-in-six figure above and the "subjective classification" refer to subjects who were "arrested *or* identified"—or merely "encountered"—in sting operations. No data is given in *What Happened* solely on the arrest of fences, subjectively or objectively classified as such.

(3) *Most subjects have a prior arrest record and many have lengthy criminal histories, while some had long escaped police attention because of their cautious approach to criminal activities.*

As was the case with the second major finding of *What Happened*, the third major finding also seeks to establish that it is the more serious, experienced, and professional criminal that the sting operation manages to "encounter" (i.e., arrest *or* identify). Again, *What Happened* provides no data that differentiates between arrests and identifications of subjects encountered. It does, however, support its third major finding with Table 5.2.

The problem with Table 5.2, as any first semester statistics student should be able to explain, is that the intervals chosen mask the distribution they should be designed to express. With more than half the cases in the "1 to 5 prior arrests" category, it is impossible to know, absent measures of central tendency or dispersion (which are absent in *What Happened*), what the distribution of prior arrest records of encountered subjects really was.

As if the problem of deciphering the concept of "encountered" subjects combined with a choice of intervals patently designed to hide the distribution of the prior arrests were not enough, *What Happened* adds, "It was not possible to distinguish between felony and misdemeanor arrests. However, a cursory examination of the charges reveals that the subjects encountered with previous records had been arrested for serious crimes, not petty or traffic offenses." If a cursory examination of the charges can reveal that the subjects had serious prior arrest records, one wonders why a sample, even a small one, could not have been drawn as evidence in support of this revelation.

TABLE 5.2
Prior Arrest Records of Subjects Encountered in 19 Operations

Prior arrest groups	(Sample = 1620 subjects) Percent
No prior arrests	16
1 to 5 prior arrests	52
6 to 10 prior arrests	17
Over 10 prior arrests	15

(4) *Prosecutors enjoy a very high conviction rate for subjects arrested in antifencing operations.*

The construction of an exemplary police image for the sting requires not only that it avoid the reputation of targeting juvenile offenders and concentrate its attentions on serious, professional criminals, but also that it do so successfully or at least more successfully than conventional police methods. In support of this aspect of an exemplary police image, one would think that stings, armed with videotaped records to support their charges, would easily surpass the success of conventional prosecutions based upon less exotic evidence. On the basis of the data presented in *What Happened*, which we have composed and included in Table 5.3, along with certain comparable national data, it would appear that stings do in fact produce higher conviction rates than conventional methods, but this statement requires some quite important qualifications.

The most important of these qualifications is that the claim in *What Happened* of a "very high conviction rate" (91%) is based on 750 completed cases, 609 of which were settled early by guilty pleas. Of the 197 cases that went to trial, 76 (38%) ended in convictions, 27 (14%) were acquitted or dismissed, and 94 (48%) remain pending. It may well turn out that all 338 pending cases (those not included in the above conviction rates) will end in convictions, in which case the 17 sting operations the cases upon which finding four is base will have achieved a 94% conviction rate. But should only half of the pending cases result in convictions, the sting will have achieved a conviction rate no better than the national average for larceny-theft and only slightly (8%) better than the national rate for burglary.

(5) *The antifencing projects examined showed decreases in property crime at the termination of their operations.*

(6) *Further analysis focusing on the impact on incidence of*

TABLE 5.3
Disposition of 1,088 Subjects Arrested in 17 Sting Operations as Compared with National Rates for Selected Property Crimes

	Persons arrested	Cases pending	Guilty pleas	Guilty (trial)	Guilty (total)	Referred to juvenile court
Sting operations	1088	338 (31%)	609 (56%)	76 (7%)	685 (63%)	Less than 3%
Total						
UCR burglary	26,821				30.9%	57%
UCR larceny-theft	161,450				49.1%	37.7%
UCR auto theft	17,726				23.5%	64.8%
Adult						
UCR burglary	11,534				71.8%	—
UCR larceny-theft	100,583				78.8%	—
UCR auto theft	6,240				66.7%	—

individual types of property crime is strongly indicated.

(7) *The assumption that the impact is maximized at termination may be questionable since adjudication and sentencing often take place over an extended period of time.*

With the fifth, sixth, and seventh findings above, *What Happened* seeks to establish what is to the general public perhaps the most important aspect of an exemplary police effort, that in the long run, or even the short run, it serves to lessen the chance of victimization and makes our person or property more secure—in brief, that it makes a difference that justifies the risks, dangers, deceptions, and expenditures it necessitates. In fact, so strong is the need to demonstrate this effect that *What Happened* seeks to do it and implies it has, at least in finding 5 above, in the face of almost overwhelming odds against it. Who could believe that a single sting operation or even a series of them, netting an average of 80 subjects, could show an appreciable decrease in property crime rates in any city or county of sizable proportions?

In order to test this hard-to-believe finding, the authors of *What Happened* perform a time-series analysis of property crime rates at three project sites: an unidentified western city of population 385,000, a second western city of population 331,000, and a third "midwestern jurisdiction" of population 746,000. The lags were computed from monthly UCR reports submitted between January 1974 and September 1978. True to the letter of finding 5 above, analysis of the property crime rate at the first western city site showed a decrease after the third sting operation in that city. However, the decrease was not statistically significant.

The second site examined, the midwestern city of population 331,000, also enjoyed the benefits of three sting operations. There the analysis showed no statistically significant reduction in the property crime rate after the first operation; an increase, but not a statistically significant one, after the second; and a statistically significant decrease ($p < .05$, one tail) after the third.

The third site examined, the jurisdiction of 746,000 people, showed a decrease in the property crime rate that was marginally significant ($p < .1$) after the termination of one sting that resulted in the arrest of "more than 100 subjects . . . including 27 fences."

While one cannot fault finding 6, which calls for further study (except to say that it is not a finding), and it is hard to argue with the logic of finding 7 (which asserts that an "assumption," which is by definition questionable, "may be" and is also not a finding), finding 5, asserting that "antifencing projects examined showed decreases in property crime at their termination," seems to be based on the also questionable assumption that readers of *What Happened* would not read further. For within *What Happened* they would find that of the seven sting operations conducted in three cities and that were subject to analysis, one was followed by a statistically insignificant *increase* in property crime rates, five were followed by statistically insignificant decreases ($p < .05$), and one was followed by a statistically significant decrease. On the basis of those results, finding 5 ought to have read: *No evidence exists to show that sting operations produce declines in the rate of property crime, either at their termination or at any time thereafter.*

(8) *Undercover personnel have paid a very small percentage of the fair market value for stolen property recovered.*

The eighth finding above addresses two facets of the exemplary police image that stings seek to maintain. The first facet is defensive and aspires to deflect the charge of entrapment. The stings must demonstrate that their willingness to buy stolen property does not encourage people to steal in response to the encouragement of the market they create. The second facet of the exemplary image finding 5 seeks to support is the reading of sting operations, by victims of theft and the public alike, as economically responsible. Stings need to demonstrate their bargain rates.

We have composed the data on sting bargaining offered in *What Happened* into Table 5.4. But before we analyze its image-making and defending properties, some notes on the figures that compose it are in order. First, the data range in their precision from figures correct to the nearest hundred thousand or million (numbers 8, 15, 16), through figures correct to the nearest thousand (numbers 1, 4, 9), to those that appear accurate to the final dollar. This variability is understandable in estimation of the value of property purchased, but surprising for the six projects (numbers 4, 7, 8, 14, 15, 16) that apparently could not account for buy money with any more precision than the closest thousand.

Second, the inclusion of stings 15 and 16 skews the table (and were excluded from the tabular presentations in *What Happened*), but the reason for their skewing and exclusion reveals some further problems in accounting. According to *What Happened*, sting 15 was excluded because it managed the purchase of $4 million worth of heroin, a product not identifiable as stolen and classed as "contraband." Likewise, *What Happened* says of sting 16:

> Approximately $42 million of stolen [sic] property was recovered in Operation 16 of which $23 million proved to be stolen. Again much of the remainder apparently was contraband.

These comments indicate some difficulty in evaluating the data reported on the 14 other sting operations. For example, it would appear that sting 1 either purchased no drugs or contraband (e.g., illegal destructive devices made from legitimate materials) or failed to exclude them from property classified as "stolen." The same appears likely to be true of sting 3, and possibly 9 and 12 as well, in that they report an unusually large percentage of property purchased identifiable as stolen.

The third qualification that must be registered before we subject the data to analysis is that the appraisal of the value of property was, to quote *What Happened*, a "subjective" process. It was, however, likely to be influenced by a policy endorsed by LEAA instructing stings to strive to pay less than 10% of the fair market value of goods they purchased. The extent to which this directive influenced sting bargaining policies is difficult to separate from the extent to which it

TABLE 5.4
Value of Property Purchased, Property Identified as Stolen, Property Not Identified as Stolen, Buy Money Expended, and Buy Money Expended per Dollar of Property Purchased in 16 Sting Operations

Sting =	Value of property purchased	Value of property identified as stolen	Value of property not identified as stolen	Buy money expended	Buy money per dollar of property purchased
1	$ 3,335,000	$ 3,335,000	$ 0	$ 155,929	.05
2	1,488,760	1,449,210	39,550	73,604	.05
3	1,049,983	1,047,215	2,768	75,283	.07
4	1,020,000	1,008,000	16,000	41,000	.04
5	897,794	841,576	56,218	91,812	.10
6	1,244,022	1,217,974	26,048	74,289	.06
7	502,019	425,000	77,019	67,000	.13
8	1,500,000	1,300,000	200,000	137,000	.09
9	989,000	985,000	4,000	74,745	.07
10	264,835	221,320	43,515	47,421	.18
11	1,000,293	989,548	10,745	59,516	.06
12	747,791	746,318	1,473	18,533	.02
13	947,682	903,700	43,982	60,717	.06
14	890,153	849,041	41,112	115,000	.13
15	6,300,000	2,200,000	4,100,000	99,000	.02
16	42,000,000	23,000,000	19,000,000	504,000	.01
Totals (1-16)	$63,175,332	$40,518,902	$23,662,430	$1,694,849	.03
Totals (1-14)	$15,875,332	$15,318,902	$ 562,000	$1,091,849	.07

influenced "subjective" evaluations of the fair market value of purchased goods.

These deficiencies in the data from *What Happened* notwithstanding, it is on the basis of the 7% of the value of the stolen property figure that the image of an exemplary police officer, careful not to entrap and efficient in the use of moneys, that sting operations need to defend and maintain. Let us first consider what seven cents on the dollar means on the purchase price of some commonly stolen property. It means that one can buy a carton of cigarettes for 70¢, a $100 stolen suit for $7, a $50 Timex quartz crystal watch for $3.50, a $90 case of decent scotch whiskey for $6.30, and a new $150 stolen Schwinn 10-speed bicycle for $10.50. Any two-bit thief in any city in the United States on any day of the week can do better than that.

This is so because there are large and ready markets for such goods and most thieves, like most people, are smart enough to know it and steal accordingly. Some, of course, are not smart enough to understand this and others steal whatever is available when the opportunity presents itself, coming up with some quite unusual things for which finding a buyer is no small problem. Consider the predicament of the thief who steals three 1977 Ford Pinto carburetors. This thief is unlikely to know three people who own such vehicles, much less three who are having or anticipate carburetor problems. Even so, tracking them down, showing them the wares, and getting any sort of decent price, even if it was "good luck" that gave the opportunity to the theft, is simply not worth the effort. That, I suggest, is one kind of product and one kind of thief from whom one is going to be able to buy at 7¢ on the dollar.

There are, though, others. Consider the thief who steals a truck, a car, or a van. Although there is a large legitimate market for such items, few people are willing to buy a stolen car because they have no idea how to go about dealing with title and registration problems, altering serial numbers, and so on. So while the streets are filled with vehicles in the $8,000 to $10,000 range, and many costing more, most of which are simple to steal, the vast majority that are stolen are found abandoned. However, should a budding young car thief find a fence who is foolish enough to pay 7¢, or even 3¢, on the dollar for stolen cars, trucks, or vans, the thief can, in short order, make a fortune. Two $8,000 cars a night, easily within the range of even a lazy thief, will bring $1,120 a night at 7% and $480 a night at 3%.

Third, one can appear, in the final accounting, to buy at 7% of the fair market value of stolen property in one other situation that deserves emphasis. On those occasions when an undercover operative (police officer or informant) accompanies a thief at work and splits the profits on the sale of the goods to the sting fence, it is possible to buy at 14¢ on the dollar and, assuming an equal divvy and the subsequent return of half, end up showing a buy ratio of 7%.

Do we show with these examples that stings seduce certain types of thieves and encourage them to steal in an effort to comply with the directive that instructs them to strive for a 10¢-on-the-dollar buy rate? Do we show that in their desire to appear as economically efficient, exemplary police officers, sting operatives are obliged to operate in ways that more modest aspirations might have prevented? The possibility exists that such practices are beneath the surface of the image of the accounting that the stings have offered of themselves. But in point of fact, the accounting itself is so poor that it makes access to what happened highly speculative at best. If, however, stings did manage to buy property at an average rate of 7¢ on the dollar, our experience suggests that they and those who fund them have some serious accounting to do.

(9) *The recovered property usually has been returned to the victim or insurance company.*

There is one group of people who are least disposed to demand an accounting of the costs, social or economic, of fence police officers. We refer, of course, to victims, who, if the price is right, are inclined to welcome the recovery of their stolen property "no questions asked."

Unfortunately, there is no evidence in *What Happened* to support finding 8 above, other than the line that reads:

> A cursory examination of the disposition of the recovered stolen property reveals that the overwhelming majority of it was returned to the owner (or appropriate insurer) in a timely fashion.

While maintenance of an exemplary police image requires only the demonstration that one has recovered stolen property and made its return possible, nothing can be said on the basis of the evidence of "cursory examination" except that for *What Happened* it is true to form. It would, though, have been most interesting to know what proportion of the victims refused to accept their recovered stolen property and preferred to keep their insurance money, what proportion took it back and neglected to inform their insurer, what proportion of insurers refused the trouble of taking it back and trying to get rid of it, and what proportion of insurers got it back, recovered their "loss," made a profit at taxpayer's expense, and raised their clients' rates anyway.

(10) *The property recovered in antifencing operations has ranged from small auto parts to Rembrandt paintings.*

The immediate inclination of the reader to this last of *What Happened*'s major findings might well be "so what?" regarding it as but another failure of *What Happened* to disclose detail that would make knowing what happened possible. While *What Happened* gives no information whatsoever on the distribution of type of property purchased, it would, I think, be incorrect to see this last major finding as merely a vague, defensive claim. Rather, I think it is intended to sponsor the impression of the egalitarian impact of sting policing. It seems to claim that stings succeed in serving everybody, rich and poor, recovering both small auto parts and priceless Rembrandts.

Both types of owners deserve to be served, of course. But it is possible that stings tend to work on behalf of one group more than another, and one interpretation of the data in *What Happened* may suggest that it does. *What Happened* reports that 18 sting operations made a total of 4791 transactions in which stolen property or contraband was purchased. They do not report the total amount of buy money expended in all 18 operations, but we do have a total figure for 16 operations from the data in Table 5.4. If we assume that the average number of transactions in these two additional sting operations were not grossly different from those in Table 5.4, we can arrive at a rough approximation of mean amount paid by stings per transaction. Using all 16 operations from Table 5.4, we arrive at a figure of $398 by dividing the total amount of buy money expended in those 16 operations by sixteen-eighteenths of 4791 transactions. Following the same procedure, but excluding operations 15 and 16, which tend to skew the table, our calculations yield an average of $293 in buy money per transaction. Using the lower figure and taking sting police at their word in spending an average of 7¢ on the dollar for property purchased, we estimate that the average sting purchase was for property valued in excess of $4,000 ($4,186). That is quite a few small auto parts.

We must, however, remember that the $293 and $4,000 figures are only means and give no indication of the distribution of transactions that compose them. It may be that the median transaction is at or near that level and most buys are for that amount and recover that much stolen property. It may also be that while most transactions are for much smaller amounts, a few big purchases raise the mean substantially and take up an inordinate share of the buy money. If the latter distribution proves to be the case, it might suggest that those who have the most to lose, owners of large quantities of merchandise and single items of great value who now enjoy the benefit of having them bought back for them at public expense, should be the major source of funding for stings in the future. But before they offer their support, they would, we think, do well to consider the virtues of holding back their funds—and perhaps the funds of others—in order to force the market for their special kinds of stolen goods still lower than its present 7%.

REFERENCES

BITTNER, E. (1971) The Function of Police in Modern Society. Washington, DC: Government Printing Office.
MANNING, P. (1977) Police Work: The Social Organization of Policing. Cambridge: MIT Press.
SHAFFER, R., K. KLOSE, and A. E. LEWIS (1977) Surprise! Surprise! New York: Viking.
U.S. Department of Justice, Criminal Conspiracies Division (1978) Taking the Offensive. Washington, DC: Author.
U.S. Department of Justice, Criminal Conspiracies Division (1979) What Happened? Washington, DC: Author.
WEBSTER, W. (1979) Uniform Crime Reports for the United States. Washington, DC: Federal Bureau of Investigations.

PART III
Controversial Issues in the Courtroom

6

The Defense of Insanity

RITA J. SIMON and DAVID E. AARONSON

The assassination attempt by John Hinckley on President Reagan and the subsequent verdict that the would-be assassinator was insane at the time he committed the act and therefore not responsible for his outrageous behavior produced great protests and demands that we either do away with the insanity defense completely, or redefine the legal criterion so as to make it much less likely for a jury to find a defendant such as Hinckley not guilty by reason of insanity. Indeed, over the past four centuries, the legitimacy of the defense of insanity has been a topic of controversy and debate. Francis Allen said of it:

> The issue of criminal responsibility has attracted more attention and stimulated more controversy than any other question in the substantive criminal law [Allen, 1964: 105].

This article briefly highlights the historical background of the various legal criteria that have been used in defense of insanity trials, examines the role of the jury in such trials, assesses the moral and legal bases for the insanity defense, and summarizes its current status.

INSANITY DEFENSE STANDARDS: PRE-M'NAGHTEN TO THE INSANITY DEFENSE REFORM ACT OF 1984

The earliest record of a jury acquitting a defendant on grounds of insanity in Anglo-Saxon law occurred in England in 1505. But even earlier than that, during the reign of Edward III (in the fourteenth century), complete madness was recognized as a defense to a criminal charge. By 1581, the doctrine of the lack of a guilty mind, or felonious intent, and hence lack of criminal responsibility, was well established.

The year 1723 marked the instigation of the "Wild Beast Test." An English judge declared, in the trial of one Edward Arnold, "In order to avail himself of the defense of insanity, a man must be totally deprived of his understanding and memory so as not to know what he is doing, no more than an infant, a brute, or a wild beast" (Simon, 1967: 17). The "Wild Beast Test," along with an ability to distinguish good from evil, remained the standards for determining responsibility for three quarters of a century, until a landmark trial in 1800 set a new standard. That trial also involved an assassination of a head of state.

James Hadfield was a former soldier who attempted to assassinate the reigning English monarch, George III, because he (Hadfield) believed he was the savior of all mankind. Hadfield thought that in order to gain world recognition it was necessary that he sacrifice himself as had Jesus Christ. The defendant concluded that an assault of the life of the king would attain his execution and, through it, martyrdom. The prosecution argued that the defendant's behavior (in the purchase of pistol, powder, and slugs, and in his concealment of the weapon) indicated that he was neither an idiot nor a madman "afflicted by the absolute privation of reason" (Simon, 1967: 18).

In his opening statement, Lord Erskine, in fact, anticipated both the *Durham* rule (adopted by the Appellate Court of the District of Columbia in 1954) and the *American Law Institute Rule* (the rule used by the jury in the Hinckley trial) some 150 years later, and argued that a person could know right from wrong, could understand the nature of the act that he or she was about to commit, could manifest a clear design, foresight, and cunning in the planning and executing of it, but that if his mental condition produced or was the cause of the criminal act, he should not be held legally responsible for it.

Lord Kenyon, the Chief Justice, recommended to the jury that Hadfield's trial be terminated. The jury accepted the court's suggestion and acquitted the defendant, because "he was under the influence of insanity at the time the act was committed" (Simon, 1967: 19). The decision in the Hadfield case was considered a landmark because it rejected two concepts previously accepted by the court. It denied that the defendant must be totally deprived of all mental faculty before he or she could be acquitted, and it severed the tie between insanity and the ability to distinguish good from evil, or right from wrong.

In the next dozen years, three cases were heard in which the defendants were charged with murder and pleaded insanity. In each case, the English courts returned to the law of criminal responsibility formulated by Mr. Justice Tracy in the Arnold case of 1723. All three of the defendants were found guilty and executed. In one of the trials, Lord Chief Justice Mansfield charged the jury as follows:

> It must in fact be proved beyond all doubt, that at the time he committed the atrocious act with which he stands charged, he did not consider that murder was a crime against the laws of God and nature [Simon, 1967: 19].

We come, in 1843, to the trial of *The Queen Against Daniel M'Naghten,* one of the most thoroughly discussed and controversial cases in English and American law. Briefly, here are the facts of the M'Naghten case. Daniel M'Naghten was a Scottish woodcutter who assassinated Edward Drumond, secretary to the prime minister, Sir Robert Peel, in the mistaken belief that the secretary was the prime minister. M'Naghten, who was described during the trial by nine medical witnesses as "an extreme paranoiac entangled in an elaborate system of delusions" (Simon, 1967: 20), believed that the prime minister was responsible for the financial and personal misfortunes that were continually plaguing him. So convincing was the defense's plea that at the end of the testimony, Lord Chief Justice Tindal, sitting with two other judges, came close to directing the jury's verdict. He told the jury:

> I cannot help remarking in common with my learned brethren that the whole of medical evidence is one side — that it seems almost unnecessary that I should go through the evidence [Simon, 1967: 20].

He then instructed the jury:

> The point I shall have to submit to you is, whether on the whole of the evidence you have heard, you are satisfied that at the time the act was committed... the prisoner had that competent use of his understanding as that he knew that he was doing, by the very act itself, a wicked and a wrong thing? If the prisoner was not sensible at the time he committed the act, that it was a violation of the law of God or of man, undoubtedly

he was not responsible for that act or liable to any punishment flowing from that act.... If on balancing the evidence in your minds, you think the prisoner capable of distinguishing between right and wrong, then he was a responsible agent and liable to all the penalties the law imposes. If not... then you will probably not take upon yourselves to find the prisoner guilty. If this is your opinion, then you will acquit the prisoner [Simon, 1967: 21].

The jury found the defendant not guilty on the grounds of insanity. Daniel M'Naghten was committed to Broadmoor mental institution, where he remained until his death about 20 years later.

Queen Victoria, the House of Lords, and the newspapers of the day disapproved of the verdict in angry and bitter tones. Broadmoor, for example, was described by the press as a retreat for idlers. M'Naghten's attempted assassination of the prime minister had marked the fifth attack on English sovereigns and their ministers since the turn of the century. The government and newspapers interpreted the court's action to be a direct disregard of the dangerous and threatening state of affairs.

The case of Daniel M'Naghten probably would have had a place of distinction in English criminal law even if the uproar had ended on this note of public indignation. But more was still to come. The House of Lords called upon the 15 judges of the common law courts to respond to a series of questions on the law that the lords would ask them. In effect, the judges were being asked to account for a miscarriage of justice. Their actions had been severely criticized by the Crown, the House of Lords, and the press, and now they were being confronted directly with their misdeeds.

The responses that the judges gave to the lords established a criterion of criminal responsibility of the insane. From that time until the present, every case heard in English courts was, and is still, decided along the principles established by the judges' responses to the House of Lords interrogation.

Less than a decade later, in 1851, what have become known as the *M'Naghten Rules* were adopted in the federal and most of the state courts of the United States. In later years, only one state, New Hampshire, adopted a rule that was not in line with the M'Naghten formula. In 1868, a New Hampshire jury that was trying to decide whether the defendant who killed his victim with an ax in the course of a robbery was insane, was instructed by Chief Justice Perley along the following lines:

> If... [the jury] found that the defendant killed Brown in a manner that would be criminal and unlawful if the defendant were sane—the verdict should be "not guilty by reason of insanity" if the killing was the offspring or product of mental disease in the defendant; that neither delusion, nor knowledge of right and wrong, nor design, nor cunning in planning and executing the killing, and escaping or avoiding detection, nor ability to recognize acquaintances, or to labor or transact business or manage affairs, is, *as a matter of law* a test of mental disease; but that *all* symptons and *all* tests of mental disease are *purely matters of fact* to be determined by the jury [Simon, 1967: 25].

Under such instructions, the issue of the accused's mental condition, whether that person had the capacity for criminal intent, became a question of fact, and therefore a matter for the jury to determine, not for the court to define.

The New Hampshire court a few years later made this point even more explicit when it used the following analogy in its instructions to the jury:

> Whether the defendant had a mental disease seems as much a question of fact as whether he had a bodily disease; and whether the killing of his wife was the product of that disease was also as clearly a matter of fact as whether thirst and a quickened pulse are the product of a fever [Simon, 1967: 26].

The decision in *State v. Pike* (1868) and *State v. Jones* (1870) are today the law in New Hampshire. But the New Hampshire rule has had little impact outside the borders of that state, and failed to gain adoption in any other jurisdiction for almost a century. Other jurisdictions continued to adhere to the M'Naghten "right from wrong" formula.

In 1954, the United States Court of Appeals for the District of Columbia handed down its decision discarding the M'Naghten rule and introducing a different legal basis for determining criminal responsibility in *Durham v. United States.*

Unlike most trials involving a defense of insanity, Monte Durham's crime was housebreaking, rather than murder. The defendant, a 26-year-old resident of the District of Columbia, had a long history of mental disorder and petty thievery. He had been committed on several occasions to mental hospitals and had served time in prison for passing bad checks. He received a medical discharge from the Navy.

On at least two occasions he attempted suicide. The judge in the district court instructed the jury along the lines of the M'Naghten rule, and the defendant was found guilty.

An appeal was granted, and the case was heard before a three-man bench of the appellate court. Having decided to grant the defendant a new trial on other grounds, the court went on to announce its new rule for insanity. Speaking for the court, Judge David L. Bazelon stated the new formula:

> The rule we now hold must be applied on the retrial of this case and in future cases is not unlike that followed by the New Hampshire court since 1870. It is simply that an accused is not criminally responsible if his unlawful act was *the product of mental disease or mental defect*. We use "disease" in the sense of a condition that is considered capable of either improving or deteriorating. We use "defect" in the sense of a condition that is not considered capable of either improving or deteriorating and that may be either congenital, or the result of injury, or the residual effect of a physical or mental disease....
>
> Thus your task would not be completed upon finding, if you did find, that the accused suffered from a mental disease or defect. He would still be responsible for his unlawful act if there was not a causal connection between such mental abnormality and the act. These questions must be determined by you from the facts that you find to be fairly deducible from the testimony and the evidence in this case [Simon, 1967: 31-32].

The adoption of the Durham rule in the District of Columbia was widely hailed in most psychiatric and some legal circles as the beginning of a new era. Halleck said of it in 1960, "It is doubtful whether any single case in the criminal law has stirred more comment and controversy than Durham. The Durham decision was regarded as a sign that the law would recognize the growing prestige and knowledge of psychiatry, and would work with it in the disposition of criminal cases, especially those in which the issue of insanity was introduced.

But the Durham rule did not gain wide acceptance. In the decade following its adoption in the District of Columbia, it was reviewed by 30 state and five federal courts and rejected by all of them. Two states, Vermont and Maine, adopted it for civil actions but retained M'Naghten for criminal cases.

Some 28 years later, in the District Court in Washington, D.C., a jury found John Hinckley not guilty by reason of insanity under still another set of legal rules. The Hinckley jury was instructed along these lines:

> A person is not responsible for criminal conduct if at the time of such conduct, as a result of mental disease or defect, he lacks substantial capacity either to appreciate the wrongfulness of his conduct or to conform his conduct to the requirement of law [American Law Institute, 1962].

With slight alterations, this formulation, which was written by the American Law Institute, is the law in a majority of the states and, until the passage of the Crime Control Act of 1984, all but one of the federal circuits. In 1984, the Fifth Circuit judicially altered its standard. In the words of Judge Irving Kaufman of the Appellate bench:

> This test focuses not only on the defendants' understanding of his conduct, which remains a key element in any inquiry into mental capacity, but also on the defendant's ability to control his actions. It would absolve from criminal punishment an individual who knows what he is doing yet is driven to crime by delusions, fears, or compulsions. This result conforms to the modern view of the mind as a unified entity whose functioning may be impaired in numerous ways ["The insanity plea on trial," *New York Times Magazine,* August 8, 1982].

The Insanity Defense Reform Act of 1984 is the first federal codification of the insanity defense. It states that a defendant may be found not guilty only by reason of insanity if the defendant, "as a result of a severe mental disease or defect, was unable to appreciate the nature and quality or the wrongfulness of his act." The 1984 Federal Act changes the insanity defense standard from a standard patterned on the American Law Institute (ALI) test to a standard patterned on the M'Naghten rule by requiring that the mental disease or defect be "severe," thus changing the definition of mental disease or defect. Further, by using the phrase "unable to appreciate" instead of "lacking substantial capacity to appreciate," it modifies the so-called "cognitive" prong of the ALI test, apparently requiring a total lack of ability to appreciate the nature and quality or the wrongfulness of the criminal act.

The Insanity Defense Reform Act of 1984 also makes substantial changes in the presentation of the insanity defense, including (1) shifting the burden of proof to the defendant, who must now prove insanity by a standard of clear and convincing evidence, (2) amending the Federal Rules of Evidence to prevent expert witnesses from testifying on "ultimate issues," and, (3) changing the verdict form to a special verdict of "not guilty *only* by reason of insanity." Finally, the act establishes for the first time a federal procedure for mandatory commitment of persons who have been found not guilty only by reason of insanity.

THE ROLE OF THE JURY

The findings from the experimental jury project at the College of Law at the University of Chicago indicated that during their deliberations, juries spend most of their time reviewing the court record, that is, the evidence they heard during the trial. By the time the juries finish their deliberations, they usually consider every bit of testimony, expert as well as lay, and every point offered in evidence. Indeed, the most consistent theme that emerged from the study of several hundred deliberations was the seriousness with which the jurors approached their job and the extent to which they were concerned that the verdict they reached was consistent with the spirit of the law and with the facts of the case.

In the instructions most juries receive about expert testimony, they are told by the court that they are *not* bound to accept such testimony; that they should give it such weight as in their judgment it is fairly entitled to receive. But, if a jury is satisfied that it does not accept the expert's testimony, it is not bound to do so.

One of our most consistent observations of the juries' behavior on defense of insanity cases was that they were very loath to declare a defendant insane on the basis of the act itself. In other words, no matter how bizarre or perverse the defendant's behavior appeared, the jury still insisted upon reviewing all of the specific details surrounding the crime and all of the information it had about the defendant's background and personal circumstances.

Many distinguished members of the bench and bar believe that juries lack the intelligence to decide cases involving a defense of insanity. The findings of the Chicago jury project dispute the practitioners' judgment. On the whole, those data demonstrate that the jury recognizes the distinction between a clinical diagnosis and the application of a moral, legal criterion, and that they understand it is the latter that they must use in deciding the case.

It is partly because the jurors recognize the separateness of the clinical and the legal questions that they are most frustrated by psychiatric testimony. The jurors realize that the expert is emphasizing only one aspect of the problem, the clinical part, and that his or her testimony contributes little or nothing to the main dilemma facing the jury—that of placing the clinical or purely medical facts about the defendant into a moral-legal context.

Most of the jurors, most of the time, recognize that the final responsibility for the defendant's fate rests with them. The data suggest that they were both proud of and a little awed by their responsibility, and most of them did not seek ways of avoiding it.

In most states and in all federal jurisdictions, a person who is acquitted on grounds of insanity is immediately confined to a mental institution until medical authorities determine that he or she is recovered or is restored to sanity. In some jurisdictions, however, the jury is not instructed as to what the consequences of a not-guilty-by-reason-of-insanity verdict would be. Some lawyers believe that jurors assume that the defendant would go free and they argue that the lack of information prejudices the defendant's right to acquittal. The Chicago Project study of the jury showed that it assumed that a defendant found not guilty by reasons of insanity would be automatically committed to a mental institution and his or her subsequent release would be determined by medical authorities. For example, in mock jury experiments, juries that received no instructions from the court on this issue were as likely to make that assumption as were juries that were specifically instructed on the commitment issue (Simon, 1967: 89).

MORAL AND LEGAL BASES
FOR THE INSANITY DEFENSE

The underlying premise of our criminal law is that a person will generally conduct him or herself in accordance with the acceptable range or norms of conduct adopted by society. There is an underlying assumption that a person in the exercise of free will should be held accountable for his or her conduct because individuals do in fact have at least a minimum capacity for making the voluntary and rational choice required for criminal responsibility. Thus the ordinary criminal defendant is viewed as "culpable" or "blameworthy" or "responsible" because that person could have chosen to abide by the dictates of the law. There are, however, those few who cannot be held accountable because of a mental disability or disease, which deprives them of the minimal capacity for rational and voluntary choices upon which the law's expectation of responsibility is predicated. Because of their incapacity to comply with the law, such persons are not held culpable, nor are criminal sanctions invoked or applied consequent to their conduct.

The insanity defense, therefore, is the exception that "proves" the rule of free will. Supporters of the defense view it as vital to a healthy society that uses its criminal law to build and buttress self-reliant action on the part of citizens affected by the law. It is this vision of law that has, throughout history, rallied supporters to resist efforts to abolish the insanity defense. Eliminating the insanity defense would remove from the criminal law and the public conscience the vitally important distinction between "illness" and "evil" or, as one scholar noted, would tuck it away in an administrative process.

Also, for those few who cannot be held accountable because of mental disability or disease, social control may be served by confining, especially those who are dangerously insane, in a secure hospital setting. Similarly, the general deterrence theory underlying punishment is that a person's awareness and fear of unpleasant consequences will restrain him or her from engaging in criminal behavior. This can be effective only with persons who can understand the signals directed at them by the criminal code, who can respond to warnings, and who can understand the significance of sanctions imposed upon violators. Thus punishment is not likely to deter seriously disturbed individuals from future antisocial conduct.

Further, the insanity defense is seen by supporters to be quite consistent with the notion of specific deterrence or restraint because, if the defense is successfully invoked, the defendant is not merely incarcerated for a fixed period of time but, instead, can or should be committed until such time as he or she is no longer dangerous.

On the other hand, a number of arguments have been advanced by those who favor abolishing or severely limiting the insanity defense. Supporters of abolition argue that the key terms in the various insanity tests are so vague that they invite semantic jousting, speculation, and intuitive moral judgments in the guise of factual determinations. Also, there is little or no basis in psychiatry for expert witnesses to testify, often in conclusory terms, to differentiate between persons who are personally blameworthy from those who are not. Further, some believe that it is therapeutically more desirable to encourage treatment of persons as responsible for their conduct rather than as involuntary victims "playing a sick role." In addition, the insanity defense discriminates against persons who commit crimes because of influences on their personalities other than mental disease or defect. Opponents of the defense argue that if it is therapeutically desirable to provide a medical-custodial disposition, then such a decision should be made directly, immediately following the defendant's conviction, rather than indirectly during the trial. Finally, opponents of the insanity defense claim that it is in practice a "rich person's defense" because it is usually only the wealthy who can afford the array of experts needed to mount a convincing defense. These scarce psychiatric resources, they argue, should be spent in treatment of those who have been committed or imprisoned.

The intense interest and attention that the insanity defense provokes is somewhat odd when we consider that it is introduced in less than 1% of all criminal trials. Steadman et al., for example, report the results of a mail survey conducted in 1978 of all 50 states and the federal system, in which they found that there were 1,554 persons admitted as not guilty by reason of insanity (Steadman, 1985). This figure represents an average of 31 insanity acquittals per state. The number of NGI admissions per state, however, varies widely from 169 in California to zero in Delaware, Iowa, North Dakota, South Dakota, West Virginia, and Wyoming. On any given day in 1978, they report that there was an average of 3,140 persons detained as not guilty by reason of insanity. California had the highest daily census of 589 and, on an average day, seven states had none.

Steadman et al. also compared the number of persons found not guilty by reason of insanity and committed to mental hospitals against the overall number of persons in such institutions. For example, on June 30, 1978, there were 147,283 patients in state and county mental hospitals (Steadman, 1985). The 3,140 NGIs thus represent only 2% of all such residents.

Of more than 32,500 cases handled by the New Jersey State Office of the Public Defender in fiscal 1982, defendants entered not guilty by reason of insanity pleas in only 50 cases, less than one-sixth of one percent (Rodriquez et al., 1983). In a Connecticut study, only 25 persons were identified as having been adjudicated NGI during the three-year period between January 1, 1970, and December 31, 1972. Nine of these persons were found NGI in 1970, ten in 1971, and six in 1972 (Phillips and Pasewark, 1980).

Of perhaps equal significance in terms of public policy and not generally known by the public, almost all of the successful insanity defense acquittals result from a prosecutor agreeing with defense counsel to enter into a formal stipulation or tacit agreement for an acquittal by reason of insanity. Almost always this results from a report of the government or state psychiatrists that the defendant meets the criteria for insanity. For example, in a letter to Senator Strom Thurmond dated November 4, 1982, then Assistant Attorney General Robert McConnell wrote that the Justice Department information in calendar year 1981 indicated that only *four* federal defendants were actually acquitted of charges on the basis of a successful insanity defense. In Maryland, of the 150 to 200 cases each year in which the state psychiatrists classify the defendants as sane, only two or three defendants are found NGI in a contested trail. The state psychiatrists find about 40 defendants to be insane each year and most, if not all, are subsequently found by the court to be not guilty by reason of insanity (Maryland Governor's Task Force Report, 1984).

Thus the legal process that results from most of the successful insanity defense pleas—often a formality—is an uncontested bench trial before a judge where formal findings are made and not a contested jury trial. A recent statistical study found that the most critical factor determining the successful outcome of an insanity plea is the forensic evaluation of the defendant by the prosecutor's mental health experts (Steadman et al., 1983).

The publicity surrounding the trial and acquittal by reason of insanity of John Hinckley—and occasional well-publicized local cases in various states—suggests to the public a totally different picture of the insanity defense than shown by careful statistical studies. Even before the Hinckley case, public opinion polls confirm that there is a profound public misunderstanding of the frequency of use and success of the insanity defense. As the above empirical data suggest, the frequency and success rate of the insanity plea has significance only from the fact that it is of no statistical significance. As the American Psychiatric Association concluded, the insanity defense is empirically unimportant (American Psychiatric Association, 1982).

Perhaps the best brief explanation for the intense interest and attention that it attracts is that the insanity defense touches on ultimate social values. It was established on the foundation of the concept of individual responsibility as a prerequisite for criminal punishment. In the words of Allan Stone, the defense of insanity

> purports to draw a line between those who are morally responsible and those who are not, those who are blameworthy and those who are not, those who have free will and those who do not, those who should be punished and those who should not, and those who can be deterred and those who cannot [Stone, 1975: 218].

Additionally, historically the insanity defense has been used to avoid the harshness of the death penalty. Since the U.S. Supreme Court has given the green light to the states to proceed with executions, the insanity defense is likely to take on new practical significance during the 1980s and beyond.

CURRENT STATUS OF THE INSANITY DEFENSE

The jury's acquittal of John Hinckley aroused the anticipated protests. Responses to that decision have taken the form of bills in state legislatures to outlaw the defense of insanity, to revise the legal criteria and/or the burden of proof, and to change the verdict forms. It has led to the adoption of a federal statute on the legal criteria for the defense of insanity, and it has resulted in position statements by such professional associations as the American Bar Association, the American Medical Association, and the American Psychiatric Association that indicate their support or opposition to the validity and legitimacy of the defense of insanity as well as to related procedural and substantive issues. At least eight state legislatures have enacted forms of guilty-but-mentally-ill verdicts: Alaska, Delaware, Georgia, Illinois, Indiana, Kentucky, Michigan, and New Mexico. Under the Michigan statute, enacted in 1975, well before the Hinckley trial, the defendant is sentenced under the statutory provisions as if found guilty, committed to prison to serve out the sentence, but is supposedly treated for mental illness during the period of incarceration at a prison facility.

CONCLUDING REMARKS

The insanity defense touches on ultimate social values. Whenever it is introduced, whatever the result of a particular trial, it arouses controversy, protest, and a clamor for reform. The jury's decision in the Hinckley trial that the defendant was not guilty on grounds of insanity aroused the anticipated protest.

In our opinion, the principle that guilt should only be placed upon those who are capable of assuming responsibility for their behavior is too important a value to give up, even in the face of a tragic incident. As we continue to struggle with the question of what should be done with people who are mentally ill and violate the law, it is very important that we do not discard the connection between responsibility and guilt, and extract revenge from those who offend us by heinous and violent behavior. Justice Kaufman, in a recent article, reminds us of the words of wisdom offered by Justice Brandeis when he said, "We must be ever on our guard lest we direct our prejudices unto legal principles" ("The insanity plea on trial," *New York Times Magazine,* August 8, 1982).

REFERENCES

ALLEN, F. (1964) The Borderline of Criminal Justice. Chicago: University of Chicago Press.
American Law Institute (1962) Model Penal Code Section 4.1, Philadelphia.
American Psychiatric Association (1982) Statement on the Insanity Defense (p. 5).
Comprehensive Crime Control Act (1984) 18 U.S.C. 20.
HALLECK, C. (1960) "Insanity defense in the District of Columbia: a legal lorelie." Georgia Law Journal 294.
Maryland Governor's Task Force to Review the Defense of Insanity (1984) Report to the Governor (p. 20).
PHILLIPS, B. L. and R. A. PASEWARK (1980) "Insanity plea in Connecticut." Bulletin of the American Academy of Psychiatry and Law 8: 335-344.

RODRIQUEZ, J. H., L. M. LEWINN, and M. L. PERLIN (1983) "The insanity defense under seige! Legislative assaults and legal rejoinders." Rutgers Law Journal 14: 397-430.

SIMON, R. J. (1967) The Jury and the Defense of Insanity. Boston: Little, Brown.

STEADMAN, H. J. (1985) "Empirical research on the insanity defense." Annals of the American Academy of Political and Social Sciences 477: 58-71.

STEADMAN, H. J., L. KEITNER, J. BRAFF, and T. M. ARVANITES (1983) "Factors associated with a successful insanity plea." American Journal of Psychiatry 140, 4: 401-405.

STONE, A. (1975) Mental Health and the Law: A System in Transtition. DHEW Pub. (ADM) 75-176. Rockville, MA: National Institute of Mental Health.

7

Convicted But Innocent
False Positives and the Criminal Justice Process

C. RONALD HUFF and ARYE RATTNER

Item: Steven Titus and his girlfriend have just left a restaurant, where they were celebrating her twenty-first birthday. While driving, they are stopped by police, who ask if he minds their taking his photograph. He agrees, joking that it is a good chance to be photographed with his girlfriend. The next day, a 17-year-old rape victim picks his photo out of a "photo lineup." Saying, "This one is the closest, it has to be the one," she identifies Titus as the man who raped her on a secluded road near the Seattle-Tacoma airport. Titus is convicted and nearly goes to prison before his innocence is established through his own efforts and the investigative reporting of a *Seattle Times* reporter. The reporter wins a Pulitzer Prize; Titus is still trying to put his life back together ("Cleared of Rape, Seattle Man Still in Hell," *Los Angeles Times,* January 4, 1983: 9).

Item: Lenell Geter, a young black engineer employed in the Dallas area is at work one day when a fast-food restaurant is robbed some 50 miles away. A white woman informs police that Geter has a "suspicious" habit of reading and feeding ducks in a park near her home. Several witnesses to the crime identify Geter from photos, even though their previous descriptions of the robber were quite different. Despite the testimony of his coworkers that he was at work at the time of the crime, and despite the absence of any physical evidence linking Geter to the crime, he is convicted and sentenced to life in prison. He is finally released in December 1983, following intense national publicity, including a feature story on CBS's "60 Minutes" ("The Bad and Good Luck of Lenell Geter," *New York Times*, March 28, 1984).

Item: Juan Venegas, a Mexican-American youth, is convicted of murdering Bill Staga, an old man, in Los Angeles. Venegas spends two and a half years in California prisons for a crime actually committed by his friend Lawrence Reyes, with whom Venegas was staying on the night of the murder. Venegas is subsequently awarded $1 million in a civil trial that reveals a police frameup, intimidation of witnesses to perjure themselves, questionable decisions by a trial judge hearing his first murder case, and other irregularities (Granelli, 1980: 9-11, 20).

These three cases of wrongful conviction illustrate a problem that poses enormous questions for the criminal justice system of any democratic nation. In a society that values the freedom of its citizens, it is a sobering thought that a citizen can be convicted and perhaps imprisoned for a long period of time for a crime he or she did not commit. While most of us express concern about guilty persons who "beat the system" and go free (the "false negatives"), comparatively little attention has been paid to those who are innocent, yet convicted (the "false positives").

Clearly, both types of error are damaging to the criminal justice system's credibility and, ultimately, to society. What is often ignored, or not realized, is that these two types of "system error" are actually interrelated. That is, when a guilty person is arrested but not convicted, it leaves open the possibility of convicting an innocent person for that crime (not to mention the fact that the guilty person is still free to commit more crimes). Likewise, when an innocent person is convicted, it means that the real criminal is still at large, posing a potential threat to public safety.

Most people, upon reading about cases such as those above, tend to be surprised, shocked, even outraged. They frequently wonder how such miscarriages of justice can occur in our legal system, which seems to go so far in protecting suspects' and defendants' rights. They may even wonder whether such a nightmare could happen to them. This article represents an attempt to analyze wrongful conviction in the context of the criminal justice process to determine those factors that seem most directly related to the production of these false positives.

IDENTIFYING CASES OF WRONGFUL CONVICTION

Our discussion and analyses are based on our research on wrongful conviction over the past three years. During this time, we have been able to assemble what we believe is the largest systematic data base ever developed on this subject. Due to the controversial nature of the subject matter, we have insisted from the outset on very conservative criteria for inclusion in our sample—that is, only those convicted of a felony and later officially cleared beyond doubt. Official acknowledgement of error includes cases in which (1) a pardon was granted due to new evidence, (2) a new trial was permitted and the defendant found not guilty, (3) innocence was established on the basis of overwhelming evidence, rather than a technicality or "reasonable doubt," or (4) appellate court review proved innocence beyond doubt.

We utilized a two-stage process in identifying cases of wrongful conviction that met our criteria: (1) literature review and retrospective analyses of both old and recent legal cases, and (2) survey research via mailed questionnaires designed to identify additional cases, improve our understanding of the dynamics of wrongful conviction, and elicit estimates of the magnitude of the problem and suggested policy reforms.

The literature review generated cases from throughout the United States, while the questionnaire sample (N = 353) consisted of both national (state attorney generals) and Ohio respondents (presiding judges of common pleas courts, prosecuting attorneys, public defenders, sheriffs, and police chiefs), with emphasis placed on the 88 counties of Ohio. Our decision to focus on Ohio in the latter phase of the survey was made for three principal reasons: (1) Ohio is the seventh largest state in the nation, with a population in excess of 10 million (U.S. Bureau of the Census, 1981) and is representative demographically, (2) the use of a single state serves to "control" for legal code, while still allowing for great diversity of jurisdictions, and (3) Ohio's criminal justice system is fairly representative of American criminal justice processes.

While space limitations preclude a full discussion of methodology, research instruments, and methods of analysis, it is important to note that both qualitative and quantitative data have been utilized in our study. Based on our ongoing review of books, articles, newspaper clippings, and legal documents, as well as our survey questionnaire, we have identified more than 500 cases of wrongful conviction that meet our conservative criteria for inclusion.

MEASURING THE TIP OF AN ICEBERG

If ever the metaphor "like the tip of an iceberg" applied to a research problem, wrongful conviction surely qualifies! In estimating the magnitude of crime in America, for example, we talk about the "dark figure" (unreported crime), but we have developed alternative methods of estimating actual crime (most notably, crime victimization surveys). But consider the phenomenon of wrongful conviction—there is simply no known method of determining how many wrongful convictions occur. The basic problem is that we generally don't become aware that a conviction is erroneous until it is officially acknowledged as such. In many cases, to be sure, there is a lingering feeling of uncertainty about the guilt of the accused, but reasonable doubt is not the same thing as proof of innocence. Such cases cannot be included in our sample, since they are not "pure" cases of clearcut wrongful conviction.

Certain types of cases have a much higher probability of coming to public attention than do others. For example, we are much more likely to learn about a wrongful murder conviction than to hear about an erroneous misdemeanor conviction. Similarly, a wrongful conviction is more likely to be uncovered in cases where the innocent defendant is still alive and has others working to clear him or her of the charges than if the unfortunate person has died, leaving those who believe in his or her innocence wondering if it is worth the trouble to clear his or her name. As Judge Frank (1957: 248) has remarked:

> No one knows how many innocent men erroneously convicted of murder have been put to death. . . . Once a convicted man is dead, all interest in vindicating him usually evaporates.

Even though we have eliminated from consideration all misdemeanor convictions (where the sanctions are less severe and the convicted person therefore less likely to press an appeal), we are left with the realization that even for felony convictions carrying severe sanctions, there is no certain way to identify the universe of false positive errors. Anyone who has worked in the criminal justice system can attest that a substantial proportion of those charged with, and even convicted of, serious crimes deny that they actually committed those offenses. If, for example, we were to accept as factual all the claims of innocence made by prisoners, we could quickly solve this nation's prison overcrowding simply by releasing all these "innocent" prisoners! Most such claims, however, are found upon closer examination to be without merit.

One of the goals of our exploratory study has been to derive an *estimate* of the magnitude of wrongful felony convictions. Most of the authors who have written on the subject are convinced that such errors were not infrequent. Radin (1964), for example, quotes a highly respected judge who estimated that there may be as many as 14,000 wrongful convictions in the United States in a given year (a 5% false positive rate at that time). However, the judge's definition of wrongful conviction was a legalistic one that included reasonable doubt. Our review of the literature revealed estimates ranging from a very few cases each year up to 20% of all convictions.

Our own preliminary estimate, based on data provided by criminal justice officials (N = 229) is that wrongful conviction constitutes less than 1% of all felony convictions. When our respondents were asked to estimate the magnitude of this phenomenon in the United States, nearly three-fourths of them indicated that it occurs in less than 1% of all felony cases, while one-fifth placed their estimate at 1% to 5%. When asked about *their own jurisdictions,* more than half of our respondents estimated a false positive rate of less than 1%, while 37% said it never happens in their jurisdictions. The collective experience of this group of 229 criminal justice officials suggests, in other words, that of every 200 persons convicted of felonies in the United States, one or two may well be innocent. While this level of accuracy may not seem terribly alarming to some, consider the following: According to the U.S. Department of Justice (1983), the total number of persons arrested and charged with index crimes in 1981 was 2,291,560. It is reasonable to assume that at least one half of them were convicted. This means that even a 0.5% error rate, when multiplied by the huge base of felony convictions in the United States, would produce about 6,000 convictions of innocent citizens in that year alone.

WHAT CAUSES WRONGFUL CONVICTION?

Major published works on the subject of wrongful conviction in America (Borchard, 1932; Gardner, 1952; Frank and Frank, 1957; Radin, 1964; MacNamara, 1969) and in England (Brandon and Davies, 1973), coupled with our own survey data, enables us to identify the major factors responsible for convicting innocent defendants.

Eyewitness Error

Item: William Bernard Jackson is convicted of rape and sentenced to a term of 14 to 50 years in prison after being positively identified by two rape victims. After serving four and a half years in prison, Jackson is finally freed when the arrest and subsequent investigation of a look-alike, Dr. Edward Franklin Jackson (no relation), proves that the "wrong Jackson" is innocent of all charges. Dr. Jackson, an internist, is indicted on 94 charges, including 36 rapes and 46 burglaries ("Ohio Physician Charged with 36 Rapes," *Atlanta Constitution,* September 23, 1982: 1A; "We're Sorry," *Time,* October 4, 1982: 45; "Mistaken Identity Not Rare Error," *Columbus Dispatch,* September 25, 1983: B1).

The single most important factor contributing to wrongful conviction is eyewitness misidentification. This source of error was involved in 52% of the cases in our data base, ranging from mistaken identification in cases of close physical resemblance to the erroneous identification of innocent persons who bear little or no resemblance to the actual offenders. While jurors tend to attach great significance to the testimony of eyewitnesses, an increasing number of experts and judges share the view of Judge Lumbard of the Second Circuit:

> Centuries of experience in the administration of criminal justice have shown that convictions based solely on testimony that identifies a defendant previously unknown to the witness is highly suspect. Of the various kinds of evidence, it is the least reliable, especially where unsupported by corroborating evidence [*Jackson v. Fogg,* 1978].

Major published research on eyewitness misidentification (Loftus, 1979; Buckhout, 1974, 1977; Brigham and Barkowitz, 1978), in addition to our own data, suggests that there are three major types of factors contributing to such errors: (1) psychological factors (affect, perception, information retention under stress, information retrieval), (2) systemic factors (the mechanics of "photo lineups," "suggestions" provided to the witness), and (3) societal factors (subcultural bias, personal prejudice, cross-racial misidentification).

One of the most bizarre cases in recent memory involved eyewitness error. In this case, a man was convicted without even having been arrested for the crime!

Item: Jeffrey Streeter is convicted and sentenced to a year of incarceration for beating up an old man. Witnesses in court point to Streeter, sitting next to the defense attorney, and say he is the person who attacked the old man. However, it is actually Lee Marvin Anderson, not Streeter, who has been arrested and charged with the crime. Streeter had been sitting outside the courtroom when the defense attorney asked him to sit next to him in order to test the credibility of the eyewitnesses. Even though Anderson, the defendant, was in the courtroom at the time, the eyewitnesses identified the innocent Streeter, who was merely trying to be helpful ("Court Stand-In Is Convicted of Crime He Didn't Commit," *Atlanta Constitution*, July 17, 1980: 12A).

Unethical Police/Prosecutors

Most of us are familiar with the problem of coerced confession, which was especially prevalent prior to the expansion of suspects' rights by the federal courts. Such abuses by police continue, sad to say, though hopefully at a lower level of frequency. Another type of abuse that still stains the image of police on occasion is the practice of coaching witnesses, showing photographs of a suspect to witnesses prior to a lineup, and similar efforts to "get their man." Perhaps less widely known are cases involving unethical prosecutors.

Item: A prosecutor secures a conviction by bringing in a piece of dramatic evidence linking the defendant to the crime—a pair of men's undershorts found a mile from the crime scene. The prosecutor alleges that the shorts are heavily stained with blood—the same type as the victim's blood! A chemist swears that this is true, and despite the defendant's protests that the shorts are not his and his attorney's request to examine the evidence (denied), the defendant is convicted.

The convicted prisoner later petitions for a writ of habeas corpus, and a microanalyst testifies that the brown stain on the shorts is paint, not blood. The prosecutor later admits knowing in advance that the stains were paint, and the Supreme Court rules that the prosecutor deliberately misrepresented the truth in the case (*Miller v. Pate,* 1967).

In a number of cases with which we are familiar, the police and/or the prosecutor were convinced of the suspect's or defendant's guilt and sought to buttress their case by prompting witnesses, suggesting what actually happened at the time of the crime, fabricating or concealing evidence, and even perjuring themselves in court. We are not claiming that this is common behavior, but we have found that it is not as rare as one might hope. It appears that such unprofessional behavior is often motivated by a sincere desire on the part of the police or prosecutor to strengthen the case against a defendant who, in their eyes, is clearly guilty but who just might be acquitted by the "twelve rocks in the box" (a derogatory term sometimes used in referring to juries).

Probably the single most important contribution to false conviction made by prosecutors is not the fabrication of evidence, as in the case above, but their failure to advise the defense of exculpatory evidence (evidence that may prove the innocence of the defendant). The pressure to obtain convictions sometimes leads prosecutors to ignore their professional obligations. In fact, it is likely that most Americans believe that the prosecutor's duty is to secure convictions, when in fact it is not. Rather, it is to seek justice. Rule 3.8 of the American Bar Association's Model Rules of Professional Conduct outlines the special responsibilities of the prosecutor:

(1) to refrain from prosecuting a charge that the prosecutor knows is not supported by probable cause
(2) to make a reasonable effort to assure that the defendant has been advised of the right to counsel and has been given reasonable opportunity to obtain counsel
(3) not seek to obtain from an unrepresented defendant a waiver of important pretrial rights, such as the right to a preliminary hearing
(4) to make reasonable effort to seek all evidence, whether or not favorable to the defendant, make timely disclosure to the defense of all evidence known to the prosecutor that supports innocence or mitigates the offense, and, in connection with sentencing disclose to the defense and to the tribunal all unprivileged mitigating information known to the prosecutor [American Bar Association, 1979].

Community Pressure for Conviction

This factor is especially prevalent during periods of perceived "crime waves" or at the time of a particularly heinous crime, such as the murder of a child. The history of the United States contains numerous examples of the persecution of innocent people, and even entire groups of people, when hatred replaces reason and due process. The lynch mobs bent on vengeance, the persecution of Japanese-Americans during World War II, the racial hatred of the Ku Klux Klan—these are but a few of the soiled pages in the American history book.

Item: In 1948 a New Jersey newspaper launched a campaign to increase the use of capital punishment as a result of an "intolerable crime wave" exemplified by the killing of an old man. In an editorial titled "The Idle Electric Chair," the *Trenton Times* noted that the State of New Jersey had not executed anyone in over two years. As a result of this inflammatory editorial, police officers organized a special squad with orders to shoot, kill, or arrest any "suspicious-looking" person. In a subsequent editorial, the newspaper called on police to solve cases "through one means or another." Within a few days six blacks were arrested without warrant. Even though all six had alibis for the murder of the old man and there were no witnesses to the crime, they were nonetheless convicted and sentenced to death by an all-white jury. Eventually, through the efforts of the American Civil Liberties Union, four of the prisoners won acquittal in a second trial; the fifth won his freedom via commutation of his sentence; the sixth died in prison, the innocent victim of public hysteria (Lofton, 1966).

Certainly, pressure from the public and the mass media in many instances is to be credited with forcing public officials to behave more responsibly and making them more accountable for their actions. One can only wonder how much the public would know of Watergate, the "Pentagon papers," and other covert activities were it not for investigative journalists. On the other hand, these same democratic forces can create tremendous obstacles to the fairhanded administration of justice. Significant conflict and tension can exist between two equally desirable democratic goals—for example, "a free press" and "a fair trial." The latter tension often emerges in local trials of despised defendants and/or where an atmosphere of hysteria prevails. Even a change of venue may not suffice, because simply moving a trial to a new location does not always guarantee an atmosphere free of bias toward the defendant.

A related issue, one that we plan to explore in future research, is the extent to which society is willing to tolerate wrongful convictions in the belief that a high conviction rate helps deter crime. Are such errors regarded as an unavoidable cost of the "war on crime?" Also of interest to us is the question of whether societal tolerance for false positives changes over time. For example, are people more willing to tolerate convictions of the innocent during "crime waves?" During economic depressions?

Knowledge of Criminal Record

Many people apparently believe that "where there's smoke, there must be fire." This is illustrated by the tendency to think that if the police have arrested someone, he or she must be guilty. It is also apparent in the belief that if someone has been convicted of a crime in the past and is rearrested, he or she must be guilty again. This becomes a factor in some cases of wrongful conviction, since the past criminal record of the accused may be divulged when the defendant voluntarily takes the stand, or may be brought out through the questioning of other defense witnesses. In some cases, it is common knowledge in the community and even among jurors. Where this occurs, it makes it much more difficult to be certain that the verdict is based solely on the present charges and that the defendant is not being convicted for *who* he or she is, since that person has a deviant status in our society as an "ex-con" (a status that, ironically, is based on a *former* status).

False Accusations

Item: On September 19, 1981, Nathaniel Carter is arrested in the brutal stabbing death of Clarice Herndon, his ex-wife's foster mother. The prosecution's key witness is Carter's estranged wife, who testifies that she watched helplessly while Carter attacked her foster mother, whose body was found to have suffered 23 stab wounds. Even the witness herself had apparently been attacked by Carter, since police found her with cuts on her hands. What a witness! Carter is convicted and sentenced to 25 years to life in prison. After serving two years, he is freed when the former Mrs. Carter admits that she, in fact, killed her foster mother in a domestic argument ("How Errors Convicted the Wrong Man," *New York Times*, March 15, 1984: B1ff).

This case illustrates one type of false accusation, in which a crime has actually occurred and someone deliberately and falsely accuses an innocent person. A second type of false accusation we found among our cases occurs where there never was a crime. There are, in fact, several documented cases where innocent men have served prison terms for "murders" that were never committed.

Item: Local citizens were understandably angered over the murder of poor John Cameron. Dutifully, they avenged his killing by convicting his murderer and hanging him in the yard of the county jail. Ten years later, the "murder victim," Cameron, was found alive and well, living in another city (" A Legal Murder," *Daily Nebraskan State Journal*, August 4, 1892).

Plea Bargaining

One of the least understood aspects of wrongful conviction is the role sometimes played by the plea bargaining process. Numerous convicted but innocent defendants agreed to negotiated guilty pleas, even though protesting their innocence to counsel and others. Why would an innocent person decide to plead guilty? A recent experiment provides some insight into this question. Utilizing a role-playing process, it was found that innocent "defendants" were more likely to accept a plea bargain when they faced a number of charges or when the probable severity of punishment was great (Gregory, 1978).

Item: A defendant in Richmond, Virginia, anxiously awaits the jury's verdict in a first degree murder trial. He is convinced that they believe he is guilty. Moments before the jury completes its deliberations, he changes his plea to guilty, hoping that he will not follow Frank Coppola to the electric chair. The jury returns and reads its verdict: "Not guilty!" ("Convict Blames Lawyer for Pleas," *Columbus Dispatch*, September 26, 1982).

A number of factors operate to make a plea bargain look attractive to a defendant, even an innocent one. If the defendant is in jail, the plea bargain may include immediate freedom on probation. If a defendant has little understanding of legal processes and is represented by an attorney who wishes to expedite the case (perhaps because of a low fee), the attorney may convince the defendant that the plea bargain is "the best he can do." Finally, being found not guilty in court is not all that certain, even if it is the correct verdict. Some observers have compared legal outcomes to a game of chance. Alan Dershowitz, one of the nation's leading defense attorneys and a member of the Harvard law faculty, recently commented, "There has been almost no correlation between the guilt or innocence of my clients and whether they served time or got off" (1982: xiv).

Inadequacy of Counsel

One of the most popular bases of appeal in recent years has been "inadequacy of counsel." Fuelled in part by an appeal in the Scottsboro case (*Powell v. Alabama*, 1932), the basic rationale in such an appeal is that the original defense counsel, perhaps due to inexperience, inadequate investigative resources, or other factors, did not adequately represent his client's interests in the case. Examples of errors made by counsel include failure to file discovery motions; poor judgment in placing a defendant on the stand; and failure to challenge vigorously the contentions of the prosecutor in court. Appeals based on inadequate counsel are not easy to win, despite the fact that there is increasing concern, shared by the Chief Justice of the U.S. Supreme Court, that many attorneys are inadequately prepared for trial work.

Other Factors

In addition to the more common factors listed above, occasionally cases of wrongful conviction are found to involve other factors, such as judicial error, bias, or neglect of duty; voluntary and deliberate false confession; and the mental incompetency of the accused (especially a low I.Q., which may make it very difficult for the defendant to assist his or her attorney in preparing the defense).

In analyzing the cases in our data base, we are struck by the realization that, in most cases of wrongful conviction, more than one factor is involved. Eyewitness misidentification may be combined with poor investigative work, or even unethical practices, by police.

An inattentive judge may fail to detect evidence of unethical prosecutorial behavior or inadequate representation by defense counsel. For the most part, wrongful conviction seems to occur when more than one part of the system "breaks down."

POLICY IMPLICATIONS

Our research has generated data that seem to support a number of policy reforms aimed at reducing the number of wrongful convictions and compensating the innocent victim of these miscarriages of justice. We recommend:

(1) Based on proved innocence, victims of wrongful conviction should be granted financial compensation, with the amount of the award to be set by (a) the trial judge or jury at the time of exoneration, (b) a compensation board, or (c) civil action. At present, victims of wrongful conviction typically must seek passage of special compensation bills in the state legislature.

(2) In cases where eyewitness identification is the sole evidence and there is no corroborating evidence, a jury or judge should hear all information related to the issue and should decide the adequacy, validity, and reliability of the eyewitness identification. The court should permit the use of expert witnesses in examining the credibility of such evidence and should issue cautionary instructions to juries.

(3) Law enforcement investigations of eyewitness and victim reports should be conducted as soon as possible in order to minimize the problems of memory distortion.

(4) No identification procedure (pre- or postindictment) should be conducted in the absence of the defense attorney.

(5) People at high risk of being victimized by crime (e.g., bank tellers, gas station attendants) should be trained to record their observations immediately after the event.

(6) New trials should be granted where reasonable concern about errors exists.

(7) Postconviction appeals for justice by reason of innocence should be permitted.

(8) Postconviction appeals on the basis of prejudicial error should be permitted.

(9) Stronger sanctions should be invoked against unethical practices by

police, prosecutors, and others who contribute to wrongful conviction by their unprofessional or negligent acts.

The problem of wrongful conviction is one that affects all citizens, not just the victims of such miscarriages of justice. It is a two-edged sword that injures the innocent victim and simultaneously exposes society to increased risk, since the *real* offender remains free while authorities are preoccupied with the wrong suspect. Police, perhaps more than anyone else, can help prevent this problem by continuing to pursue all available evidence and not prematurely closing their investigations. Prosecutors can make a positive contribution by pursuing justice, not just convictions. Defense attorneys must be held accountable for providing adequate representation to their clients. Judges can insist that all of these things happen by critically examining the evidence in each case. And we must hold them all accountable.

REFERENCES

American Bar Association (1979) Model Code of Professional Responsibility and Code of Judicial Conduct. Chicago: American Bar Association.
BORCHARD, E. M. (1932) Convicting the Innocent: Sixty-Five Actual Errors of Criminal Justice. Garden City, NY: Doubleday.
BRANDON, R. and C. DAVIES (1973) Wrong Imprisonment: Mistaken Convictions and Their Consequences. London: Allen & Unwin.
BRIGHAM, J. C. and P. BARKOWITZ (1978) "Do they all look alike? The effects of race, sex, experience, and attitudes on the ability to recognize faces." Journal of Applied Psychology 8: 306-318.
BUCKHOUT, R. (1974) "Eyewitness testimony." Scientific American 231: 23-31.
BUCKHOUT, R. (1977) "Eyewitness identification and psychology in the courtroom." Criminal Defense 4: 5-10.
DERSHOWITZ, A. (1982) The Best Defense. New York: Random House.
FRANK, J. and B. FRANK (1957) Not Guilty. New York. Doubleday.
GARDNER, E. S. (1952) Court of Last Resort. New York: William Sloane.
GRANELLI, J. S. (1980) "Trials—and errors." National Law Journal, December 15: 9ff.
GREGORY, W. L. et al. (1978) "Social psychology of plea bargaining: applications, methodology, and theory." Journal of Personality and Social Psychology 36: 1521-1530.
Jackson v. Fogg (1978) 589 F.2d 108 (2d. Cir.).
LOFTON, J. (1966) Justice and the Press. Boston: Beacon.

LOFTUS, E. F. (1979) Eyewitness Testimony. Cambridge, MA: Harvard University Press.
MacNAMARA, D.E.J. (1969) "Convicting the innocent." Crime and Delinqueny 15: 57-61.
Miller v. Pate (1967) 386 U.S. 1.
Powell v. Alabama (1932) 287 U.S. 45.
RADIN, E. D. (1964) The Innocents. New York: William Morrow.
U.S. Bureau of the Census (1981) Census of Population and Housing (Ohio).
U.S. Department of Justice (1980) Sourcebook of Criminal Justice Statistics.

PART IV
Controversial Alternatives to Prison

8

Home Incarceration with Electronic Monitoring

RICHARD A. BALL and J. ROBERT LILLY

Within the past two decades, the need for alternatives to institutional incarceration of offenders has become more and more pressing, and the problem has gained international attention (Dodge, 1979; *Removing Children From Jails*, 1980; Austin and Krisberg, 1981; Warren, 1981; Cohen, 1985). In the United States, this trend has been referred to as "the new justice" (Aaronson et al., 1977). Jails and prisons have become too costly to build and maintain, and there is a persistent and dangerous problem of overcrowding (*Overcrowded Time*, 1982). More recently, there has appeared a new trend toward an alternative we have termed "Home Incarceration" (Ball and Lilly, 1985, 1986).

Although we have been instrumental in the development of such programs, we have become increasingly concerned with their larger implications for the changing nature of social control. Our intention here is to examine home incarceration as an alternative, to consider its possible advantages, and to investigate certain of these larger issues with respect to major trends in the ideology and strategy of social control.

Although we concentrate on the United States, it is clear that the trend toward home incarceration is part of a more global movement. Denmark, for example, has moved toward the "depenalization" of minor property crimes through what are termed "anti-institutions" involving collective housing for staff and "clients" outside traditional correctional facilities (Brydensholt, 1980: 41). In Scotland and South Australia, Juvenile Aid Panels have been developed to offer assistance to youth within a family setting as an alternative to court proceedings (Sarri and Bradley, 1980). As early as 1970, France introduced the concept of *control judiciare* as a form of pretrial detention, which could include detention in the home (Gerety, 1980). In 1975, Italy initiated *affidamento in provo ai servizio sociale* as a form of parole after an abbreviated period of three months incarceration (Gerety, 1980). In the United States, "home detention" came into use as an alternative at about the same time, generally as a "curfew" alternative for use with juveniles (*Removing Children From Jails*, 1980).

Home incarceration seems to have both theoretical and practical advantages. The problem with many alternatives to institutional incarceration is that the public is deprived "of the symbolic value of an official finding of offender accountability" (Aaronson et al., 1977). Home incarceration takes account of this symbolism. According to our theoretical perspective (Ball, 1979), punishment is a symbolic statement of reprobation in the form of an official denunciation of an offense. As such, it combines aspects of retribution, social utilitarianism and the hope of reformation. Key to this theoretical perspective is the goal of reconciliation of offender and community.

Official confinement to the home for a specified period would appear to provide, at least for certain offenses, a clear statement of retribution, a utilitarian form of incapacitation, and the possibility of reformation within a more "normal" environment.

We have proposed, for example, that home incarceration be considered as a sentencing alternative for drunken drivers (Ball and Lilly, 1986). This proposal is based upon an analysis indicating that, while the current "slammer laws" mandating jail time for those convicted of DWI (Driving While Intoxicated) are counterproductive, public sentiment demands that something more effective than the typical fines or license suspensions be employed to deal with the problem. Home incarceration for a reasonable period of time would seem to offer sufficient retribution to satisfy the sense of public indignation by "grounding" the offender. It would serve the incapacitation function and thereby protect the community. And it would allow the community to deal with the "drinking problem" of the offender in a setting that might be expected to add to the probability of "rehabilitation" and "reintegration."

Whether such advantages outweigh a number of possible disadvantages must be left for later consideration. The fact is that the trend toward home incarceration rests upon its perceived *practical* advantages. These we have also laid out in some detail elsewhere (Ball and Lilly, 1985). Home incarceration has a good *degree of fit* to a variety of circumstances in such a way that it could be employed alone or in concert with other programs, tailored to certain hours of the day, and perhaps even combined with incarceration in a traditional jail with home incarceration on weekends in certain cases. It also offers the possibility of practical use at various *stages* of the correctional process from pretrial detention through parole. Our early hope was that this alternative might be structured to allow for initiation either by the court or by the offender, especially in the case of offenders with such special problems as mental retardation or terminal illness, which could be faced much more easily while confined to the home rather than jail. This we considered an alternative that might be made available by law to certain offenders and not simply an alternative to be used only as the discretion of the court.

Home incarceration appeared from its earliest development to possess practical features that would provide a high likelihood of actual adoption (Ball and Lilly, 1985). According to the National Advisory Commission on Criminal Justice Standards and Goals (1973), these include communicability, a satisfactory complexity level, a reasonably clear potential impact, reasonable cost, reversibility, divisibility, compatibility with existing programs, and perceived relevance to organizational goals. Such an alternative is simple to explain and is certainly not of forbidding complexity. Its potential impact in terms of reduction of jail overcrowding, protection of the community through the effective incapacitation of selected offenders such as drunken drivers, and avoidance of the "crime school" effects of jailing seems fairly obvious. As to reversibility, any agency adopting home incarceration as we had originally envisioned it would have been in position to retreat if significant public sentiment arose against the policy, if offenders failed to cooperate, or if other unforeseen problems appeared.

Home incarceration offers an extremely flexible and divisible alternative, far from the "all or nothing" options. A particular offender might be confined for weeks, for certain hours of given days, or in any of a number of configurations. This alternative seemed from the beginning to be compatible with ongoing programs in agencies such as probation departments, particularly those moving in the direction of intensive supervision. If the goals of organizations such as the police and courts can be summarized as protection of the public while doing the least damage to the offender and yet providing the forceful symbolic denunciation desired by the community, then home incarceration also appeared to offer a perceived relevance to such ends.

From the beginning of our own efforts, however, we have assumed that the most crucial advantage of home incarceration as an alternative to jailing lay in its relatively low cost. If community volunteers were used to monitor compliance by telephone and occasional unannounced visits, the savings would be enormous. This is an especially important consideration given the fact that many communities face increasingly severe fiscal problems. Even if there were doubts as to potential impact, questions as to relevance to organizational goals, or simply reluctance to try something new, the lure of cost reduction appeared to give home incarceration good prospects for adoption.

Our interest in the development of home incarceration as a formal sentencing alternative was triggered in part by a recognition that something similar had been practiced informally in many jurisdictions, especially with juveniles, and a concern with issues of due process and the protection of public employees such as probation officers. The National Advisory Commission on Criminal Justice Standards and Goals for Courts (1973) has expressed a concern here and has suggested that a court-approved agreement be required whenever "diversion" involves actual deprivation of liberty, as is true of home incarceration. Formal adoption through enabling legislation would appear to provide the offender with much more due process protection than has been the case under the tradition of informality. At the same time, public employees such as probation officers would seem to benefit by formal legitimization, including specified guidelines for implementation.

POTENTIAL PROBLEMS

Our original analysis of home incarceration as a possible sentencing alternative was confined to examination of two categories of potential problems: legal and administrative. We described the legal issues in fairly narrow terms, dealing with questions of sanctions for noncompliance, eligibility of different categories of offenders, and responsibilities of others within the home, particularly as potential accessories in any possible violations of the conditions of home incarceration set by the court. Although we did address the best means of structuring such an alternative so as to reduce the danger of widening the net to include offenders who would have been released prior to the development of this new "alternative" (Ball and Lilly, 1985) and pointed to such intrusion as a possible threat to the "home as castle" tradition (Ball and Lilly, 1986), our analyses concentrated on narrower administrative issues. These included questions of effective screening for offenders placed in home incarceration, issues of monitoring strategies, and suggestions for probation contracts specifying the conditions to which the offender would be expect to adhere. The time is now ripe for a deeper examination of potential problems, especially in view of the rapid proliferation of home incarceration programs.

By early 1986, at least 30 states were experimenting with home incarceration, with offenders in home incarceration programs numbering as many as 4,750 in Florida (Petersilia, n.d.). Although some jurisdictions were following the model advocated in our early work, employing volunteers as monitors, the trend was clearly toward electronic monitoring. This issue deserves closer examination.

The use of volunteers to monitor compliance was suggested for both practical and theoretical reasons. In practical terms, volunteers could reduce the pressures on probation officers, who tend to be caught between the surveillance and counselor roles. It is difficult to provide guidance to an offender who resents the probation officer as someone who is constantly "checking up on" or "spying on" him or her. With the surveillance and monitoring function in the hands of volunteers with a home incarceration program, the probation officer might find this problem less troublesome. And the low cost of employing volunteers appeared as another very important practical inducement.

The use of community volunteers was also considered of significant value in terms of our theoretical perspective, which seeks to facilitate the reconciliation of offender and community. Under these conditions, the offender would be involved with representatives of his or her community rather than only with official functionaries representing some governmental bureaucracy. At the same time, the use of volunteers would contribute to the further involvement of the public in the systems of juvenile and criminal justice, fostering community penetration into these rather closed systems. According to this perspective, home incarceration ought to provide a powerful symbolic denunciation of the offense in community rather than bureaucratic terms, saying in effect, "If you continue to endanger the community (e.g., by driving while intoxicated), your liberty to participate in the community will be restricted, even while you are permitted to remain within the boundaries of that community (i.e., inside your own home)." Such a reaction was regarded as fitting our theoretical perspective in that it symbolized a repudiation of the act rather than the actor.

Given these advantages in the use of community volunteers, the extent to which the home incarceration has tended to use electronic monitoring is something of a puzzle. In fact, close consideration of this development may lead to a rethinking of home incarceration, partly in terms of recent criticisms of the failed promise of community corrections and partly in terms of a much larger and more complex question of the real functions of such policies. Before undertaking this examination, however, it will be necessary to describe the current state of electronic monitoring itself.

Several electronic monitoring systems are now on the market. In general, they involve a "bracelet" that attaches to ankle or wrist, serving as a transmitter emitting signals to a receiver located in a telephone within the home. If the offender wearing the bracelet moves further than a specified distance (e.g., 150 feet) from the telephone, this signal is broken and another signal alerts a central computer, located perhaps in the local probation agency, which provides a printout indicating a violation. The computer can be programmed with the incarceration parameters set for that particular offender so that if, for example, he or she is permitted to leave the home during specified time periods, the computer will take account of this and disregard any break in the bracelet signal during these approved time frames. As of 1983, Albuquerque, New Mexico, was paying $100,000 per year for 25 GOSSline monitor/bracelet sets with additional sets leasing at $1,000 per year (Berry, 1985).

Because we expected that cost reduction would be the most attractive advantage of home incarceration to those willing to consider it, we have been struck by their eagerness to embrace the more expensive electronic monitoring systems in lieu of the use of volunteers. Much of our theoretical perspective has rested upon the concept of reconciliation between offender and community, and we had been troubled by data suggesting that the community might resist such reconciliation, calling into question the entire enterprise of community-corrections (Greenberg, 1975). The rapid development of electronic monitoring now suggests that the systems of juvenile and criminal justice may be more interested in maintaining bureaucratic control over offenders than in involving the community in the monitoring of compliance with home incarceration, even at the cost of sacrificing other goals to the budget squeeze. But if the public resists reconciliation and reintegration of offenders and if the bureaucracies charged with offender surveillance and control prefer to remain aloof, this lends substance to the argument that the very term "community" is often meaningless rhetoric (National Institute of Mental Health, 1971).

Home incarceration may be caught in the common pattern of the "dialectics of reform" in which the entrenched agents of social control, such as judges, sheriffs, prosecutors, and the like, permit reforms only at the expense of certain libertarian traditions (Austin and Krisberg, 1981). The question of a possible "widening of the net" so as to place even more people under official social control is only one of the issues here. Despite the assertion of the National Advisory Commission on Criminal Justice Standards and goals for Corrections (1973: 222) that "the humanitarian aspect of community-based corrections is obvious," developments within the home incarceration movement suggest otherwise. There is the additional danger that the use of the home as a jail may contribute to the further erosion of the distinction between the private and public realms, which some have argued would leave the community more and more open to the extension of control by the state (Cohen, 1979). As Hylton (1982) points out, the President's Commission on Law Enforcement and Administration of Justice (1967) recognized two decades ago that any blurring of lines between institutional treatment and community treatment might affect the rights of offenders. This is, however, only part of what may be a much larger danger.

Apart from the general question of home incarceration as a sentencing alternative, there are specific questions about the use of electronic monitoring. Some of these questions have been addressed, but developments have moved so quickly that considerable confusion seems to have arisen. Berry (1985), for example, devotes an entire article to a critique of electronic monitoring, reviewing and attempting to apply a body of literature dealing with surreptitious surveillance. Yet there is nothing surreptitious about strapping an ankle bracelet on an offender and explaining that the computer will be notified if he or she moves outside a certain distance from the home telephone. Indeed, the key question may actually have to do with the effect upon the offender of operating under the constant realization that movement is being monitored by a computer operated by a faceless bureaucracy in some distant location.

Considered in a larger context, home incarceration seems to demand the deeper examination of two related issues. First, there is the question of the nature and meaning of privacy. Secondly, there is the question of the true drift of community-based corrections, including the trend toward home incarceration. Is home incarceration really a humanitarian reduction of social control, or is it further intrusion into private life under a humanitarian guise?

THE SOCIAL MEANING OF PRIVACY

The legal concept of privacy in American Constitutional law is usually traced to an 1890 article, "The Right to Privacy," by Charles Warren and Louis D. Brandeis (Beany, 1966). In common law there are four categories of privacy. These include (1) protection from public disclosure of personal facts, (2) protection from intrusion upon a person's seclusion, solitude, or personal affairs, (3) protection from the appropriation of one's name or likeness for the personal advantage of another, and (4) protection from being cast in a bad light publicly (Miller, 1972). Home incarceration, particularly with electronic monitoring, may represent a challenge to the first and second of the categories of privacy.

According to Westin (1967: 254), "Privacy is the claim of individuals, groups, or institutions to determine for themselves when, how, and to what extent information about themselves is communicated to others." In their empirical study of the social meaning of privacy, Wolfe and Laufer (1974) found that privacy carries the meanings of (1) controlling access to information about oneself, (2) being alone, (3) "no one bothering me," and (4) controlling access to spaces. All of these meanings seem relevant to an examination of home incarceration, particularly with electronic monitoring. The political import comes through very clearly in the definition of privacy as "the negation of potential power-relationships between a person or group and others" (Altman, 1974: 6).

In general, it can be said that while social science considerations of the meaning of privacy take account of the perceiver's definition of the situation, the law usually does not (Levin and Askin, 1977). One exception is the Katz decision (*Katz v. United States*, 1967), which involved the bugging of a public telephone booth. Here the Court ruled that the bug constituted an illegal search and seizure under the Fourth Amendment, with the two-fold requirement that the person involved must have shown an actual expectation of privacy (as shown, for example, by his closing the door of the telephone booth) and that this expectation must be one that society would regard as reasonable under the circumstances. In another decision, *Camara v. Municipal Court of San Francisco* (1967), the Court held that a welfare recipient has no significant expectation of privacy from a caseworker who wants to inspect the home to verify eligibility, taking the benevolence of the welfare worker for granted while making it clear that a policeman would not be permitted entry. In a later case (*Wyman v. Jones*, 1971) the Court ignored a dozen affidavits from welfare recipients claiming embarrassment or unease amounting to a breach of privacy when welfare workers entered their homes. Levin and Askin (1977) consulted 15 social scientists, all of whom disagreed with the Court's operating assumption that people should perceive and define the situation in a way consistent with the prescribed role of the caseworker.

It is important to note that the very concept of a private self appears to have developed in conjunction with the emotional seclusion made possible by the construction of the home in such a way as to separate certain areas from the public domain (Shorter, 1977). This sense of self is sustained by a zone of personal space extending about an arm's length from the body (Sommer, 1969). Fischer (1975) has argued that such personal privacy is the very manifestation of authentic consciousness in an "existential-phenomenological" sense. Thus it is that the elimination of opportunities for privacy has been associated with various techniques for breaking down the self (Goffman, 1959). What does this imply for a policy that converts the private dwelling place into a mode of official incarceration and monitors compliance by attaching an electronic device to the body of the individual so incarcerated?

As Marx (1981: 242) has shown, "It would appear that modern society increasingly generates ironic outcomes, whether iatrogenic effects . . . unintended consequences of new technologies . . . or the familiar sociological examples found in prisons and mental hospitals, or in the careers of urban renewal and various other efforts at social reform." This increase in ironic outcomes stems from the increasing complexity and interdependence of social life and the increased effort at intervention based upon the expansion of professionalism and expertise (Marx, 1981). As others have shown, the legal concept of the right of individual privacy is based on the person's right to challenge invasion rather than the institution's responsibility to avoid it. Defense of privacy would thus seem to require considerable self-identity and a strong sense of personal autonomy on the part of those threatened (Levin and Askin, 1977). If it is true that individual autonomy is being eroded by more general social trends (Foucault, 1977), then this tilt in favor of the institutions of social control may greatly reduce possibilities for the "negation of potential power-relationships between a person or group and others." Such a possibility would make a mockery of the famous quotation from William Pitt:

> The poorest man may in his cottage bid defiance to the crown. It may be frail—its roof may leak—the wind may enter—but the King of England cannot enter—all his force dares not cross the threshold of the ruined tenement [quoted in Glasser, 1974: 100].

What is so sacred about the home? The answer is that it has come to represent the social significance of the nuclear family and the personal dignity of the individual. The home is much more than an organized pile of bricks and mortar; it is a phenomenological domain. Thus it is of vital importance that the law give more attention to the phenomenological experience of the perceiver, especially with respect to legal conceptualizations of privacy. What the law takes for the "facts" of the matter may correspond not at all to the experience of the individual concerned. To breach the walls of the home electronically is to alter the nature of interpersonal boundaries and hence the nature of intersubjectivity within society.

The experience of privacy is closely associated with a phenomenologically delimited field of *copresence* (Goffman, 1963: 22) in which there are strict limits on the manner in which individuals are accessible to one another and in which the sense of personal autonomy is augmented. This is so important that access to privacy scenes is governed by tightly defined access rituals (Goffman, 1971). Only those who submit to the rituals of entrance and exit and thereby affirm the dignity of the individual(s) within the context are permitted to share in the experience of mutual copresence. Furthermore, the interpersonal boundaries are more like screens than walls in that they tend to transform the consciousness of those who pass through them, providing for a different manner of interaction and intersubjectivity (Goffman, 1963).

To take one example of the way in which the boundaries composing the home are structured, it may be useful to examine the dwelling place in terms of a set of concentric circles. These concentric circles define three distinct zones of the typical home in Western industrialized societies: the *surround,* the *region,* and the *nucleus* (Scheflen and Ashcraft, 1975). The area between the property line and the walls of the house makes up the zone termed the *surround.* It may be limited to the hallway in an apartment building. The domestic zone termed the *region* is made up of the living room, the parlor in older homes, and the dining room and kitchen. The innermost zone, the *nucleus* of the home, is comprised of bedrooms and the "private" bathroom if there is more than one. Although there are differences in the way certain rooms may be defined and accessibility to them limited (e.g., differences in the phenomenological "privacy" of the kitchen or downstairs bathroom), these three zones may be taken as prototypical.

The nature of copresence varies enormously across these three zones. The surrounding tends to be "off-limits" to casual passersby, but it is available to those delivering messages or groceries, those seeking certain relatively public information (e.g., asking directions), and others with a socially legitimate reason to be there. It is characterized by a form of sociability quite similar to that of the public domain, although some may attempt to deny copresence entirely and insist upon extreme privacy even in the surround, perhaps by use of walls and locked gates if these can be afforded, or through the posting of "No Trespassing" and "Beware the Dog" signs if there is less to spend. Only a few of those to whom the surround is accessible are permitted access to the region, where a much more intimate intersubjectivity prevails. The tradition of inviting guests to enter this domestic zone and perhaps to share a meal there is one example of the way in which the boundaries of the home are manipulated to enhance sociability by extending privileges to some that are denied to others.

As for the nucleus of the home, it is available only to a selected few who are admitted into the inner circle of domestic privacy by limited social gestures, such as showing off a new piece of bedroom furniture, or more extensive gestures, such as an invitation to stay overnight.

The phenomenological sanctity of the home, and its intense salience to the self and to the status on one's relationships with other, is captured nicely in the following remarks on the emotional impact of boundary breaches:

> Doors provide boundaries between ourselves (i.e., our property, behavior, and appearance) and others. Violation of such boundaries imply a violation of selfhood. Trespassing or housebreaking, for example, is unbearable for some not only because of the property damage that might result but also because they represent proof that the self has lost control of its audience; it can no longer regulate who may and who may not have access to the property and information that index its depths. The victim of a Peeping Tom is thus outraged not only at having been observed naked but also for having lost control of the number and type of people who may possess information about her body. To prove this, we note that no nakedness need be observed to make Peeping Tomism intolerable [Schwartz, 1968: 747].

From the beginning of our own work with home incarceration, we have been concerned about the social psychological impact of employing the home as a surrogate jail. Even the use of volunteers to monitor compliance by telephone presents problems, for it is clear that the intrusion of the telephone itself into the home represents a more complex phenomenological situation than may be apparent at first glance (Ball, 1968). But the electronic bracelets are of a different level of intrusion, not only because they operate continuously and impersonally, but because they are actually strapped to the *body* itself, which, as the above quotation suggests, is even more intimately associated with the sense of selfhood than is the home.

The body is so crucial to selfhood because it is "our anchorage in the world" (Merleau-Ponty, 1962: 144). "The world experienced comes at all times without body as its centre, centre of vision, centre of action, centre of interest" (James, 1 42: 170). Some of the phenomenological import of the meaning of the body is apparent in the following:

> My embodied space mediates between the other and me, it defines my "spatiality of situation" as a spatiality of *social* situation. The other is

present to my space. I cannot avoid taking him into consideration . . . Consciousness is always contextualized in the deployments of the lived body, and embodiment always provides the *vicinity* for consciousness . . . Consciousness and body interpenetrate . . . Alienation is present when the world of objective nature becomes an overpowering reality no longer subject to man's calculation and control; when technology develops into technocracy and the tools that man has made rise up to enslave him; when the incarnated other gazes upon one's body . . . to achieve undisputed sovereignty over one's lived space . . . The body is a *way of being embodied,* menaced by threats of alienation and struggling for transcendence as incarnated consciousness, is not a sign of who I am but veritably *is who I am.* I am my body. I exist as embodied. [Schrag, 1969: 132-133; emphasis in the original].

HOME INCARCERATION AS TROJAN HORSE

Expectations about the future of home incarceration depend largely on how one reads the history of corrections over the past century. Several interpretations are possible, and it is likely that there is some degree of validity to each. But which is most valid? Is it fundamentally a history of progress, of benevolent intent leading to unanticipated consequences, or the inexorable outcome of deeper structural trends toward total social discipline and suppression of individuality? Such social control techniques as torture, branding, mutilation, flogging, and hanging represented brutal, public spectacles of the past. Although social control has tended to become less coercive in a physical sense, it has become both more specialized and technical, as well as more penetrating and intrusive, and thus more subtly coercive in a different sense (Marx, 1981). As Cohen (1985: 26) has put it, "The new power was not to punish less but to punish better, to punish more deeply into the social body."

The repudiation of corporal punishment and capital punishment in favor of imprisonment was regarded as an immensely progressive step. The much later movement from institutional to community-based correction was regarded as even more progressive. Yet there is more and more data suggesting that the potential problem of "widening the net" to bring an increasing proportion of the population under state control has become a reality (Greenberg, 1975;

Austin and Krisberg, 1981; Hylton, 1982; Cohen, 1985). Cohen (1985) argues that official social control is being extended through both the *exclusion* and the *inclusion* of offenders. Policies of exclusion lead to the use of institutional incarceration to the point of severe overcrowding of jails and prisons and great pressure from the public and from correctional authorities for construction of more and more such facilities. These pressures lead to a search for "alternatives" by which the offender can be included within the "community" at the price of surrendering certain personal autonomy. Because the inclusive policy is perceived as less harsh, its use is encouraged. Thus it is extended to include a larger and larger proportion of the population.

The ironies of social control appear to be increasingly obvious. While, for example, the movement toward community-based corrections drew much of its practical impetus from the need to reduce costs, its major theoretical justification came from labeling theory (Schur, 1971). In the classic statement of this theoretical position, Lemert (1951) argued that the labeling of offenders tends to reinforce their deviance, the implication being that the less stigmatizing the label, the more likely that the deviation would be a mere passing aberration. We have advanced a similar argument in suggesting that home incarceration might provide community protection without the extreme stigma associated with jailing (Ball and Lilly, 1985). But it must be noted that Lemert (1981) himself has had second thoughts based on the use of the labeling perspective by agents of social control.

Even in our earliest papers dealing with home incarceration, we expressed concern about the possibility of widening the net to include a greater percentage of the population and gave special attention to the "Orwellian overtones" of electronic monitoring and the implications of home incarceration for the "Anglo-American tradition of 'home as castle' in which the private dwelling place is regarded as sacred ground off limits to the state except under extreme conditions" (Ball and Lilly, 1983). Developments since then have done nothing to reduce these concerns. In fact, we have become increasingly impressed by theoretical arguments such as those of Foucault (1977), who maintains that there is a fundamental structural movement by which official control is extended in very subtle ways through a spiral of knowledge and power. As the state is able, especially through more effective technologies, to attain to greater and greater knowledge of the private lives of its citizens, it is capable of extending its power in ways of considerable subtlety. This power can be used to augment the knowledge, which can then increase the power over the citizen, usually in a manner that is less obviously coercive and thereby even more effective.

According to this perspective, the talk of "progress," "benevolence," and "reform" is merely the rhetoric of those carried forward on the tide of history. For Foucault, the spiral of increasing knowledge and increasing power moves toward an end of total discipline and control. If history is read this way, the rise of the prison and the subsequent development of community-based corrections represents neither progress nor benevolence gone awry. Instead, it represents a pattern by which the urge to impress order upon social life led to increased surveillance and classification of citizens, with the penitentiary arising as a contained, dramatic model of what the perfectly rationalized and controlled "community" would become. Under such a reading of history, the final step is the imposition of this model upon the "community" at large so that the entire society becomes the equivalent of a prison. From this perspective, the reforms undertaken by the progressives had the effect of rendering prisons less artificial and somewhat more like ordinary communities, merely part of an historical process that facilitated the dispersal of the prison model back into society through the rhetoric of community-based corrections (Cohen, 1985).

One may have reservations about such a theoretical perspective, which gives little room for the motivations of self-conscious actors, treating them like puppets whose strings are pulled by history, but this approach does offer some explanation of the vast gap between rhetoric and reality. For Cohen (1985: 198), the trend is fed by the "right combination of benevolence and technology," a phrase that is strangely evocative of home incarceration when it is implemented using electronic monitoring. The key here is surveillance, as exemplified in Bentham's utilitarian vision of the panopticon. "Surveillance and not just punishment became the object of the exercise" (Cohen, 1985: 26). In this vision of social control, total knowledge is total power.

Thus Bentham's ideal prison was a tightly bounded realm in which every action of the prisoner could be monitored from a central location. As Cohen (1985: 221) says, "The current . . . control resembles much of the panopticon vision: visibility (you know about the TV screens and data banks), unverifiability (you do not know when you are being watched or checked), anonymity (it does not matter who is operating the system—it could be a computer), and the absence of force (you should want to be good)" (parenthetical remarks in the original). All this is true of home incarceration with electronic monitoring save one exception. The offender *must assume that he or she is being monitored at all times set by those supervising the program,* although one can never be completely certain that the equipment is not malfunctioning at any particular moment.

CONCLUSION

We do not accept the argument that the knowledge-power spiral is inevitable and that the individual is doomed to succumb to the increasing power of the state. As we have argued elsewhere (Ball and Lilly, 1982), historical change appears to be a product of instrumental maneuvering and expressive, symbolic perceptions as well as powerful structural trends. There is little doubt, for example, that the spread of electronic monitoring is due in large part to the salesmanship of the "social-control entrepreneurs" (Warren, 1981), who have developed the devices and merchandised them most effectively. Unlike the "moral entrepreneur," who may be motivated by deep convictions, the social-control entrepreneurs operate essentially in terms of direct, economic self-interest. At the same time, we suspect that the electronic devices evoke an almost totemic imagery of considerable symbolic force, with elemental connotations of order, efficiency, and control, rendering them "good to think," whether or not they are "good to use" in terms of cost effectiveness (Levy-Strauss, 1963). This is to say that they have what amounts to nothing less than a *mythic appeal,* part of the larger "myth of the machine" (Mumford, 1966).

Nevertheless, we are concerned that the panopticon mentality may be gaining ground, especially in view of the rapid developments in what has been termed "the new surveillance" (Marx, 1985). This concern is shared by the Office of Technology Assessment (1985), which has highlighted the proliferation of surveillance in the United States and recommended immediate legislative action to limit the use of intrusive devices. In any consideration of home incarceration, particularly with electronic monitoring, we would urge that the scope of legal concern embodied in the Katz decision be widened further in order that the perceptions of those subjected to surveillance be taken into account and its impact upon them assessed. The issue of privacy is central here, especially as the state enters the home. Foucault (1977) may be wrong in his assertion that we are headed for the totally disciplined, "carceral" society, but the spread of home incarceration with the use of electronic monitoring provides little hope for those who disagree with this dim view.

REFERENCES

AARONSON, D. E., B. H. HOFF, P. JASZI, and D. SARRI (1977) The New Justice: Alternatives to Conventional Criminal Adjudication. Washington, DC: Government Printing Office.
ALTMAN, I. (1974) "Privacy: a conceptual analysis," pp. 87-96 in D. H. Carson (ed.) Man-Environment Interactions: Evaluations and Applications. Washington, DC: Environmental Design Research Association.
AUSTIN, J. and B. KRISBERG (1981) "Wider, stronger and different nets: the dialectics of criminal justice reform." Journal of Research in Crime and Delinquency 18, 1: 165-196.
BALL, D. (1968) "Toward a sociology of telephones and telephoners," pp. 59-75 in M. Truzzi (ed.) Sociology and Everyday Life. Englewood Cliffs, NJ: Prentice-Hall.
BALL, R. A. (1979) "A theory of punishment: restricted reprobation and the reparation of social reality," pp. 135-149 in P. J. Brantingham and J. M. Kress (eds.) Structure, Law, and Power: Essays in the Sociology of Law. Newbury Park, CA: Sage.
BALL, R. A. and J. R. LILLY (1982) "The menace of margarine: the rise and fall of a social problem." Social Problems 29, 5: 489-498.
BALL, R. A. and J. R. LILLY (1983) "Home incarceration for drunken drivers." Presented at meetings of American Society of Criminology, San Francisco.
BALL, R. A. and J. R. LILLY (1985) "Home incarceration: an international alternative to institutional incarceration." International Journal of Comparative and Applied Criminal Justice 9, 2: 85-97.
BALL, R. A. and J. R. LILLY (1986) "The potential use of home incarceration for drunken drivers." Crime and Delinquency 32, 2: 187-196.
BEANY, W. M. (1966) "The right to privacy and American law." Law and Contemporary Problems 31, 2: 326-341.
BRYDENSHOLT, H. H. (1980) "Crime policy in Denmark: how we managed to reduce the prison population." Crime and Delinquency 26, 1: 35-41.
Camara v. Municipal Court of San Francisco (1967) 387 U.S. 523.
COHEN, S. (1979) "The punitive city: notes on the dispersal of social control." Contemporary Crises 3, 4: 339-363.
COHEN, S. (1985) Visions of Social Control. Cambridge, England: Polity.
DODGE, C. R. (1979) A World Without Prisons. Lexington, MA: Lexington.
FISCHER, C. T. (1975) "Privacy as a profile of authentic consciousness." Humanitas 11, 1: 27-44.

FOUCAULT, M. (1977) Discipline and Punish (A. Sheridan, trans.). New York: Random House.

GERETY, P. (1980) "A French program to reduce pretrial detention." Crime and Delinquency 26, 1: 22-34.

GLASSER, I. (1974) "Prisoners of benevolence: power versus liberty in the welfare state," pp. 97-168 in W. Gaylin et al. (eds.) Doing Good: The Limits of Benevolence. New York: Pantheon.

GOFFMAN, E. (1959) The Presentation of Self in Everyday Life. New York: Doubleday.

GOFFMAN, E. (1963) Behavior in Public Places. New York: Free Press.

GOFFMAN, E. (1971) Relations in Public. New York: Harper & Row.

GREENBERG, D. F. (1975) "Problems in community corrections." Issues in Criminology 10, 1: 1-10.

HYLTON, J. H. (1982) "Rhetoric and reality: a critical appraisal of community correctional programs." Crime and Delinquency 28, 3: 314-373.

JAMES, W. (1942) Essays in Radical Empiricism. New York: Longmans, Green.

Katz v. United States (1967) 389 U.S. 347.

LEMERT, E. M. (1951) Social Pathology. New York: McGraw-Hill.

LEMERT, E. M. (1981) "Diversions in juvenile justice: what hath been wrought?" Journal of Research in Crime and Delinquency 18, 1: 34-45.

LEVIN, H. A. and F. ASKIN (1977) "Privacy in the courts: law and social reality." Journal of Social Issues 33, 3: 138-153.

LINDESMITH, A. R. and A. L. STRAUSS (1956) Social Psychology. New York: Henry Holt.

MARX, G. T. (1981) "Ironies of social control: authorities as contributors to deviance through escalation, nonenforcement and covert facilitation." Social Problems 28, 3: 221-246.

MARX, G. T. (1985) "I'll be watching you." Dissent 30, 1: 26-34.

MERLEAU-PONTY, M. (1962) Phenomenology of Perception (C. Smith, trans.). New York: Humanities.

MILLER, A. R. (1972) The Assault on Privacy. New York: New American Library.

MUMFORD, L. (1966) The Myth of the Machine, 1: Technics and Human Development. New York: Harcourt Brace Jovanovich.

National Advisory Commission on Criminal Justice Standards and Goals for the Criminal Justice System (1973) Report of the National Advisory Commission on Standards and Goals for the Criminal Justice System. Washington, DC: Government Printing Office.

National Advisory Commission on Criminal Justice Standards and Goals for Corrections (1973) Report of the National Advisory Commission on Criminal Justice Standards for Corrections. Washington, DC: Government Printing Office.

National Advisory Commission on Standards and Goals for Courts (1973) Report of the National Advisory Commission on Criminal Justice Standards and Goals for Courts. Washington, DC: Government Printing Office.

National Institute of Mental Health (1971) Community Based Correctional Programs: Models and Practices. Washington, DC: Government Printing Office.

Edna McConnel Clark Foundation (1982) Overcrowded Time. Chicago: Author.

PETERSILIA, J. (n.d.) Exploring the Option of House Arrest. Santa Monica, CA: Rand Corporation.

President's Commission on Law Enforcement and Administration of Justice (1967) The Challenge of Crime in a Free Society. Washington DC: Government Printing Office.

Removing Children from Jail: A Guide to Action (1980) Washington, DC: Government Printing Office.

SARRI, R. and P. W. BRADLEY (1980) "Juvenile aid panels: an alternative to juvenile court processing in South Australia." Crime and Delinquency 26, 1: 42-62.

SCHEFLEN, A. E. and N. ASHCRAFT (1975) Human Territories. Englewood Cliffs, NJ: Prentice-Hall.

SCHRAG, C. O. (1969) Experience and Being. Evanston, IL: Northwestern University.

SCHUR, E. M. (1971) Labeling Deviant Behavior. New York: Harper & Row.

SCHWARTZ, B. (1968) "The social psychology of privacy." American Journal of Sociology 73, 6: 741-752.

SHORTER, E. (1977) The Making of the Modern Family. New York: Basic Books.

SOMMER, R. (1969) Personal Space. Englewood Cliffs, NJ: Prentice-Hall.

WARREN, C. (1981) "New forms of social control: the myth of deinstitutionalization." American Behavioral Scientist 24, 6: 724-740.

WESTIN, A. (1967) Privacy and Freedom. New York: Atheneum.

WOLFE, M. and R. S. LAUFER (1974) "The concept of privacy in childhood and adolescence," pp. 260-286 in D. H. Carson (ed.) Man-Environment Interactions: Evaluations and Applications. Washington, DC: Environmental Design Research Association.

Wyman v. Jones (1971) 400 U.S. 309.

9

Probation Reform

JOAN PETERSILIA

Probation, hailed only a decade ago as the "brightest hope for corrections," is experiencing unprecedented strain. On the one hand, its supporters argue that probation can reduce crime by reforming criminals, and can cut prison costs by supervising low-risk offenders in the community. But its opponents say that probation does not represent punishment, that its rehabilitation methods are ineffective, and that sentencing felons to probation presents a serious threat to public safety.

Until the last few years, the probation debate remained at an impasse. Caseloads continued to increase, budgets stabilized or declined, and public and judicial support remained low. It appeared that probation had been left to wither on the vine.

But policymakers have begun to pay renewed attention to probation, specifically with an eye toward the role it might play in easing prison crowding. Prisons have become so overcrowded that in all but six states they have been declared unconstitutional. And prison commitments are continuing to rise sharply. At the present rate of growth, officials need to build the equivalent of two new 500-bed prisons every week simply to keep pace with the expanding inmate population (Prisoners in 1984, 1985). Obviously, this represents a staggering expenditure by all standards. Consequently, the courts are seeking other alternatives to prison, and in many jurisdictions probation offers the only option.

Probation is now being asked to implement control-oriented programs designed for prison-bound offenders. The underlying objective is simple: to create intermediate-level sentencing options whereby nondangerous offenders can be supervised in the community, thereby saving expensive prison beds. The goal is not offender *rehabilitation*, but offender *control*, with public safety the central concern.

Several probation departments have begun implementing such programs. Oklahoma, Florida, Texas, and Alabama, for example, use a model that relies heavily on house arrest, offender employment, and community service. Kentucky, Utah, Michigan, Oregon, and New Mexico have begun experimenting with electronic monitoring devices. Intensive probation supervision is the cornerstone of the programs in Georgia, Connecticut, Ohio, New Jersey, Illinois, Oregon, Massachusetts, and New York. Several other states are experimenting with police-probation cooperative teams, urinalysis testing, shock imprisonment, third-party supervision, and so forth.

Whether these programs can adequately control the participants' future criminality is unknown at this point; the programs are too new to tell. What is certain is that probation is being forced into the limelight of modern corrections policy, and that its performance over the next few years will be closely scrutinized.

This article provides an overview of probation today—its responsibilities, its need for resources, and its evolving programs. It discusses the emerging issues that must be addressed if these newer probation programs are to be implemented successfully. It concludes by noting that if probation documents its ability to supervise prison-bound offenders adequately in the community, probation will probably return to public favor. If it fails, the public is likely to further embrace incarceration as the only sure way to forestall crime, driving prison populations even higher.

THE CURRENT CONTEXT OF PROBATION IN THE UNITED STATES

Probation is a criminal sentence whereby the convicted offender is allowed to remain in the community, subject to imposed conditions. Probation is commonly confused with parole, which is the conditional release of an offender after having served a prison term. Probation is an *alternative* to a prison term.

This confusion reflects probation's core problem: lack of understanding about what it does and for whom. Even though probation is responsible for supervising two-thirds of all convicted felons in the United States, it receives very little public or policy attention, and proportionately few of the resources allocated to corrections.

By any measure, probation has become the sentence of choice in criminal convictions: 80% of all persons convicted of misdemeanors and about 60% of those convicted of felonies are sentenced to probation. That results in 1.9 million adults being on probation on any given day—four times the number who are in prison in the United States. And each year, the probation population grows about 30% faster than the prison population.

Not only has the number of probationers increased, but those granted probation have committed more serious crimes. Misdemeanants on probation once outnumbered felons three to one, but the ratio is reversing. Last year, half of the adults sentenced to probation had been convicted of felony crimes (Probation and Parole 1984, 1986).

Comparisons of this type cannot fully indicate the level of risk that probationers now pose to the public. Some probation officials say that the risk from probationers has increased because probationers today are more likely to be drug-involved, to have committed crimes at an earlier age, to be more violent, and to be gang-affiliated. The overloading of court calendars has created increasing pressure to plea-bargain cases, resulting in reduced conviction charges that sometimes bear slight resemblance to the original arrest crime. The defendant pleads guilty to a reduced charge, perhaps a misdemeanor, and is placed on probation.

Resources

Financial support for probation agencies has not kept pace with the growing number of probationers. Indeed, since the mid-1970s, probation has fallen on hard times.

Probation is often promoted as being primarily rehabilitative, thus increasing the perception that these programs coddle and give breaks to criminals. As the mood of the county has grown more punitive, the public has increasingly demanded consistent, harsher sentencing, not "lenient" probation. Consequently, policymakers have devoted more of their attention and their criminal justice budgets to prisons and jails.

Of every criminal justice dollar expended, only a quarter is allocated to corrections, and only three cents of that quarter to probation. Further, while total expenditures for criminal justice have increased over the past decade, probation has actually experienced decreases in many states. In California, for example, total expenditures for criminal justice have increased since 1975—in real terms, by 30%—but expenditures for probation actually declined by more than 10%. Last year alone, California courts sentenced 30,000 more people to probation than the year before—an 11% increase—with virtually no increase in dollars to support their supervision. These people simply had to be "absorbed" by already scanty probation resources.

California is not unique in this regard. A recent study of the effects of fiscal restraint concluded that probation departments experienced larger budget cuts than other criminal justice agencies during the last decade. In fact, probation is the *only* criminal justice function to have experienced budget *declines*—police, court, and prison budgets have all increased significantly since 1975.

Given this context, many people question whether probation practices are seriously jeopardizing public safety. How is probation handling all those felons placed under its care? How many probationers ultimately recidivate, and to what crimes do they return?

The Effects Of Felony Probation Practices

In 1985, the Rand Corporation released a study undertaken to answer such questions. Our final report, titled *Granting Felons Probation: Public Risks and Alternatives,* by Petersilia et al., attracted considerable professional and media interest. Tracking a group of adults who had been convicted of felonies in Los Angeles and Alameda counties, we found that during the 40 months while most of them were on probation, 65% were rearrested and 34% were sentenced to jail or prison for new crimes. Of those arrested again, 75% were charged with burglary, robbery, or other violent crimes.

These results led us to believe that the majority of felons who are placed on probation in California constitute a serious threat to the public and that the increasing use of probation to punish felons is a "high risk gamble." Our findings also showed that with information currently available to (or legally usable by) the courts, it is not possible to make prediction of recidivism more than 70% accurate. Under the circumstances, we concluded that "probation is intended for offenders who pose little threat to society and can, ideally, be rehabilitated through a productive, supervised life in the community . . . it is not an effective sentencing alternative for most felons."

It became clear to us that routine probation, as administered in the two study counties, did not work. Caseloads were so large that probation officers were often unfamiliar with many of those placed under their care. Many probation officers could do no more than give these people a stack of postcards to mail in at required intervals. In these instances, probation actually meant freedom, with few constraints and little supervision. Today's probationers, who appear to pose a more serious threat to public safety than in the past, should have more supervision, not less.

We argued in the report that the current troubles are self-perpetuating. Without some sanction that is intermediate in severity between incarceration and probation for serious offenders, prison populations will continue to grow and the courts will be forced to consider probation for more and more serious offenders. Probation populations will increase, petty offenders will be increasingly ignored by the system (possibly creating more career criminals), and recidivism rates will rise. In short, probation will become increasingly unable to supervise offenders adequately.

We recommended that probation develop alternative, intermediate forms of punishment, programs that change the perception of probation as a "slap on the wrist" to that of a viable alternative to prison. The core of such an alternative must be intensive surveillance, coupled with substantial community service and/or restitution. It must be structured to satisfy public demands that the punishment fit the crime, to show criminals that crime really doesn't pay, and to control potential recidivists.

A number of counties are experimenting with intermediate sanctions. Rand recently conducted a nationwide mail survey of the characteristics of such programs, and the next section describes some of the more popular programs and discusses the issues they raise for probation's future.

A NEW GENERATION OF PROBATION ALTERNATIVES

Results from the Rand "Innovations in Probation" survey show that all states are now developing community-based alternatives to prison, motivated by the lack of prison space to house all convicted felons. These programs are "intermediate" in severity—tougher than routine probation but less harsh than prison.

On the surface, some of these programs resemble the older reform efforts of the 1970s. But the resemblance is more apparent than real. The "rehabilitation" programs operated by probation in the 1970s are being modified and expanded to exert greater control over participants. This is done primarily by increasing the requirements, penalties, and monitoring of probationers. The overriding goal of the newer probation programs is offender control, accountability, and supervision. If rehabilitation occurs, so much the better.

Variations on the theme include intensive probation supervision, electronic monitoring, shock incarceration, community diversion centers, police-probation surveillance teams, community sponsors, and house arrest.

Intensive probation supervision. The most common new probation program spreading across the nation is intensive probation supervision (IPS). IPSs were recently called "the future of American corrections" by the New York Times. The Rand survey shows that 40 states are now developing IPS programs to serve as alternatives for offenders otherwise likely to be incarcerated. While IPS programs differ in their specifics, all of them are designed to test whether an intermediate form of punishment, one that is less costly than prison but much more onerous (and much more restrictive) than traditional probation, will achieve the objective of deterrence—general and specific.

IPS programs usually promise continuous monitoring to ensure that the offender is complying with court-ordered probation conditions, and immediate incarceration if failure to comply is detected.

Statewide IPS programs now exist in New York, Florida, Texas, Georgia, Massachusetts, New Jersey, Illinois, and Ohio. Most of these programs have been modeled after Georgia's program, implemented in 1982. Georgia's IPS standards include the following:

— five face-to-face contacts per week
— 132 hours mandatory community service

— mandatory curfew
— mandatory employment
— weekly check of local arrest records
— automatic notification of arrest elsewhere via State Crime Information Network listing
— routine and unannounced alcohol and drug testing

According to Georgia officials, "These standards are designed to provide sufficient surveillance to control risk to the community, while at the same time providing the framework for treatment-oriented counseling designed to encourage law-abiding behavior" (Erwin, 1986).

An evaluation of the recidivism rates of the 2,300 offenders who have participated in Georgia's IPS to date shows that 16% have absconded or been revoked, and that none has been revoked for a crime involving bodily injury. Furthermore, probation supervision fees have paid for the total cost of implementing Georgia's IPS program. Hence, it appears that Georgia's IPS has demonstrated that prison-bound offenders can be supervised under strict surveillance programs with relatively little risk to the public, and at considerable cost savings.

House arrest. Oklahoma, Alabama, Connecticut, Delaware, Indiana, Florida, New York, California, Texas, and South Carolina have recently begun to operate house arrest programs, and a dozen more states are planning to implement such programs next year.

The goal of house arrest is to restrict the offender's movements. In some instances, curfews are simply added on to the offender's court-ordered probation conditions. More typically, offenders participating in Intensive Probation Supervision programs are required to be in their residences during the evening hours and on weekends.

While curfews permit individual freedom in the community except for particular hours, more direct home incarceration programs totally restrict the offenders freedom *in all but* court-approved limited activities. For example, a judge in New York recently sentenced a woman, convicted of a major insurance fraud, to spend the next two years confined to her home. She is allowed to leave her home only for medical reasons, employment, religious services, or to conduct essential food shopping. Another judge sentenced a landlord who had been convicted of repeated health and safety violations to live for

30 days under house arrest in a Los Angeles building he owns.

Some house arrest programs have begun to use computers to help monitor compliance. In New Jersey, for example, the telephone numbers of house arrest participants are programmed into an automatic telephone call-back system. The computer continues to call the offender until contact is made. Some telephonic systems even ask the offender a prerecorded question. If the individual is not there to answer the computer-generated phone call, or fails to provide the correct answer to the question (verified by a probation officer), then a violation is recorded.

Electronically monitored house arrest. The most stringent of the house arrest programs are those using electronic monitoring devices. One form of the technology—popularly referred to as "active" monitoring—requires the probationer to wear a small transmitter. The transmitter emits a radio signal that is picked up by a receiver attached to the probationer's telephone. During curfew hours (which can be 24-hours per day), the computer automatically dials the offender's phone at random intervals to determine whether the receiver is receiving a signal from the transmitter. If so, the computer assumes the probationer is at home. If not, the computer registers a potential curfew violation.

As of this writing, several agencies are using active electronic monitoring. These include correctional agencies and private service corporations in Florida, Idaho, Kentucky, Michigan, New Jersey, Oregon, Utah, Indiana, California, and Virginia.

Another version of the technology uses a passive wrist band instead of a transmitter. In this case, a computer dials the probationer's home during curfew hours, the probationer then inserts an identification bracelet worn on the wrist into a receiver attached to the phone, and the receiver sends a signal back to the computer. If the telephone is not answered, or the bracelet is not inserted into the receiver, the computer notes a potential violation.

Shock imprisonment. Several states are developing or, in some cases, expanding their shock imprisonment programs. The purpose is to offer the courts an alternative to long-term incarceration, usually reserved for young offenders or those convicted of a felony and facing their first adult prison term. These programs combine a brief prison experience (usually an average of 3 months) with intensive probation supervision. Some of the newer programs, for example, those in

Georgia and New York, combine hard physical work with a strict regimen of discipline and drill, much like military basic training.

Community service sentencing. Many counties are reinstituting community service sentencing, which requires offenders to perform unpaid services for the community in a public or private agency for a specified period of time. While many states have had community service as an optional condition of probation, some legislatures are beginning to pass bills providing (and in some cases mandating) community service as a sentencing option. Such legislation will increase dramatically the use of community service, and many offenders in the near future will likely be sentenced to 40 hours per week at community service in lieu of incarceration in jail.

Community sponsors and network teams. Given the scanty resources available to probation, many agencies have begun looking for ways to increase surveillance over probationers without increasing costs. In the past, this has meant recruiting volunteers to serve as aides, usually serving in "big brother" or "big sister" helping capacities. Some probation offices have begun to recruit probation "sponsors" whose primary responsibility is to assist the probation officer in monitoring court-ordered probation conditions.

For example, in New Jersey, each IPS applicant must obtain a community sponsor "who will be responsible for the applicant's actions" while in the program. The sponsor's responsibilities include monitoring compliance with curfews and other special conditions of the offender's plan, assisting the offender in obtaining community resources, and maintaining regular contact with the offenders' probation officer. The IPS participant must also identify additional community members who will assist the community sponsor. Members of this "network team" help supervise the offender's community service work, monitor work attendance, work with the offender during free time on weekend nights, and randomly call and visit the offender to check on curfew or home detention status.

In some counties, the police department is playing a larger role in assuring compliance with probation conditions. Police in Long Beach, California, carry the names, addresses, and probation conditions of each adult on probation in their area. Police are encouraged by the probation department to make random and unannounced visits to probationer's homes and places of employment. If violations are detected, they immediately notify the probation department, where a special team of prosecutors streamline revocation proceedings.

ADVANTAGES AND UNRESOLVED ISSUES

The programs cited above and others along similar veins, are thought to be highly cost effective. Intensive supervision programs cost between $2,000 and $5,000 per year. If electronic monitoring is used, the cost rises to about $8,000 to $10,000 per year. That is still quite a bit less than the cost of sentencing an offender to prison, which has been conservatively estimated to be $25,000 per year per offender (when construction and operational costs are considered (Zedlewski, 1985). If the offender were truly prison bound, then the state would be saving, at a minimum, $15,000 per year per offender.

And there are indirect cost savings as well. Offenders with families can contribute to their support, thus saving the state welfare costs those families may have required. Many of these programs also require the offenders to be employed. Consequently, they continues to pay taxes, and may be required to pay victim restitution and probation supervision fees.

These community-based programs are also thought to be "socially cost effective." Treating the offender in the community can prevent the breakup of the offenders family, with its consequent psychological and physical disruption, which may traumatize the family as well as the offender. Further, any "criminogenic effects" associated with prison would be avoided.

Given these considerations, these programs seem ideally suited to the pressures facing corrections today. Because several of these sanctions target high-risk offenders who might be imprisoned, they should help alleviate crowding, and because they involve strict supervision, they are responsible to community pressures to control offenders. But these programs are not without difficulties, and should not be implemented without a great deal of forethought.

Victims' advocates argue that placing convicted offenders back in the community, however stringent the conditions, trivializes the nature of their crimes. Civil rights groups fear that electronic monitoring will be abused, and that the private sector will begin selling the equipment to extend surveillance not only to convicted criminals, but to "undesirables" (e.g., persons with AIDS).

Some probation officers worry that these programs, particularly those that utilize electronics, will be the final blow to the "rehabilitation ideal." As probation officers focus more heavily on surveillance, rehabilitation-type activities are diminished. Most probation officers monitoring house arrestees or those on intensive probation admit they have little time for one-to-one counseling.

It is also true that intensive supervision programs easily fall into the pattern of detecting a large number of minor violations and generating revocations to an unmanageable degree. That can become almost as significant a problem in managing the program as the felony arrests and convictions that are bound to occur in any community-based program. For instance, when Georgia randomly tested probationers for drug use using urinalysis methods, 46% of those tested produced positive results (Erwin, 1985). What is the appropriate response to positive drug screens? If incarceration is called for, then the county's incarceration rate could increase significantly after such intensive surveillance programs are implemented.

Some people seriously question whether these programs can adequately protect the public. Regardless of stringency, these programs cannot guarantee that offender will go "straight" and relies for the most part on the offender's willingness to comply. Can a criminal really be trusted to refrain from further crime if allowed to remain in the community? Even under house arrest, what is to stop him from simply escaping or using his home as a base of criminal operations?

While current statistics on recidivism and escape in these programs don't cause particular alarm, the low rates are due in part to the fact that such programs select the best risks. As these programs become more widespread and incorporate other offender types, the public safety question will resurface.

While these programs may cost less overall, that cost savings is not necessarily being passed on to probation departments. If offenders who would normally be serving time in state prison are being diverted to local communities to serve intensive probation, who should bear the costs? The state saved a prison or jail bed, but probation picked up an additional client—who requires intensive, costly community supervision.

In states operating centralized probation departments, reallocating a portion of the overall corrections budgets to correct this imbalance is rather straightforward (although not necessarily easy to accomplish). But in many states, prisons are state funded and probation is county funded. Hence a savings in the state-level prison budget does not necessarily translate into an "add on" to the county-level probation budget.

Should the state reimburse the county to offset some of the additional costs incurred? This is a core issue, and unless it is addressed, probation is likely to find itself again in a no-win situation—responsible for supervising high risk felons with little resources to do the job adequately. Recidivism rates will likely rise, and probation will again come under fire for its ineffectiveness.

Furthermore, these programs will not reduce costs if, rather than diverting offenders from prisons, they serve offenders who are not prison bound, and thus result in a widening of the net of social control. These programs are designed as *alternatives* to prison. However, the possibility exists that the emphasis of such programs will shift from diverting those who truly face prison terms to dealing with lesser offenders more harshly. Intensive supervision programs in Georgia, Washington, Texas, and New York allow judges to sentence an offender directly to the programs, opening the possibility that intensive supervision will be applied to offenders who would otherwise receive routine probation. New Jersey, on the other hand, imposes so many requirements on offenders that they have difficulties locating enough prison-bound offenders who qualify. In short, as Kay Harris (1983-1984) recently noted, "Reformers have not yet developed alternative programs that clearly avoid net-widening while maintaining an effective impact on incarceration.

And, the organization of probation itself is going to need changing. In moving from primarily rehabilitative to restrictive supervision, structural and organizational changes must inevitably follow. Most dramatically, probation departments may need to change from 8-to-5 organizations, closed on weekends, to 24-hour, 7-day-a-week services. Essentially, the argument is that the schedules of probation officers ought to more closely correspond to the schedules of those they are presumed to service and deter. Furthermore, probation may need to staff and monitor surveillance programs differently. Probation may soon consisted largely of mandatory monitoring and enforcement— writing court-ordered presentence reports, making sure offenders report for drug testing or alcohol programs, and checking for new law violations. Probation agencies may need to recruit and train different types of personnel.

Many probation officers will find this surveillance role uncomfortable, while others will argue for even more policing powers. Probation unions are already discussing the desirability of carrying firearms, having search and seizure powers, being able to impose house arrest, and having authority to revoke probation. Some believe these powers are essential to protect the officers themselves, enable them to secure evidence of criminal activity, and minimize the risk to public safety. An evolving issue is how far probation agencies wish to go in supporting "quasipolicing" roles for their officers.

The effectiveness of these programs will depend on the ability of the system to resolve these very complex and controversial problems.

CONCLUSIONS AND IMPLICATIONS

Probation has fallen on hard times. Its caseloads are increasing and it is serving more serious offenders, while its budgets are being cut. But prison overcrowding has forced states to find alternatives to prison, and probation is the most viable one. Hence, states are moving to restructure probation services away from offender treatment and toward control and surveillance. A number of innovative programs are being implemented across the country along these lines. And while such programs appear to hold some promise, a number of unresolved issues remain. Most important perhaps is, for whom should these programs be targeted? If participants were not truly prison-bound, then we have simply expanded the net of social control and increased the dollars expended on crime control.

These programs are, for the most part, not being systematically evaluated. And since many programs have focused initially on minor offenders (to avoid opposition and establish credibility), we have little notion of how such programs might effect more serious offenders.

But these intermediate sanctions deserve serious attention. The public has become increasingly skeptical that anything other than prison constitutes real punishment. If probation's new programs prove successful over time and across jurisdictions, probation will have demonstrated that it can design and operate community-based programs that are safe, hold offenders accountable, and do not compromise public safety. Probation's credibility will be restored and, perhaps more important, such programs may well have rehabilitated at least some of the offenders who participated.

REFERENCES

Bureau of Justice Statistics (1985) Prisoners in 1984. Washington, DC: Department of Justice, April.
Bureau of Justice Statistics (1986) Probation and Parole 1984. Washington, DC: Department of Justice, February.
ERWIN, B. (1985) "Evaluation of urinalysis project report." Atlanta: Georgia Department of Corrections.
ERWIN, B. (1986) "New dimensions in probation: Georgia's experience with IPS." Atlanta: Georgia Department of Corrections.
HARRIS, M. K. (1983-84) "Strategies, values, and the emerging generation of alternatives to incarceration." New York University Review of Law and Social Change 12, 1: 141-202.
PETERSILIA, J., S. TURNER, J. KAHAN, and J. PETERSON (1985) Granting Felons Probation: Public Risks and Alternatives. Santa Monica, CA: Rand Corporation.
PETERSILIA, J. (1987) Expanding Options for Criminal Sentencing. Santa Monica, CA: Rand.
ZEDLEWSKI, E. W. (1985) "When have we punished enough?" Public Administration Review, November: 771-779.

PART V
Controversies in the Penal System

10

Prison Crowding
The Dimensions of the Problem and Strategies of Population Control

SANDRA EVANS SKOVRON

In the past decade, prison crowding has become one of the most critical issues confronting state correctional systems. Demographic shifts placing the "baby-boom" generation in an age bracket more prone to commit offenses, rising crime rates and law-and-order mandates of the 1960s and 1970s, changes in punishment philosophies, and changes in sentencing and correctional policies that swept the nation have contributed to the crowding problem in our prisons. Major sentencing revisions by state legislatures, including instituting longer prison sentences, mandatory incarceration, and determinate sentences, have increased the prison population. Policy revisions that reduce good time, narrowly constrain parole eligibility, and eliminate certain classes of offenders from parole consideration have also helped to raise prison populations to unprecedented levels.

Nationally, prison crowding has reached serious levels. In 1984, the rosters of state and federal prisons increased by 26,618 inmates, bringing the total prison population to 463,866. The incarceration rate in the United States reached 188 per 100,000, an unprecedented level (Bureau of Justice Statistics, 1985). The prison population has grown rapidly. The total growth in the state and federal prison populations from 1980 to 1984 was 134,000 inmates, a 40% increase. By 1984, at least 29 states had formed task forces to address the problem of prison crowding (Ney, 1984).

Prison crowding has had legal repercussions in a number of states. In 1984, the entire prison systems of seven states and the District of Columbia were operating under court orders or consent decrees. In 25 other states, at least one major institution was operating under a court order or consent decree concerning crowding and other conditions. In four additional states, legal challenges were pending.

A number of states house state inmates in local jail facilities because of the severely crowded conditions in the prisons. Holding state prisoners in local jails exacerbates the often already severe crowding problem in local facilities. In 1984, more than 11,500 prison inmates in 18 states were housed in local jails due to prison crowding. Some states were housing a substantial proportion of their state inmates in local jails. Over 10% of the inmates under state jurisdiction in New Jersey, Kentucky, and Tennessee were housed in local jails. More than 20% of the state prisoners in Louisiana and Mississippi were backed-up into local jails (Bureau of Justice Statistics, 1985).

Prison crowding resulted in the emergency early release of over 17,000 state inmates in 1984. These inmates were released early from prisons in 14 states due to emergency crowding conditions. Some 90% of these early releases were from crowded state facilities in three states: Georgia, Michigan, and Tennessee (Bureau of Justice Statistics, 1985).

Prison crowding has resulted in great increases in expenditures for corrections. Expenditures have increased for both operating costs and construction of new facilities. Fiscal year 1984 operating budgets for state correctional systems increased by nearly $1.2 billion and approached a record $7.2 billion. More than 67,000 prison beds were added nationwide through renovation and construction from 1981 to 1983. The 1984 gain of 26,618 inmates implies a need to increase available beds nationally by 500 each week simply to accommodate new prisoners. In 1983, the 50 states reported capital expenditures greater than $780 million and bond issues and other financing mechanisms totaling nearly $1.2 billion to support prison capital improvements (Bureau of Justice Statistics, 1985). In 1985, 35 states and the Federal Bureau of Prisons were involved in construction or planning approved construction totaling 61,975 beds (Contact Center, Inc., 1985).

In recent years there have been increases in the use of all types of adult corrections; jails, prisons, community supervision, probation, and parole. However, the greatest increases have occurred in the prison population. What factors account for the rapid increase in the prison population?

A common assumption is that prison populations have increased as a result of high crime rates. The serious crime rate did increase in the 1960s and 1970s. However, the prison population continues to grow rapidly despite declines in the serious crime rate since 1981. The ratio of prison admissions to the number of serious crimes significantly increased from 1981 to 1984 (Bureau of Justice Statistics, 1985).

Demographic trends may have played a role in the increases in the prison population witnessed to date. Males between the ages of 20 and 29 have the highest incarceration rate of any demographic group. The size of this age group has increased rapidly. Austin and Krisberg (1985: 24) note that from 1930 to 1981, the number of males aged 20 to 29 in the general population increased by 105% and prison admissions grew by 143% in the same time period. The size of this age group began to decline in 1984.

Not only may an increase in the size of the age group at-risk have contributed to the prison population increase, but there also has been an increase in the use of imprisonment as compared to other types of adult corrections. From 1970 to 1982, the jail population increased by 30% while the prison population increased by 110%. From 1979 to 1982, there was a 25% increase in offenders on probation and a 12% increase in offenders on parole. The prison population increased by 34% during this same time period (Austin and Krisberg, 1985: 23).

The principle factor responsible for the rapid increase in the prison population to date has been increased admissions to prison. These increases resulted from demographic trends, crime trends, and increased reliance on prison as opposed to other sanctions. However, given current demographic and crime trends, prison admissions should begin to level off or decline in the late 1980s.

Despite declines in the at-risk population, crime rates, and prison admissions, prison populations are projected to continue to grow throughout the 1980s and 1990s as a result of increases in the length of prison terms. Inmates are serving longer periods of time as a result of changes in sentencing and release practices. The increases in length of prison terms are projected to fuel future population increases.

LEGAL ISSUES

The federal courts have intervened in a number of jurisdictions in efforts to relieve problems of crowding through issuing court orders and consent decrees. As noted above, in 33 jurisdictions, either the entire correctional systems or at least one major correctional institution was operating under court order or consent decree in 1984.

Court intervention of this magnitude has had a dramatic influence on efforts to control prison crowding. The focus of the federal courts on prison crowding has created visibility for the problems of crowding and generated a recognition of prison crowding as a nationwide crisis in corrections. Correctional systems and institutions that have not been sued are affected by litigation in other jurisdictions. Many jurisdictions have voluntarily settled lawsuits alleging crowding to avoid court orders. The anticipation of lawsuits has led others to undertake efforts to reduce prison crowding.

Two recent crowding cases have established the approach taken by the courts in crowding cases. *Bell v. Wolfish* (1979) and *Rhodes v. Chapman* (1982) established the standards to be used in evaluating prison crowding cases.

Bell v. Wolfish was the first case to reach the Supreme Court in which crowding was the central and critical issue. The Supreme Court was asked to decide whether or not it was constitutional to "double bunk" pretrial detainees at the Federal Bureau of Prisons Metropolitan Correctional Center in New York City. Double bunking is the practice of housing two prisoners in a cell originally designed for one. The Metropolitan Correctional Center was a new facility (opened in 1975) and was very modern in design and operation.

The federal district court had found it unconstitutional to double bunk inmates in cells designed for single occupancy. The Court of Appeals had affirmed this decision. The Supreme Court noted that since the prisoners housed at the Metropolitan Correctional Center were pretrial detainees and had not been convicted of a crime, the cruel and unusual punishment clause of the Eighth Amendment did not apply. The Court held that under the due process clause of the Fifth Amendment, a federal pretrial detainee could not be punished prior to conviction. To demonstrate that a condition of confinement constituted punishment, either an intent to punish or the absence of a legitimate governmental purpose to which the condition was related must be demonstrated (*Bell v. Wolfish*, 1979). Evaluating the conditions in accordance with these standards, the Supreme Court reversed and ruled against the inmates, stating:

> We disagree with both the District Court and the Court of Appeals that there is some sort of "one man, one cell" principle lurking in the Due Process Clause of the Fifth Amendment. While confining a given number of people in a given amount of space in such a manner as to cause them to endure genuine privations and hardship over an extended period of time might raise serious questions under the Due Process Clause . . . nothing even approaching such hardship is shown by this record. Detainees are required to spend only seven or eight hours each day in their rooms, during most or all of which they presumably are sleeping. The rooms provide more than adequate space for sleeping. During the remainder of the time, the detainees are free to move between their rooms and the common area. . . . Nearly all of the detainees are released within 60 days. . . . We simply do not believe that requiring a detainee to share toilet facilities and this admittedly rather small sleeping place with another person for generally a maximum period of 60 days violates the Constitution [*Bell v. Wolfish*, 1979].

The Supreme Court held that double bunking in and of itself was not a violation of due process rights. Rather, the Court reinforced the "totality of conditions" approach to ruling on prison conditions. The totality of conditions theory provides that prison conditions must be taken as a whole in considering whether a constitutional violation exists. A specific condition, such as double bunking or exceeding design capacity, may not alone be evidence of unconstitutional conditions. The total environment must be considered.

The 1982 case *Rhodes v. Chapman* focussed on the Eighth Amendment rights of convicted inmates, rather than the due process rights of pretrial detainees considered in *Bell v. Wolfish*. *Rhodes v. Chapman* involved the Southern Ohio Correctional Facility, a modern maximum security male institution constructed in the early 1970s and designed to house inmates in individual cells of 63 square feet. The institution quickly became crowded and approximately two-thirds of the inmates were housed in cells that were double bunked.

As in *Bell v. Wolfish*, the federal district court had found it unconstitutional to double bunk inmates in cells designed for single occupancy and the Court of Appeals had affirmed this decision. The

Supreme Court reversed and ruled against the inmates, indicating that

> the double celling made necessary by the unanticipated increase in prison population did not lead to deprivations of essential food, medical care, or sanitation. Nor did it increase violence among inmates or create other conditions intolerable for prison confinement . . . although job and educational opportunities diminished marginally . . . limited work hours and delay before receiving education do not inflict pain, much less unnecessary and wanton pain; deprivations of this kind simply are not punishments. . . . The five considerations on which the District Court relied also are insufficient to support its conclusion. The court ruled on the long terms of imprisonment served by inmates at SOCF; the fact that SOCF housed 38% more inmates than its 'design capacity'; the recommendation . . . that each inmate have at least 50-55 square feet of living quarters; the suggestion that double celled inmates spend most of their time in their cells with their cellmates; and the fact that double celling at SOCF was not a temporary condition. . . . These general considerations fall far short in themselves of proving cruel and unusual punishment, for there is no evidence that double celling under these circumstances either inflicts unnecessary or wanton pain or is grossly disproportionate to the severity of the crimes warranting imprisonment [*Rhodes v. Chapman*, 1982].

The Supreme Court opinion held that double bunking itself does not violate the Eighth Amendment and that prisoners are not entitled to any set minimum square footage of cell space. The Court stated that single-celling may be an aspiration of an ideal prison environment but "the Constitution does not mandate comfortable prisons" (*Rhodes v. Chapman*, 1982). In *Rhodes v. Chapman* the Court repudiated any notion that crowding per se would be a basis for court intervention. The Court reinforced that crowding suits would be decided based on the "totality of conditions." When crowding does not result in "unnecessary or wanton pain," inmates do not suffer cruel and unusual punishment as prohibited by the Eighth Amendment.

Rhodes v. Chapman and *Bell v. Wolfish* both reinforce the "totality of the conditions" theory and establish the constitutional boundaries of crowding. Double bunking and exceeding design capacity are not in and of themselves impermissible. Recommendations of capacity and minimum correctional standards established by such organizations as the American Correctional Association have no constitutional basis. The opinion in *Bell v. Wolfish* held that the due process rights of pretrial detainees are violated when crowding causes "genuine privations and hardships over an extended period of time" (Bell v. Wolfish, 1979). *Rhodes v. Chapman* indicated that when crowding leads to "deprivation of basic human needs" and "unnecessary or wanton pain" (*Rhodes v. Chapman*, 1982), Eighth Amendment rights are violated.

Numerous jail and prison crowding cases have been litigated since the *Bell v. Wolfish* and *Rhodes v. Chapman* decisions. The lower federal courts apply the standards established in *Bell v. Wolfish* and *Rhodes v. Chapman* to the fact situations in crowding suits. The courts must examine a broad range of prison conditions to determine whether their combined effects result in an unconstitutional totality. The courts must consider to what extent crowding has created deprivations in a variety of other areas including but not limited to, vocational, educational, and recreational opportunities, medical and mental health services, food services, and sanitation. The courts also consider the extent to which prison crowding leads to increases in prison rule infractions, violence, stress, illness, psychological disturbances, suicide, and mortality, among other negative conditions. The deprivations and negative conditions identified above have been determined in empirical studies and by the courts to result from prison crowding (Thornberry and Call, 1983; Toch, 1985).

A case in which this approach was clearly articulated by the district court judge is *Ruiz v. Estelle,* 1980). In this case, the federal court declared that the crowded conditions in the Texas prison system violated the Eighth Amendment prohibition against cruel and unusual punishment. The district court provided a clear discussion of the need to demonstrate harmful effects of crowding:

> Defendants have steadfastly maintained that crowding cannot be found to violate the Eighth Amendment, unless there is a showing of "a concrete injury prescribed [sic] by the Eight Amendment that is directly caused by crowded conditions." Defendants argue for an exceedingly strict standard of proof on these points; they criticize plaintiffs' evidence, for its alleged failure to demonstrate with a high degree of specificity and certainty that harms have been caused to the inmates by overcrowding.

It is clear . . . that the unconstitutional characterization of the plaintiffs' burden of proof is erroneous. Detailed scientifically exact proof of harm has never been required. Courts have reached conclusions concerning the extent of harm from overcrowding based on common sense reasoning from observable facts, such as population levels, space per inmate, incidence of violence, and staffing levels [*Ruiz v. Estelle*, 1980].

The Court heard testimony and reviewed evidence of the consequences of prison crowding in the Texas prison system. The Court indicated:

Included among the consequences were the spread of disease and the enhancement of stress, tension, anxiety, hostility, and depression. Among the distinguishable manifestations of hostility and depression . . . were increased blood pressures, aggressive behavior, and extreme psychological withdrawal . . . Overcrowding . . . substantially contributed to increased rates of disciplinary offenses, psychiatric commitments, and suicides . . . all of these effects are counterproductive to rehabilitation and are creative of serious behavioral and disciplinary problems [*Ruiz v. Estelle*, 1980].

Judicial decrees in crowding suits are difficult to formulate and enforce. State departments of corrections have little control over the size of the prison population. The number of inmates and the length of prison terms is determined much more by the courts and state legislatures, whose decisions are in turn influenced by public attitudes. However, the courts, state legislatures, and the public are not parties to crowding litigation. Remedying crowding conditions is therefore rendered more difficult.

The federal courts have taken a number of approaches in their orders to reduce crowding. The simplest and least drastic approach has been to limit the amount of time that an inmate may suffer crowded conditions such as double celling, or crowded dormitory or corridor housing. Courts have also banned, limited, or otherwise restricted certain forms of crowded housing. More drastic orders, such as imposing population caps (specifying a maximum number of inmates that may be housed in a facility) or ordering the closing of facilities, have also been issued. The closure of facilities is reserved for antiquated, deteriorated institutions that can no longer constitutionally house inmates (Angelos and Jacobs, 1985). Some of these court rulings may have drastic consequences. An example is the 1985 order that the Tennessee Department of Corrections could accept no new inmates until the prison population was reduced to a specified level. In effect, the prisons were ordered to accept no new inmates. Actions such as these contribute to the enormous back-up of state prisoners into already crowded local jails. In Tennessee, one sheriff, exasperated with the situation, left his convicted offenders refused by the state handcuffed to the prison gates.

Federal court intervention to reduce prison crowding has had an impact. The federal courts have been described as the best weapon correctional administrators have to fight crowding. Court intervention forces states to confront their prison crowding problems and forces the legislative and executive branches to undertake efforts to reduce crowding. The intervention of the federal courts has reduced the rate of growth in the prison population. The rate of prison population growth in states under court supervision is significantly lower than in states without court intervention (Bureau of Justice Statistics, 1985: 4).

STRATEGIES TO REDUCE PRISON CROWDING

States have undertaken a number of strategies to reduce prison crowding. The various approaches to reducing prison crowding may be grouped into three basic strategies: "front-end" strategies, "back-end" strategies, and capacity expansion.[2]

Front-end strategies refer to policies that either reduce the number of offenders admitted to prison or reduce the sentence lengths of those admitted. Back-end strategies are policies that increase the numbers of offenders released from prison, typically by changes in good time credits or parole policies. Capacity expansion refers to increases in the institutional ability to house inmates through prison construction and/or renovation projects. States may attempt to alleviate their prison crowding problems by using elements of one or all of these strategies. Typically, however, the efforts of most states have been focussed on changes in release practices, a back-end strategy, and capacity expansion (Austin and Krisberg, 1985).

Front-End Strategies

Front-end strategies are policies that either reduce prison admissions or reduce sentence lengths. A reduction in the number of offenders admitted to prison is typically attempted through an increase in the use of community-based correctional programs such as intensive probation supervision, community service orders, restitution programs, and nonsecure residential facilities. The increased use of these nonprison penalties has not been a major strategy relied upon to reduce prison crowding. The reasons for this will be discussed below.

In the 1970s, there was great enthusiasm for community-based corrections. The emphasis on community corrections was called for by the 1973 National Advisory Commission on Criminal Justice Standards and Goals, the American Bar Association, the American Correctional Association, and the National Council on Crime and Delinquency, among others. In the decade of the 1970s, numerous community-based correctional programs were developed throughout the United States. However, the proliferation of these programs did not lead to reductions in the prison population. Rather than these community correctional programs being used as substitutes to imprisonment, they were applied to offenders already being sentenced to nonprison penalties. They were typically used as alternatives or supplements to sentences of probation or fines.

Community-based correctional programs have been challenged on the basis of cost effectiveness. One argument that had supported community corrections is that these programs were less costly than imprisonment. However, prison populations were not reduced; populations and costs of institutional confinement continued to increase. The costs of corrections not only had continued to increase, but there was also a whole array of new community programs that added to the expenditures for corrections. Not only had the programs failed to reduce the overall costs of corrections, but their effectiveness was also challenged. As the effectiveness of rehabilitation programs was challenged in reports such as that of Martinson[3] (1974), support for community-based programs was also undercut. As faith was lost in the rehabilitative ideal and attitudes became more oriented toward punishment, community programs were viewed as being too "soft" on crime.

These factors have led many policymakers to view community-based correctional programs as ineffective tools for reducing prison crowding. It is thought that nonprison penalties will not lead to decreases in the prison population and that the public and policymakers view these programs as too lenient and ineffective. There are, however, strategies to combat these perceptions and to implement nonprison penalties as available options to help reduce prison crowding.

Harris (1985) has identified a number of strategies currently being utilized to implement nonprison penalties more effectively. Introducing the alternatives at more points in the criminal justice system may more effectively target the programs to prison-bound inmates. Most community programs were originally introduced as sentencing options for judges. More innovative and recent approaches have been to introduce community alternatives at sentence review or resentencing hearings after a prison sentence has been imposed, at probation and/or parole revocation hearings, and at other points throughout the system, thereby more effectively targeting the prison-bound inmate.

Another technique is to select program participants from offenders with a high probability of receiving prison sentences. Programs are being designed in which eligibility is limited to offenders with specified characteristics (such as repeat offenders, certain categories of felons, etc.) that have a high likelihood of receiving a prison sentence.

Perceptions of community-based corrections as lenient may be combated by increasing the severity of the nonprison penalties. Programs may be designed to emphasize the punitive, deterrent, and controlling aspects of the punishments. Multiple requirements are imposed on offenders in many programs. For example, intensive supervision programs may require the offenders to pay fines and supervision costs, pay restitution to the victim, perform community service work, participate in work, education, and/or training, participate in counseling, and abide by a variety of rules.

Policymakers may also develop techniques to ensure that programs are used as intended. The primary technique utilized has been monetary incentives. Funds may be provided to localities for the development of programs and the screening of appropriate offenders into the programs. Localities may receive additional funding for reductions in the number of inmates sentenced to prison or conversely may be penalized for sending less serious offenders to prison.

As outlined above, there are strategies to develop community programs that will effectively target prison-bound offenders and that are punitive in nature. The use of community-based corrections as a strategy to reduce crowding, however, must overcome the perceptions of policymakers and the public. In addition, the impact of increases in the use of community-based corrections on the prison crowding problem is limited inasmuch as the future growth in the prison population will result from the buildup of serious felons serving very long sentences. These offenders typically are not candidates for community programs. Although community correctional programs may provide some relief from prison crowding, this strategy should be used in combination with strategies directed toward the length of stay of offenders in order to achieve effective population control.

The second major area of front-end strategies is changing sentencing policies to reduce sentence lengths. As noted above, much of the crowding problem is related to sentencing changes that swept the country in the 1970s and 1980s. These changes include instituting mandatory sentences, definite sentences, and sentence enhancements that have led to increases in sentence lengths. Changes in sentencing policies that reverse some of the effects of these new sentencing laws would lead to reductions in prison crowding.

Relatively few states have adopted this strategy. As noted above, most of the tougher sentencing laws are of relatively recent origin. Few state legislatures are willing to so quickly reconsider such a complex and comprehensive area. This strategy has the potential for dramatically affecting the prison crowding problem but in many jurisdictions is not politically feasible or popular.

The most notable sentencing strategy designed to control prison crowding is the Minnesota Sentencing Guidelines System. The Minnesota Legislature created the Sentencing Guidelines Commission that developed and adopted sentencing guidelines, providing judges with a range of permissible sentences based upon the current offense and prior record of the offender. Any sentence outside the range established by the guidelines is appealable. The guidelines were designed to result in greater uniformity in sentencing (Minnesota Sentencing Guidelines Commission, 1980). The most unique feature of the Minnesota system is that sentence length is tied to prison capacity. If the prison population increases above the limits of capacity, sentence lengths must be adjusted accordingly. In 1983, the

Sentencing Guidelines Commission did, in fact, modify the sentencing guidelines as a result of increases in the prison population.

Back-End Strategies

A number of states have focused efforts to reduce crowding on back-end strategies that increase the number of prisoners released. These strategies, which include changes in good time, changes in parole practices, and emergency release, although not politically popular, are more politically feasible than strategies such as sentencing reform. Changes in release practices are more politically feasible because they typically require incremental changes in existing policies (good time) or the institution of a new policy (emergency release), rather than a comprehensive revision of complex legislation.

A variety of back-end strategies have been developed. One form of good time policy change is the granting of additional good time to inmates for successful participation in institutional programs and industries, and for meritorious conduct. These policies have a variety of names, including incentive good time, earned credits, and work credits. Still other good time changes have been introduced in states like Michigan, which had abolished good time by public referendum. The state later adopted "disciplinary credits" to alleviate crowding (Kaufman, 1985). Disciplinary credits allow the prison administration to give offenders time off for good behavior, a policy very similar to good time.

Emergency release legislation has been adopted in a number of states. Emergency release has been adopted in a wide variety of forms. A typical emergency release act provides that the governor may declare that emergency crowding conditions exist and accelerate the release dates of inmates by a specified period of time. In some states, the emergency declaration is triggered when the population exceeds a designated percentage of capacity. In many states, the acceleration of release dates does not provide for the automatic release of inmates, but rather accelerates their parole hearings. Many emergency release statutes exclude certain categories of serious felons from the emergency acceleration of release. Emergency release has a very direct impact on the size of the prison population and is felt relatively quickly. It has been used in a number of states. In 1984, 17,365 inmates were released early in 14 states due to emergency crowding conditions

(Bureau of Justice Statistics, 1985). Emergency release, however, has become severely criticized and politically challenged in states that have invoked the emergency release powers a number of times. For example, the state of Michigan invoked its emergency release act eight times in a three-year period between 1981 and May of 1984.

Capacity Expansion

Expansion of prison capacity through construction is a common approach taken to alleviate prison crowding. As noted above, 35 states and the Federal Bureau of Prisons are involved in or planning new construction of a total of 61,975 beds (Contact Center, Inc., 1985). This is in addition to over 67,000 beds added nationwide from 1981 to 1983.

Prison construction is not, however, a panacea to the crowding problem. Construction must be viewed as a long-term strategy to reduce crowding. A prison normally takes several years to construct. It is nearly impossible for prison construction to keep pace with the growth in population. Although many states have undertaken massive construction programs, the gap between population and capacity is widening. From 1972 to 1977, over 23,000 beds were added nationwide, however population increased by 81,000. From 1978 to 1980, 7,000 beds were added, and population increased by 61,000 inmates. In 1981, 21,000 beds were added, and population grew by 39,000 (Funke, 1985: 87).

Prison construction is a very costly solution. The quoted construction costs per bed range from $50,000 to $100,000. Using an average bed cost of $75,000, an average 500-bed institution would appear to cost about $37.5 million. However, as Funke (1985) notes, many of the costs of construction are not obvious and the true costs are much higher. After all base capital costs,[4] phased construction costs, inflation costs, and financing costs are included, Funke indicates that the construction costs are more realistically $135 million over a 30-year period. Operating costs must also be included in a cost analysis. It is estimated that at current dollar values, operating costs would be about $7 million annually. The more realistic cost estimate, therefore, is nearly $350 million; $135 million for construction and $210 million for operation over a 30-year period. This is an average yearly cost of $11.5 million (Funke, 1985).

SUMMARY

Prison crowding has become a serious and costly correctional crisis. Prison populations have reached unprecedented levels and are projected to continue to grow. Crowding conditions in many states have led to severe management problems and court suits. States have been forced to reassess their imprisonment policies and have attempted to achieve solutions to the prison crowding problem. Effective correctional management necessitates a balanced approach to controlling prison population. The ability of states to achieve effective population control is frequently hampered by public attitudes and an unfavorable political environment. However, states must begin to adopt balanced, systemic strategies of population control that provide for safe and secure, constitutional prisons, public protection, and the wise use of fiscal resources.

NOTES

1. The incarceration rate includes inmates in both state and federal prisons but does not include those confined in jails.
2. These strategies have also been referred to as "front-door" strategies, "back-door" strategies, and prison construction.
3. Martinson reviewed over 200 evaluations of correctional treatment programs issued from 1945 to 1967 and concluded that "with few and isolated exceptions the rehabilitative efforts that have been reported so far have had no appreciable effect on recidivism" (1974: 22). His conclusion was quickly heralded as evidence that rehabilitation programs were not successful.
4. Base capital costs also include areas other than housing, such as administrative offices, and fees that attach to base costs, such as architectural fees, equipment, site acquisition, and site preparation.

REFERENCES

ANGELOS, C. and J. B. JACOBS (1985) "Prison overcrowding and the law." Annals of the American Academy of Political and Social Science 478: 100-112.

AUSTIN, J. and B. KRISBERG (1985) "Incarceration in the United States: the extent and future of the problem." Annals of the American Academy of Political and Social Science 478: 15-30.

Bell v. Wolfish (1979) 441 U.S. 520.
Bureau of Justice Statistics (1985) Prisoners in 1984. Washington, DC: Department of Justice, April.
CONRAD, J. P. (1985) "Charting a course for imprisonment policy." Annals of the American Academy of Political and Social Science 478: 123-134.
Contact Center, INC. (1985) "1985 prison construction." Corrections Compendium, February.
FUNKE, G. S. (1985) "The economics of prison crowding." Annals of the American Academy of Political and Social Science 478: 86-99.
HARRIS, M. K. (1985) "Reducing prison crowding and nonprison penalties." Annals of the American Academy of Political and Social Sciences 478: 150-160.
KAUFMAN, G. (1985) "The national prison overcrowding project: policy analysis and politics, a new approach." Annals of the American Academy of Political and Social Sciences 478: 161-172.
MARTINSON, R. (1974) "What works? Questions and answers about prison reform." Public Interest 35: 22-54.
Minnesota Sentencing Guidelines Commission (1980) Minnesota Sentencing Guidelines and Commentary. St. Paul, MN. (unpublished)
NEY, B. (1984) "A survey of state prison overcrowding task forces." Philadelphia, PA: National Jail and Prison Overcrowding Project, Center for Effective Public Policy. (unpublished)
Rhodes v. Chapman (1982) 452 U.S. 337.
Ruiz v. Estelle (5th Cir., 1982) 679 F.2d 1115; (S.D. Tex., 1980) 503 F. Supp. 1265.
THORNBERRY, T. P. and J. E. CALL (1983) "Constitutional challenges to prison overcrowding: the scientific evidence of harmful effects." Hastings Law Journal 35, 2: 313-351.
TOCH, H. (1985) "Warehouses for people." Annals of the American Academy of Political and Social Science 478: 58-72.

11

Career Criminals and Selective Incapacitation

MICHAEL GOTTFREDSON and TRAVIS HIRSCHI

Andrew von Hirsch (1985) has traced criminal justice policy through four phases in recent years. During the first phase, American sentencing policy pursued rehabilitation as its major goal. It was assumed that offenders could be changed into law abiding citizens by a large variety of therapeutic techniques. This assumption gives considerable discretion to those imposing sentence on offenders, allowing them to base the length of the sentence on the amount of treatment thought to be required by the offender as well as on the seriousness of the offense and the danger posed by the offender to the community.

In the middle 1970s, research was progressively interpreted as showing that treatment had little or not effect, and the rehabilitation model fell into disfavor. As von Hirsch points out, the perspective that justified rehabilitation (often called *positivism*) could have been used to justify "restraining" offenders, whether or not they could be treated (since it suggested that it was possible to predict future misbehavior), but the link between positivism and rehabilitation was so strong that the "failure" of rehabilitation led to a search for a new justification for sentencing decisions.

In the late 1970s, the deterrence school therefore rose to prominence. Although positivism had traditionally found the deterrence perspec-

---

Authors' Note: This research was supported by a grant from the National Science Foundation, SES-8500244.

tive contrary to its assumptions about human nature (and contrary to its interpretation of research on the effectiveness of punishment), positivism was no longer in control. When economists and political scientists turned their attention to crime, they brought with them the assumption that "crime could effectively be reduced . . . through sentencing policies aimed at intimidating potential offenders more efficiently" (von Hirsch, 1985: 7). In fact, interest in deterrence became sufficiently strong that the National Academy of Sciences sponsored a panel of well-known criminologists to investigate the factual basis for this policy. The conclusions of the panel were cautiously optimistic, reporting that, in general, the evidence supported the idea of deterrence over the idea that deterrence has no effect. Perhaps because the panel studied only work on the effects of criminal justice system sanctions and ignored a considerable body of research within the larger deterrence tradition, its report did not lead to increased interest in deterrence as a viable public policy. On the contrary, the panel's work on incapacitation seems to have stimulated greater interest and to have captured the interest of policymakers.

Since the early 1980s, then, incapacitation has been a major focus of theoretical and research attention. (The major alternative perspective, championed by von Hirsch, is called the "just desert" or "retributive" view. We do not deal with von Hirsch's perspective here.) This chapter discusses the origins of the idea of incapacitation, reviews the evidence about its usefulness, and explores alternative crime prevention policies.

DISCOVERY OF THE CAREER CRIMINAL

Contemporary interest in the idea of incapacitation can be traced to the rediscovery of an old idea in criminology. This old idea is captured in such terms as *chronic offender* or *career criminal*. If the crime problem is largely the work of a few highly active criminals, the crime problem can be largely controlled by identification and incapacitation of them. The question to be answered by research is thus "How general or widespread is involvement in criminal acts?"

In 1972, Wolfgang et al. published a study of the criminal records of about 10,000 boys in Philadelphia. In this study, the researchers traced the boys from birth to age 18, counting the number of times they had been arrested and convicted. The 10,000 boys had committed 10,214 offenses by age 18, an average of slightly more than one offense per boy. But these offenses were not evenly distributed among the boys in the sample. Indeed, only one third of the boys had committed any offenses at all, suggesting that the average delinquent was responsible for about three offenses. But these offenses were not evenly distributed among the delinquents in the sample. Indeed, a sixth of the delinquents were responsible for more than half of the offenses committed by all delinquents. Wolfgang refers to these boys, 6% of the entire sample, as "chronic offenders."

Such concentration of offending among a small segment of the population suggested to many that the crime rate could be cut in half by isolating such chronic offenders and preventing them from engaging in criminal acts. In other words, the rediscovery of the chronic offender redirected attention from crime prevention aimed at the population as a whole toward that small group responsible for a disproportionate share of crime.

This new direction in crime control policy has a number of attractive features. It suggests that with minimal money and effort, sizable reductions in the crime rate can be achieved. Since the focus is on chronic, habitual, or career criminals, there will be few legal or ethical problems with a policy that isolates them from society. Since the number of career criminals is small, it may be possible to reduce the scope of the criminal justice system at all levels, from police to prisons. Instead of a large and unwieldy system passively accepting a mixture of occasional, petty, and serious offenders, this new policy would create an efficient system where resources could be focused on the dangerous few. Finally, this new system would take the criminal justice system out of the business of dealing with social problems and put it to work doing what it alone can do: Identifying and removing from circulation people whose continued freedom would jeopardize the safety of the community.

EVALUATING SELECTIVE INCAPACITATION POLICY

How could such an ideal system be implemented? Clearly, the first requirement is the identification of chronic offenders before they have committed the crimes that define them as chronic offenders. It would be of little value to incapacitate such offenders after they have committed their crimes. Thus a threshold requirement for implementation of selective incapacitation policy is a scheme or mechanisms whereby we can predict with sufficient accuracy a habitual or sustained pattern of offending.

What would such a scheme look like? First, it would have to meet fairly high standards of accuracy. After all, persons with scores indicating that they are a threat to society are going to be deprived of liberty. Second, it would have to use evidence of dangerousness that is public, easily or consistently measurable, and socially and legally acceptable. Third, it would have to use evidence available prior to commission of the acts that identification is designed to prevent. Finally, the measuring device could not be subject to manipulation by potentially dangerous subjects.

What are the prospects of developing predictive procedures that satisfy these requirements? Interestingly enough, researchers had explored the prospects for predicting delinquency long before the idea of selective incapacitation came on the scene. These efforts demonstrated that delinquency could be predicted with sufficient accuracy to justify benign or minimal intervention. For example, in the Cambridge-Somerville Youth Study it was shown that boys predicted to be delinquent at 11 were considerably more likely actually to become delinquent than boys predicted at the same age to be nondelinquent (McCord and McCord, 1959). By scientific standards, these predictions are a remarkable achievement. However, a majority of those predicted to be delinquent turned out not to be seriously delinquent after 10 years, and harsh or restrictive treatment of the entire group predicted to be delinquent could by no means be justified. These predicted delinquents who turn out to be nondelinquents are known as "false positives." In the absence of perfect prediction, there will always be such false positives, a fact that has led some to argue that predictive punishments are necessarily unjust (von Hirsch, 1985). In any event, the existence of false positives in the Cambridge-Somerville Youth Study is good evidence that the best available prediction strategies do not satisfy the "accuracy" standard when they are applied before criminal acts take place.

Examination of the factors used to predict delinquency from an early age quickly reveals that these predictive schemes fail to satisfy the social-legal acceptability criterion as well. Thus, although social scientists have been able to establish reliable and valid predictors of crime and delinquency, these predictors typically do not themselves justify harsh intervention. For example, a major predictor of subsequent criminality is a tendency to push and shove other kids. Another predictor is unsatisfactory relations with one's parents or other authorities. Still another is the use of alcohol and tobacco. Another is the age of the individual, with young people being more likely than old people to commit criminal acts. Clearly, none of these traits or behavior tendencies would in and of itself justify incarceration. It is not surprising therefore that the incapacitation tradition has focused attention on behavior that lends itself more readily to intervention by the criminal justice system.

Behavior consistent with incapacitation by the criminal justice system is, by definition, illegal behavior. Thus the search for predictors acceptable on one criterion tends to lead to predictors unacceptable by another criterion. The effort to prevent illegal behavior by incapacitation must await the commission of illegal acts before it can get under way. What kinds and how much illegal behavior is required for effective prediction of subsequent illegal behavior?

It is easy to make the case that the greater the frequency of criminal activity in the past, the greater the frequency of criminal activity in the future. Thus Shannon (1981) shows that there is a strong correlation between past and future delinquent behavior, a correlation that has been reported many times in the literature. To illustrate the strength of this correlation, Shannon notes that almost two-thirds of those who have as many as five criminal offenses before age 18 will have five or more criminal offenses in the dozen or so years following. Clearly, the policy of selective incapacitation would take advantage of this relation. The problem arises, however, that the criminal justice system as it now operates and as it has always operated has reserved its harshest sanctions for those with a prior record. In fact, apart from the seriousness of the instant offense, prior record is the best predictor of the actions of the criminal justice system. That is, all things equal, those with prior records are more likely to be arrested, prosecuted, and sentenced to harsh treatment than those without such records.

Although such an outcome is consistent with all penal philosophies, and certainly comes as no surprise, it presents the idea of selective incapacitation with a special problem: How to improve on a system that is already highly selective and that uses the very criteria of selection recommended by the goal of incapacitation.

Given this problem, advocates of selective incapacitation can focus on two groups of offenders: (1) those unnecessarily incapacitated (on purely predictive grounds) by the current system, and (2) those whose behavior justifies greater incapacitation than that provided by the current system.

Focus on the first of these groups reveals an obvious problem. As mentioned, the best predictor of sentence severity or probability of incarceration is the gravity of the current offense. Thus, under the current system, those guilty of murder or forcible rape have the highest probability of incarceration, regardless of prior record. Although most such offenders do have prior records, some do not. A strict incapacitation policy would suggest that these first-time murderers and rapists not be incarcerated, a policy obviously at odds with other goals of the criminal sanction, such as "just desert."

As a consequence of this problem, selective incapacitation in practice focuses on the second group and attempts to identify high-rate or chronic offenders who now escape the notice of the criminal justice system. On its face, such an undertaking seems doomed to failure. It is instructive, therefore, to examine studies devoted to the discovery of *secret* career criminals.

The most famous example of such research is that by Greenwood of the Rand Corporation (1983). Greenwood (1983: 260) identifies seven variables in the construction of a scale for the identification of high-rate offender:

(1) incarceration for more than half of the two year period preceding the most recent arrest
(2) prior conviction for the crime type that is being predicted
(3) juvenile conviction prior to age 16
(4) commitment to a state or federal juvenile facility
(5) heroin or barbiturate use in the two-year period preceding the current arrest
(6) heroin or barbiturate use as a juvenile
(7) employment for less than half of the two-year period preceding the current arrest

This scale, intended for the prediction of high-rate offenders qualified for selective incapacitation, was constructed on the basis of interviews with a sample of imprisoned offenders. It has been the object of considerable criticism (see von Hirsch, 1985, for a full discussion). For example, there was no validation of the predictive ability of the scale, which was, the reader will note, constructed by interviews with people already incapacitated. It cannot then provide information on those people of most interest, that is, those who currently avoid incarceration. As developed, it also violates our rule that the prediction devise not be manipulable by those whose behavior is being predicted. (Interviewees might be inclined to deny behavior that would add to the length of their sentence.)

Nonetheless, it is interesting to learn what factors appear to discriminate between high- and low-rate offenders, according to the Greenwood scale. It cannot escape notice that these factors tend to overlap to the point that they may be considered measures of the same thing. This "thing" is, apparently, prior record of illegal conduct. As indicated above, decision makers in the criminal justice system now pay considerable attention to prior record in making their incarceration decisions. Explicit, mandatory attention to prior record would systematize decision making and would therefore increase its visibility and equity (Gottfredson and Gottfredson, 1987), but it would not be expected greatly to increase the system's ability to isolate the so-called career criminal.

There are, however, even more fundamental difficulties in this method of identifying targets for selective incapacitation that have heretofore escaped the notice of the criminal justice system. (One of these difficulties has to do with procedures for bringing the police power of the state to bear on persons who have done nothing to justify such intervention.) By the time such "targets" have been identified by Greenwood's procedures, they will have been incarcerated as adults; in other words, they will have moved well beyond the age of maximum offending. It is therefore doubtful that large reductions in the crime rate (the goal of selective incapacitation) could be achieved by marginal increases in their incarceration. Thus Greenwood's scale fails also to satisfy the requirement that the prediction instrument allow *prediction* of high-rate criminality.

The decline in crime with age in fact suggests that for maximum effectiveness incapacitation should be focused on the age period just prior to the rapid onset and peaking of crime. Figure 1 shows the age distribution of robbery offenders as indicated by FBI arrest statistics for 1970, 1974, and 1983. Clearly, these statistics suggest that were intervention to be made on the basis of potential incapacitation effects, such intervention would take place at an early age, probably

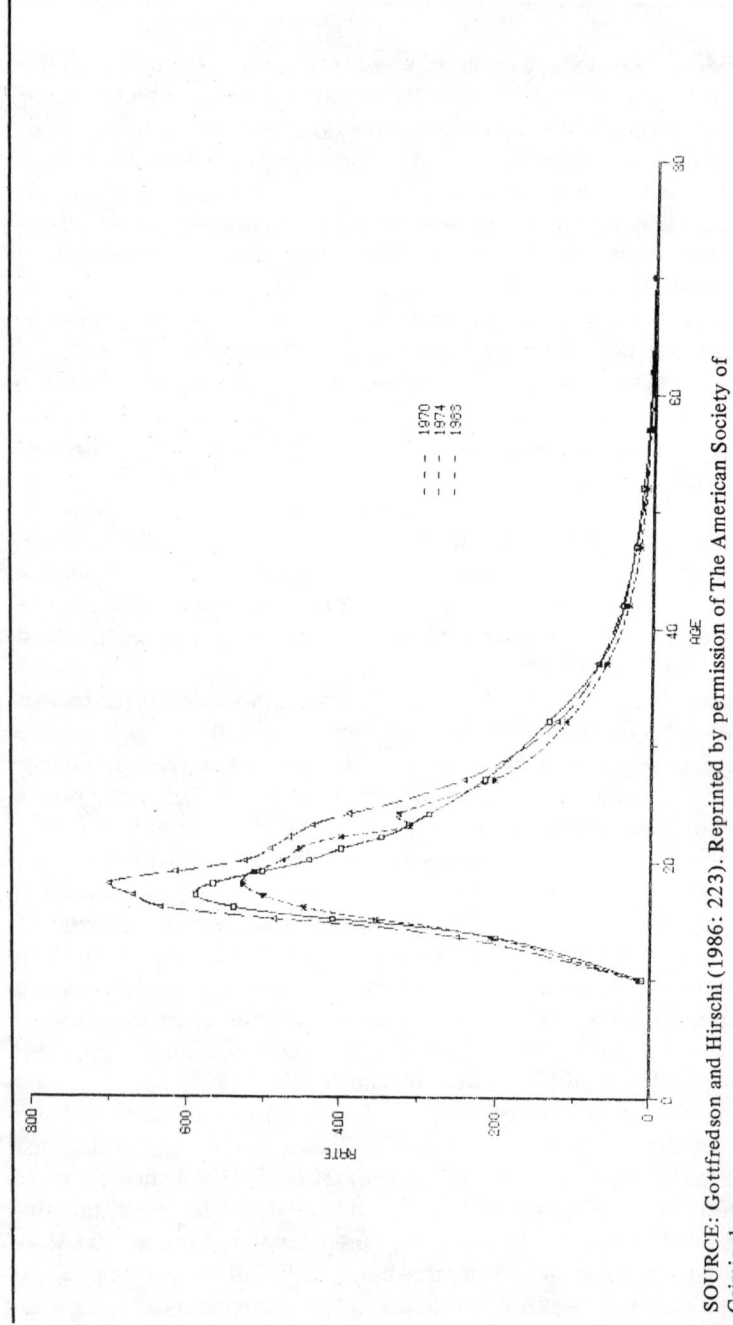

SOURCE: Gottfredson and Hirschi (1986: 223). Reprinted by permission of The American Society of Criminology.

Figure 11.1: Number of Robbery Arrests/100,000 Males.

around 13 or 14. The ethical issues raised by the apparent advantage of incapacitating young people usually preclude further investigation of the actual mechanics of such a policy. This creates the impression that selective incapacitation has an ace in the hole, a card it could play were it not prevented from doing so on ethical grounds.

Does selective incapacitation have an ace in the hole? One way to find out is to ask those favoring such policy to devise a maximally efficient policy free of ethical concerns. Incapacitate as you will, they may be told. Would they lock up youth of 13 and 14? If so, which ones?

Obviously, such predictive devices as Greenwood's would be inapplicable. What might be used instead? The Cambridge-Somerville type of scale, we have previously shown, would not achieve the required efficiency, since it would entail locking up too many nondelinquents. Apparently, the only choice left is to base the decision on prior criminal acts. So, putting these facts together, the ace in the hole becomes the policy of incarcerating 13- and 14-year-olds on their first offense. So far, so good. One problem, however, quickly surfaces. As Wolfgang et al. have shown, almost half of all offenders are one-time-only offenders, and it would again seem inefficient to incapacitate people who will, if left alone, commit no more offenses. Given the very large number of one-time offenders (a third of the Wolfgang et al. sample by age 18), such a strategy would be inconceivable in any event. We are therefore forced to move the selection point for number of offenses to two, and to consider the consequences of this selection policy.

Recall that a maximally efficient incapacitation policy does not incarcerate those who pose too little risk. This suggests that no one-time offender be incarcerated, and that all two-time offenders be incarcerated. Again, however, the policy suggested is inconceivable. No matter how little risk is posed by them, some first-time offenders must on grounds of just deserts or deterrence be punished by imprisonment. And, since more than a third of second-time offenders do not commit a third offense by the time they are 18 (Wolfgang et al., 1972), we are again treating many low-rate offenders as though they were high-rate offenders. And so on as the number of offenses increases.

At some point, of course, almost any policy will suggest that multiple recidivists merit incarceration, that enough is enough. Also note that the accumulation of a record sufficient to justify imprisonment will typically take time, that offenders with such records will not be 13 or 14, but will have passed beyond the peak age of crime. Therefore, the logic of selective incapacitation falls of its own weight. We cannot predict relative criminal activity until the absolute likelihood of such activity has declined to the point that our prediction is of little practical value.

THE 30-YEAR-OLD CAREER CRIMINAL

We find such a conclusion inescapable, and therefore neither to be celebrated nor mourned. Others find this conclusion unacceptable, and seek strategies for identifying career criminals whose patterns of criminal activity deviate from those for the general population of offenders, criminals active in crime long after their colleagues have retired. Although considerable research effort has concentrated on the search for such offenders, this effort has yielded little in the way of results (Gottfredson and Hirschi, 1986). The public policy most clearly identified with this effort is the creation of special career criminal units in prosecutors' offices and police departments. Such units seek to assign special priority to the arrest and prosecution of those with lengthy prior records. This activity has considerable appeal to the media, to politicians, and to the general public. It suggests that some segment of the offender population is worthy of concentrated, sophisticated effort. As indicated above, however, there is reason to doubt that such units are of much consequence for the crime problem.

CRIME POLICY IN LONG-TERM PERSPECTIVE

We earlier followed Andrew von Hirsch through the recent fads in justification of criminal justice policy. Rehabilitation gave way to deterrence, which was in turn replaced by incapacitation. Obviously, we do not believe that the current emphasis on the career criminal and selective incapacitation is likely to yield significant benefits in crime reduction. We do not conclude, however, that crime prevention is a hopeless aspiration of an enlightened policy, that there is nothing society can do to reduce the level of crime. On the contrary, we find considerable hope in the finding that the period of important criminal activity is very brief. Given the brevity of this period, many opportunities for significant change in the level of criminal activity in the population as a whole are available. Further, these opportunities are available in the short run. They do not require long-term incapacitation of potential offenders nor expensive rehabilitation of inveterate offenders. They do require an understanding that crime primarily occurs among youth (and it is there that it must be prevented), and that it occurs primarily in the absence of restraints. These restraints traditionally come from a variety of sources, only one of which is the criminal justice system. Deterrence research has erred in thinking that the state alone provides the restraints necessary to prevent law violation among children, and incapacitation research has erred in thinking that the state can reasonably consider controlling crime by simply locking up its children.

REFERENCES

GOTTFREDSON, M. and D. GOTTFREDSON (1987) Decisionmaking in Criminal Justice. New York: Plenum.

GOTTFREDSON, M. and T. HIRSCHI (1986) "The true value of lambda would appear to be zero: an essay on career criminals, criminal careers, selective incapacitation, cohort studies, and related topics." Criminology 24: 213-234.

GREENWOOD, P. (1983) "Controlling the crime rate through imprisonment," in J. Wilson (ed.) Crime and Public Policy. San Francisco: ICS.

McCORD, W. and J. McCORD (1959) Origins of Crime. New York: Columbia University Press.

SHANNON, L. (1981) Assessing the Relationship of Adult Criminal Careers to Juvenile Careers: Final Report. Washington, DC: NIJJDP.

Von HIRSCH, A. (1985) Past or Future Crimes. New Brunswick, NJ: Rutgers University Press.

WOLFGANG, M., R. FIGLIO, and T. SELLIN (1972) Delinquency in a Birth Cohort. Chicago: University of Chicago Press.

About the Contributors

David E. Aaronson is a Professor of Law at American University. He received a Ph.D. in Economics from George Washington University and a J.D. from the Harvard Law School. He is the coauthor of *Public Policy and Police Discretion*.

Richard A. Ball is a Professor of Sociology at West Virginia University. He has written on juvenile delinquency and, more recently, on the use of home incarceration and electronic monitoring.

John Dombrink is Assistant Professor of Social Ecology at the University of California, Irvine. His earlier research focused on gambling and the legalization of vice. More recently, he has conducted research on organized crime, including a major study for the recent President's Commission on Organized Crime.

James J. Fyfe is an Associate Professor of Justice at the American University and a Senior Fellow at the Police Foundation. He served as a New York City police officer for 16 years, has written and published extensively on police matters, and has served as an expert witness in numerous cases around the country on the police use of deadly force.

Gilbert Geis is a Professor of Social Ecology at the University of California, Irvine. He has written numerous works in criminology and the sociology of law. He is a Past President of the American Society of Criminology and received their Sutherland Award in 1985. Much of his recent work has focused on white-collar crime.

Michael Gottfredson is an associate professor in Management and Policy at the University of Arizona. He is the author of articles and books dealing with criminal justice statistics, victims of crime, and decision making. He was the coeditor of *Sourcebook of Criminal Justice Statistics* from 1977 to 1982 and has served on the editorial boards of the major journals in the field of criminology.

Travis Hirschi is a Professor of Sociology at the University of Arizona. He is author/coauthor of several books, including *Delinquency Research* and *Causes of Delinquency*. He is a former president of the American Society of Criminology and was the recipient of that society's Sutherland Award in 1986.

C. Ronald Huff is Director of the Program for the Study of Crime and Delinquency at Ohio State University, where he is also Associate Professor of Public Administration. His research has focused on criminal justice policy and management, as well as on wrongful convictions.

Paul D. Jesilow is a researcher at the University of California at Irvine. His major research interests are in deviance, deterrence, social control, and white-collar crime. He is the coauthor of *Myths That Cause Crime* (Seven Locks Press, 1984), for which he received the Academy of Criminal Justice Sciences' Outstanding Book of the Year Award.

Carl B. Klockars is a Professor in the Department of Sociology and the Program in Criminal Justice at the University of Delaware. He has conducted research on police "sting operations" and "fencing" and is the author of several books, including *The Professional Fence* and *The Ethics of Research with Human Subjects*.

J. Robert Lilly is Professor of Sociology at Northern Kentucky University. He has conducted research on juvenile delinquency, victimless crimes, and, most recently, on home incarceration. His writings have also included a critique of criminological theory, a subject on which he is currently writing a book, *American Criminological Theory: Its Content and Consequences* (forthcoming, Sage).

Joan Petersilia is a Senior Researcher in the Criminal Justice Program at the Rand Corporation. She has conducted research and published on such topics as juvenile delinquency, police, sentencing, community corrections, career criminals, and racial discrimination. She is the former Vice President of the American Society of Criminology, as well as the former President of the Association for Criminal Justice Research.

Henry N. Pontell is Associate Professor and Associate Director of the Program in Social Ecology at the University of California, Irvine. His research involves physician fraud and abuse in Medicare and Medicaid. He is a Past President of the Western Society of Criminology and the author of *A Capacity to Punish: The Ecology of Crime and Punishment* (Indiana University Press, 1984).

Arye Rattner is Assistant Professor of Sociology at the University of Haifa, Israel. A native Israeli with degrees from both Bar-Ilan University and Tel-Aviv University, he received his Ph.D. in Public Administration, with a specialization in Criminology and Criminal Justice, from Ohio State University. He is currently conducting research on wrongful convictions in Israel.

Loretta A. Schwalm received her M.A. in Sociology with a specialization in Criminology from Ohio State University. She is currently employed with the law firm of Ulmer, Berne, Laronge, Glickman, and Curtis in Cleveland, Ohio.

Joseph E. Scott is Associate Professor of Sociology at Ohio State University. His present research focuses on the effects and contents of erotic/pornographic material and its effects on society, as well as on cross-cultural perceptions of the seriousness of crime. He is author/co-author of articles and books addressing policy issues in the criminal justice system, including *Criminal Justice Planning and Ex-Offenders as Parole Officer Aides*.

Rita J. Simon is Dean of the School of Justice at the American University and a Professor of Law at that institution. She is the former editor of the *American Sociological Review and Justice Quarterly*. She is the author of several publications and books, including *The Jury and Defense of Insanity* and *Women and Crime*.

Sandra Evans Skovron is Assistant Professor in the Department of Criminal Justice and the Department of Sociology at the University of Cincinnati. She served as the Project Director for the Ohio Governor's Committee on Prison Crowding. Her research has concentrated on the perceived seriousness of crime and, more recently, on prison overcrowding.

NOTES

NOTES